The Lighthouse Devotional

COMPILED BY DR. CORNELL HAAN

Multnomah® Publishers *Sisters, Oregon*

THE LIGHTHOUSE DEVOTIONAL
published by Multnomah Publishers, Inc.

© 2000 by Dr. Cornell Haan
International Standard Book Number: 1-57673-743-8

Lighthouse image on cover by PhotoDisc
Background cover image by Doré

Scripture quotations are from:
The Holy Bible, New International Version © 1973, 1984 by International Bible
Society, used by permission of Zondervan Publishing House

Also quoted:
The Holy Bible, King James Version (KJV)
The Holy Bible, New King James Version (NKJV) © 1984 by Thomas Nelson, Inc.
New American Standard Bible (NASB) © 1960, 1977 by the Lockman Foundation
Holy Bible, New Living Translation (NLT) © 1996. Used by permission of
Tyndale House Publishers, Inc. All rights reserved.
The Living Bible (TLB) © 1971. Used by permission of
Tyndale House Publishers, Inc. All rights reserved.
Revised Standard Version Bible (RSV) © 1946, 1952 by the Division of Christian
Education of the National Council of the Churches of Christ
in the United States of America
New Revised Standard Version Bible (NRSV) © 1989 by the Division of Christian
Education of the National Council of the Churches of Christ
in the United States of America
The Message © 1993 by Eugene H. Peterson
The Holy Bible, New Century Version (NCV) © 1987, 1988, 1991 by
Word Publishing. Used by permission.

Multnomah is a trademark of Multnomah Publishers, Inc.
and is registered in the U.S. Patent and Trademark Office.
The colophon is a trademark of Multnomah Publishers, Inc.

Printed in the United States of America

Library of Congress Cataloging-in-Publication Data:
Haan, Cornell. The lighthouse devotional/by Cornell Haan. p. cm.
ISBN 1-57673-743-8   1.Witness bearing (Christianity)—Prayer-books and devo-
tions—English.   2. Evangelistic work—Prayer-books and devotions—English. 3.
Devotional calendars. I. Title.   BV4520 .H32 2000   242'.2—dc21   00-010004

00 01 02 03 04 05 — 10 9 8 7 6 5 4 3 2 1 0

Authors

Joe Aldrich

Dallas Anderson

Neil T. Anderson

Stephen Arterburn

Henry Blackaby

David Brickner

Bill Bright

Vonette Z. Bright

David Bryant

Bobbye Byerly

Paul Cedar

Evelyn Christenson

Charles T. Crabtree

Robert C. Crosby

Steve Douglass

Dick Eastman

Francis Frangipane

Steve Fry

Jonathan Graf

Dr. Cornell Haan

Ali Hanna

Jack Hayford

Jim Hylton

Wood Kroll

Larry Lewis

Max Lucado

Lowell Lundstrom

David Mains

Mary L. Marr

Bill McCartney

Ron Mehl

Luis Palau

Tom Pelton

Tom Phillips

John Piper

Rebecca Manley Pippert

Robert E. Reccord

Bob Ricker

Pat Robertson

Darrell Robinson

Moishe Rosen

Bruce Schoeman

Dr. Douglas Shaw

Alice Smith

Eddie Smith

Justin Taylor

Dr. Terry Teykl

Al VanderGriend

Thomas Wang

Jarvis Ward

Introduction

You are the light of the world. A city on a hill cannot be hidden.
Neither do people light a lamp and put it under a bowl.
Instead they put it on its stand, and it gives light to everyone in the house.
In the same way, let your light shine before men, that they may
see your good deeds and praise your Father in heaven.

MATTHEW 5:14–16

Before He ascended into heaven, Jesus commanded his disciples to "go and make disciples of all nations" (Matthew 28:19). Our Lord has charged us with the awesome responsibility—and privilege—of reaching a dying world with the gospel. No one should be left out when it comes to hearing the gospel, and none of us who already know Him should be left out when it comes to sharing it.

Most Christians have a genuine concern for the lost and a sincere desire to see people come to a saving knowledge of the Lord. The problem isn't the lack of willingness; it's the lack of knowing where to go and how to get started.

It's not as complicated or difficult as you might think.

In the past few years a movement has arisen in America that promises to change Christian evangelism profoundly and permanently. It is called the Lighthouse Movement, and it has quickly gained the support of hundreds of evangelical leaders, including the twentieth century's most influential evangelist, Billy Graham. The goal of the movement is simple: to enable Christians from all walks of life to pray for, care for, and share the gospel with people in their circles of influence—families, friends, neighbors, colleagues, as well as people they don't know.

Think about it for a minute: What better place to share God's love than where you live, and who better to share it with others than you? Beautiful in its simplicity, the Lighthouse Movement is nothing more than all of us praying for those around us, caring for their needs, and sharing with them the Good News of salvation through Jesus Christ. It gives all Christians—people with no formal ministry training, credentials, or titles as well as those in full-time ministry—a way to minister to the people around them. All it takes is a willing heart!

So why the *Lighthouse Devotional*?

I've compiled this one-year devotional to help you grow in different aspects of your relationship with Jesus Christ and to offer helpful hints on how your light can shine more brightly for Him in your sphere of influence. In 312 devotionals, fifty authors give valuable insights on important aspects of a life of faith, including prayer, fasting, Bible reading, assurance, personal evangelism, and more. Each devotional begins with a Scripture reading and ends with a Lighthouse Thought for the Day, a short reflection that challenges you to apply the principles in the devotional to your life.

I believe that if you will accept this challenge, not only will your efforts to reach those around you bear more fruit than you ever thought possible, but they will also make a difference in the world for Jesus. The light shining from you and others like you will reach far beyond your homes, neighborhoods, and workplaces—it will shine on all nations.

Dr. Cornell "Corkie" Haan
National Facilitator of Ministry Networks
Mission America

The Power of God's Word

*For the word of God is living and active. Sharper than any double-edged
sword...it judges the thoughts and attitudes of the heart.*

HEBREWS 4:12

The Word is God. The physical pages of the Bible are not God, but the
Spirit who breathes the words onto those pages is. As you read your
Bible, are you not meeting the Almighty Himself? Are you not learning
the thoughts and ways of our heavenly Father? Reading and understanding the Word of God is a vital part of any true disciple's life. It's
crucial for those who wish to be lighthouses for Jesus Christ. So how
do we get the most out of God's Word?

First, prepare your heart to receive God's Word. Before you read
your Bible, pray that your study will not merely be an intellectual pursuit. Ask the Holy Spirit to speak to your heart through the Word and
cause you to tremble when He does (Isaiah 66:2).

Second, be ready when God speaks to you through His Word.
Carry a pen and pad with you at all times—even when you aren't
actively reading the Word—and write down what the Lord speaks to
your heart. At night, put your notebook at your bedside, for God will
speak to His beloved even as we sleep.

Third, open your heart to hear new truths from God's Word. Many
Christians miss the fullness of God's heart because their study is merely
to reinforce what they already know. The Word of God is rich and full
of a lifetime of truths to be learned.

Finally, do not grow faint when God reveals the darkness of your
heart. Remember, the voice that speaks to you through the Word of
God is the same mighty voice that spoke to the pre-Creation void.
God's Word transformed the nothingness then, and He can do the
same within your heart.

LIGHTHOUSE THOUGHT FOR THE DAY

Allow God's Word to remake you and bring light to your heart. Read
the Bible not just to be informed, but to be transformed.

FRANCIS FRANGIPANE

The Abundant Life

Count yourselves dead to sin but alive to God in Christ Jesus.
ROMANS 6:11

My friend Randy had given up trying to live the Christian life. He said, "I have tried, but have failed so many times. Nothing seems to work for me."

After listening to his account of his many failures and defeats, I began to explain the ministry of the Holy Spirit. Randy interrupted: "I know all about the Holy Spirit. I've read everything I can find, and nothing works for me."

My thoughts turned to Romans 6. I asked him, "Randy, are you sure you're a Christian?"

"Yes," he answered. "I'm sure."

"How do you know?"

"By faith," he responded, then cited Ephesians 2:8–9. "Scripture promises, 'For by grace you have been saved through faith—and this not from yourselves, it's a gift of God—not by works, so that no one can boast.' I know I'm saved."

"Why," I asked him, "do you trust God for your salvation, but not for His other promises concerning your rights as a child of God?"

I read from Romans 6 and reminded Randy that every believer has access to the mighty supernatural power of the risen Christ. The same Holy Spirit who inspired Ephesians 2:8–9 also inspired Romans 6. By faith we can claim that sin no longer controls us, and we can live in the power of the resurrection as the Word promises.

That day, God touched Randy's life. His spiritual eyes were opened, and he began, by faith, to live in accordance with his God-given heritage, to be "salt and light." As lighthouses for the Lord Jesus Christ, we are to do no less.

LIGHTHOUSE THOUGHT FOR THE DAY
You cannot live an abundant Christian life by yourself, but you can trust Jesus to live His supernatural resurrected life in and through you by faith through the enabling of the Holy Spirit.

BILL BRIGHT

Assurance of God's Purposes

In all things God works for the good of those who love him,
who have been called according to his purpose.

ROMANS 8:28

Bill had tears in his eyes when I met him after the worship service. "I loved your service," he said, "but I could not see you. I am going blind."

"That must be traumatic!" I replied.

"Yes, it is traumatic, but it's okay. I don't understand it all, but I don't have to. It's one of those 'all things' that God talks about in Romans 8:28. I have served Him faithfully with my eyesight; now I will serve Him faithfully without it. I don't know how He will use it for good, but I know He will."

Not all things are good in themselves. Some are painful and hard to bear. It is not scriptural to say "all things are good," but it is scriptural to believe that in all things God works for good. What a treasure it is to know that God faithfully uses all things for good.

I see unpleasantness in life as a lot like the ingredients in a chocolate cake, which in its finished form is delicious. Imagine eating the ingredients one by one—a cup of flour, a mouthful of chocolate, a couple raw eggs, a cup of sugar. Yuck! But when you blend those ingredients together in just the right proportions and put the mixture in the oven at just the right temperature, you get something delectable.

Likewise, when we love God and know He has called us to be His, He will take every "ingredient" of our lives—pleasant and unpleasant—and blend them together for good to fulfill the greatest purpose possible: to "conform us to the likeness of his Son." He will make us like Jesus.

LIGHTHOUSE THOUGHT FOR THE DAY

The Father gives us His highest and best to make us like Jesus so that His light may shine brightly through us. It's not always easy, but it's always for the best.

DARRELL ROBINSON

Being Ready for Inspections

Examine yourselves.

2 CORINTHIANS 13:5

People who served in the Lighthouse Service in the early 1900s knew that the often lonely nature of their assignment was no excuse for a lower standard of work. Many lived and labored on islands or secluded coasts, but there was a constant sense of accountability. The importance of keeping strong, steady lights beaming to the vulnerable vessels at sea did not allow for slackness. Their work was a matter of life or death, and readiness was the daily credo.

To maintain high standards among the lighthouses that dotted the eastern seaboard, the government appointed a group of lighthouse inspectors who daily made rounds from site to site. The keepers seldom received notice that an inspector was coming, so most knew it was wise to work each day as if the inspector were arriving. Upon arrival the inspectors would judge the lighthouse in several areas: *Was everything in order? Were the wicks properly trimmed? Was the brass polished? Were there any safety violations? How well was the machinery operating? Was the keeper in full uniform? Had accurate records been maintained?*

It has been said: "You cannot *expect* what you do not *inspect*." As lights for Jesus Christ, you are called to "Examine yourselves to see whether you are in the faith; test yourselves" (2 Corinthians 13:5).

Taking time to prayerfully reflect on and consider how we are living our lives is essential for spiritual growth. Is everything in order? Are we living for Christ sincerely and representing Him authentically? Is our flame of witness burning brightly? Are we wearing the "full armor of God" (Ephesians 6)? We would also be wise to pray the prayer of the psalmist: "Teach us to number our days aright" (Psalm 90:12).

LIGHTHOUSE THOUGHT FOR THE DAY

If we *expect* to grow for God, we must remember to *inspect* our lives.

ROBERT C. CROSBY

Reasons to Fast and Pray

Declare a holy fast; call a sacred assembly. Summon the elders and all who live in the land to the house of the LORD your God, and cry out to the LORD.

JOEL 1:14

The Bible teaches that there are times for feasting and banqueting, but there are also times for fasting. Biblical reasons for fasting are national peril (Joel 1:2; 2:12); mourning (2 Samuel 12:16–17); protection (Esther 4:16); revelation (Daniel 9:3); and power in the personal life (Luke 4:1–2).

Certainly we are in a time of national peril and should be mourning for the moral condition of our country. With fasting and prayer, we plead for protection and fresh revelation from our holy God. As Christians, we need the power of the Holy Spirit in our personal lives on a daily basis.

The Christian practice of fasting tells God (and us) that we are serious. History teaches us that the early church fasted twice a week: Wednesdays and Fridays. Our sincere confession tells God that we are serious about change. While fasting, John Knox prayed, "Give me Scotland or I will perish." We fast and pray for God to stop the flood of evil and invoke His goodness into our situation. The Lord has promised to hear our cry. "He may come and shower righteousness" down upon us (Hosea 10:12, NLT).

When we fast, we must remember that it is to God that we are fasting. Fasting isn't just starving ourselves. Nor is it a hunger strike to twist God's arm. Also, there must be prayer with our fasting. True fasting is taking mealtime and using it for time on our knees in serious prayer. God will hear us when we fast and come to Him saying, "Cleanse us, O Lord. We're sorry, and we mean business with You."

LIGHTHOUSE THOUGHT FOR THE DAY

As lighthouses for Jesus Christ, we need to fast and pray for ourselves, our nation, and those in our neighborhoods. When we do this, God will hear us and act on our behalf.

PAT ROBERTSON

Love in the Berry Patch

"'You shall love the LORD your God with all your heart, with all your soul, and with all your mind.... You shall love your neighbor as yourself.'"

MATTHEW 22:37, 39, NKJV

Just as Christians have a love for God, they also have a new kind of love for other people. It's not a perfect love, and it may not be on par with those saintly people who have walked with the Lord for decades, but it's definitely love, and it's definitely different from what it used to be.

I remember when my parents demonstrated this to me. I was ten years old at the time, and our family had planted two acres of strawberries on the back field of our farm. As you may know, strawberry plants do not bear much fruit the first year, and they take a lot of care after that.

By the third year our strawberries were producing wonderfully. One evening while we were working the patch, our neighbor came out and said, "I had the surveyors here, and they've determined that ten feet of your strawberry patch is on my property. I'm here to pick my berries."

We had worked those strawberries for three years, weeding the patch, carefully placing the runners back into rows, and now we were ready to enjoy the fruits of our labor. Our neighbor had done nothing; still he came to pick our berries, and he had the nerve to do so right before our eyes.

My parents never complained. They treated this man cordially, showing nothing but Christ's love. He needed the Savior, and that was foremost in their minds. That's the way Christians express their love.

Do you want proof that God lives in you? Think back to before you were saved. Do you see any more love in yourself than you did then? If so, God's Word says that is evidence of salvation.

LIGHTHOUSE THOUGHT FOR THE DAY

Our love for our neighbors, even those we see as unlovable, affirms that we know Jesus Christ.

WOOD KROLL

Relying on the Savior

*"And I will do whatever you ask in my name,
so that the Son may bring glory to the Father."*
JOHN 14:13

Suppose you were totally paralyzed and could do nothing for yourself but talk. And suppose a strong and reliable friend promised to live with you and do whatever you needed done. How could you glorify your friend if a stranger came to see you? Would you glorify his generosity and strength by trying to get out of bed and carry him?

No! You would say, "Friend, please come lift me up, and would you put a pillow behind me so I can look at my guest? And would you please put my glasses on for me?" And so your visitor would learn from your requests that you are helpless and that your friend is strong and kind. You glorify your friend by needing him, asking him to help, and counting on him.

Jesus says, "I am the vine, you are the branches. He who abides in me, and I in him, he it is that bears much fruit, for apart from me you can do nothing" (John 15:5, RSV). So we really are paralyzed. Without Christ we are incapable of good. As Paul says, "Nothing good dwells within me, that is, in my flesh" (Romans 7:18, RSV).

But, according to John 15:5, God intends for us to do something good—namely, bear fruit. So as our strong and reliable friend—"I have called you friends" (John 15:15, RSV)—He promises to do for us what we can't do for ourselves.

How then do we glorify Him? Jesus gives the answer in John 15:7—"If you abide in me, and my words abide in you, ask whatever you will, and it shall be done for you" (RSV). *We pray!* We ask God to do for us through Christ what we can't do for ourselves—bear fruit.

LIGHTHOUSE THOUGHT FOR THE DAY
Relying on and delighting in our sovereign Savior is the key to glorifying our Father, as He promises to do for us what we cannot do for ourselves.

JOHN PIPER, WITH JUSTIN TAYLOR

An Open Invitation

"All you who are thirsty, come and drink."
ISAIAH 55:1, NCV

The most incredible invitations are not found in envelopes; they are found in the Bible. You can't read about God without finding Him issuing invitations. He invited Eve to marry Adam, the animals to enter the ark, David to be king, Israel to leave bondage, Nehemiah to rebuild Jerusalem. God is an inviting God. He invited Mary to birth His Son, the disciples to fish for men, the adulterous woman to start over, and Thomas to touch His wounds. God is the King who prepares the place, sets the table, and invites His subjects to come in.

In fact, it seems His favorite word is *come.*

"Come, let us talk about these things. Though your sins are like scarlet, they can be as white as snow" (Isaiah 1:18, NCV, emphasis added).

"Come to me, all of you who are tired and have heavy loads, and I will give you rest" (Matthew 11:28, NCV, emphasis added).

"Come to the wedding feast" (Matthew 22:4, NCV, emphasis added).

"Come follow me, and I will make you fish for people" (Mark 1:17, NCV, emphasis added).

"Let anyone who is thirsty *come* to me and drink" (John 7:37, NCV, emphasis added).

God is a God who invites. God is a God who calls. He opens the door and waves His hand, pointing pilgrims to a full table.

His invitation is not just for a meal, however; it is for life. An invitation to come into His kingdom and take up residence in a tearless, graveless, painless world. Who can come? Whoever wishes. The invitation is at once universal and personal.

LIGHTHOUSE THOUGHT FOR THE DAY
Share God's invitation to come with those around you today.

MAX LUCADO

Safety in Numbers

In an abundance of counselors there is safety.
PROVERBS 11:14, NRSV

I was honored when an internationally known evangelist called to ask me if I thought he should follow through with his plans for a ministry trip to a war-torn African nation. His heart was set on the mission: He had already printed fifty thousand gospel tracts, and his bags were packed. But this brother in Christ had the wisdom to ask for and submit to the counsel of the leaders he queried. Just three hours before he was to take off, he postponed his trip.

There is an old saying that sometimes we can't see the forest for the trees. In other words, we can get so close to a situation that we are not able to see the big picture. That's when we need the objective counsel of loving, spiritually mature friends.

It isn't always easy to discern God's will in a matter. It means hearing His voice in our hearts and through His Word. But it also may mean seeking counsel from men and women of God who have our best interests—as well as those of the kingdom—in mind.

We were never meant to be "Lone Ranger" Christians. God designed the body of Christ—our spiritual family—to help keep us accountable and protected. We've all heard Christians say, "God alone is my spiritual authority." However, spiritual authority comes in human packages, and if we are to be successful in our walk with Christ and in our ministries, we need to learn to heed their counsel.

The apostle Paul wrote in Ephesians 5:21, "Submit to one another out of reverence for Christ." Paul understood that there is safety for the individual believer in seeking the wisdom of "an abundance of counselors."

LIGHTHOUSE THOUGHT FOR THE DAY

God has put us in the body of Christ for several reasons, one of which is to seek counsel from one another when we have decisions to make.

EDDIE SMITH

Dispelling Darkness

"Neither do people light a lamp and put it under a bowl.
Instead they put it on its stand, and it gives light to everyone in the house."
MATTHEW 5:15

The title of the magazine article, "When Darkness is Allowed to Reign," caught my eye. As I read about the details of another tragic school shooting, my heart was gripped with the burning question, "How could this happen?"

When evil raises its ugly head in our society, we are quick to point the finger of blame at different aspects of our culture such as the mass media, the government, and video games. But perhaps instead of looking to place blame, we should remember that our Lord has commissioned us, His followers, to go out and be the light of the world. Are we fulfilling the commission we've been given? The darkness in our world is due to an absence of God's light.

One of the great privileges of following Christ is having Him dwelling within so that He can shine through us and spread His light to the world. When the light of Christ shines, it dispels darkness.

We can expect that the community will be changed as God's people make a commitment to be lights in this world. As you think about your circle of influence—at school, at work, or in your neighborhood—remember that although the forces of evil want to frustrate the work God seeks to accomplish, Christ is greater than the enemy. The war has already been won. The victory is ours! As lighthouses for Christ, we bring hope into the world, and the darkness is driven away.

LIGHTHOUSE THOUGHT FOR THE DAY
Shine the light of Christ into the world around you and watch as the darkness fades.

DALLAS ANDERSON

God's Call to Intercession

"Look at the nations and watch—and be utterly amazed. For I am going to do something in your days that you would not believe, even if you were told."

HABAKKUK 1:5

In 1967, God began to show me ways to pray for people, situations, and nations. This kind of prayer is called *intercession*. I did not know the term at the time, only that I sensed the Holy Spirit leading me to this kind of prayer.

For the past thirty-three years, I have cried out to God for worldwide revival, and I still believe that we will yet see His glory poured out on the nations of the world, because God wants His voice to be heard and His Son glorified everywhere. He wants to do amazing things in answer to His people's intercessory prayers. He wants to amplify His Spirit's voice within His body, the church. That will only happen as His children dedicate themselves to prayer for people, situations, and nations.

I believe these things are happening now. God's anointed are travailing in prayer for their neighbors, friends, family members, coworkers, and others within their spheres of influence.

May the Holy Spirit touch each of us with an anointing to call out to God in intercessory prayer for those who don't yet know Him. This anointing of prayer will help us to pray effectively to God for a dying, lost world.

Lighthouses of intercessory prayer are springing up all around us. As lighthouses for Jesus Christ, we can pray for our neighbors and for every neighborhood and city in our nation.

LIGHTHOUSE THOUGHT FOR THE DAY

Let us be diligent in praying for all people in all nations, that they may come to know the love of God as extended to us through the Lord Jesus Christ.

BOBBYE BYERLY

Gotta Tell Somebody

*You are a chosen generation, a royal priesthood, a holy nation,
His own special people, that you may proclaim the praises of Him who
called you out of darkness into His marvelous light.*

1 PETER 2:9, NKJV

I've seen what Jesus can do in changing a life forever. That's why I'm just like those shepherds who went to see the baby Jesus lying in the manger: "Now when they had seen Him, they made widely known the saying which was told them concerning this Child" (Luke 2:17, NKJV).

I'm like Andrew after he was introduced to the Lamb of God who takes away the sin of the world (John 1:29). I'm tracking down my brother to tell him, "We have found the Messiah" (John 1:41, NKJV).

I'm like the woman at the well who, having encountered Jesus Christ in a meaningful way, announced to her city, "Come, see a Man who told me all things that I ever did. Could this be the Christ?" (John 4:29, NKJV).

I'm like the woman at the empty tomb who saw the risen Christ and then "returned from the tomb and told all these things to the eleven and to all the rest" (Luke 24:9, NKJV).

I'm like the two on the road to Emmaus who were joined by the resurrected Jesus and had the Scripture opened to them. Once He vanished from their sight, "they rose up that very hour and returned to Jerusalem.... And they told about the things that had happened on the road" (Luke 24:33–35, NKJV).

I'm a witness because I've witnessed a change in my own life. I'm not a witness because I have received the call of an evangelist. I'm not a witness because I'm exercising the gift of evangelism. I'm a witness because things have happened in my life that only God could do.

LIGHTHOUSE THOUGHT FOR THE DAY

When we see what Jesus can do in our own lives, we can't help but be a witness for Him to our neighbors.

WOOD KROLL

Is It Real?

If any man be in Christ, he is a new creature: old things are passed away; behold, all things are become new.

2 CORINTHIANS 5:17, KJV

It may have happened to you at a Billy Graham Crusade. Perhaps it was during a telecast of *The 700 Club* or during a conversation with a friend. Maybe you were alone with God when it happened. But somehow, someplace deep within, you believed that Jesus of Nazareth, God's Son, died for your sins and rose from the dead to be your Lord and Savior. Then that belief grew into action, and you called out, "Jesus, I take You as my Savior. I surrender to You. Be the Lord of my life!"

Then something wonderful happened. A deep peace came over you. No more internal fighting. No more running. Your sins were forgiven. You were part of the family of God. It was as if you had been born all over again. Old things were gone; everything was new. For the first time, you truly understood God's love.

But now some time has passed, and you're wondering if anything has changed. It is common for new Christians to wonder if anything actually happened when they prayed. It seemed so wonderful, so easy—almost too good to be true—that many have thought that maybe it wasn't true at all.

In a court of law, the truth of a matter is established by evidence. The statements of witnesses are accepted in court as valid evidence. To prove the reality of your experience with Christ, God has given you three witnesses: His Word, His Holy Spirit, and your changed life.

As you examine the Word, as you receive the assurance provided by the Holy Spirit, and as you look at the evidence of your new life, you will know that blessed assurance that Jesus is truly yours!

LIGHTHOUSE THOUGHT FOR THE DAY

God gives us evidence that we truly know Him through His Son, Jesus Christ.

PAT ROBERTSON

How Far on One Tank?

Be filled with the Spirit.
EPHESIANS 5:18

Spiritual encouragement is a renewable resource. But like backpackers with canteens, you and I can carry just so much in our souls. Then we run dry. We must return again and again to the Lord, the never failing source of encouragement, to replenish our supply.

It *has* to be that way. If we never ran low, if we never found our little water bottles empty, we wouldn't keep coming back to Him. But we simply weren't built to carry around a two-hundred-gallon tank on our backs. It's more like a one- or two-gallon tank, and we go through it pretty fast—even on a normal day. And when it's gone, we're *discouraged*. We're out of courage, and we need to come back to Him, get on our knees in His presence, and obtain a fresh supply.

God intended that we live our lives in this way so that we would return to Him again and again in our need and in our emptiness. He wants a continual relationship with us. He wants us to walk *with* the Spirit.

When Scripture commands us to "be filled with the Spirit," as in Ephesians 5:18, a literal translation points toward a continuous, all-the-time filling of the Spirit. Be filled every hour! Be filled every day! Why?

Because this world is going to dry you up.

Everyday relationships are going to drain you.

The pressures of life are going to deplete you.

Struggles with Satan and the flesh are going to drag you down.

God says, "Be sure to come back to Me tomorrow. I'll fill you again so that you can carry on another day and give some more…love some more…lift some more…and serve some more in My name."

LIGHTHOUSE THOUGHT FOR THE DAY

Being filled with the Spirit of God is continual for the Christian. We need to go to God daily to get our tanks filled!

RON MEHL

The Gethsemane Experience

An angel from heaven appeared to him and strengthened him.
LUKE 22:43

Luke 22 tells us that Jesus' struggle in Gethsemane became so intense that an angel of the Lord had to come to encourage Him. All of Jesus' prayer and what the angel said to encourage Him are not recorded, but Isaiah 49 might give us some idea of the kind of exchange that took place.

Perhaps, in His desperation and anguish, Jesus prayed something similar to Isaiah 49:4: "I have labored to no purpose; I have spent my strength in vain and for nothing."

Perhaps the angel encouraged Jesus with words similar to God's words in verse 6: "It is too small a thing for you to be my servant to restore the tribes of Jacob and bring back those of Israel I have kept. I will also make you a light for the Gentiles, that you may bring my salvation to the ends of the earth."

Let's personalize that for a moment. Could it be that what God has done in our families and churches is "too small a thing" for God compared with His desire to make us lights to the lost?

Are you in your own personal Gethsemane right now? Does it seem you have labored to no purpose and spent your strength in vain? Does it appear that all your efforts are wasted energy?

Let God encourage you today with these words from Isaiah 49: "In the time of my favor I will answer you, and in the day of salvation I will help you; I will keep you and will make you to be a covenant for the people, to restore the land and to reassign its desolate inheritances, to say to the captives, 'Come out,' and to those in darkness, 'Be free!'" (vv. 8–9).

LIGHTHOUSE THOUGHT FOR THE DAY

God sent encouragement to Jesus so that He could complete the work He had been sent to do. The Lord will give the same encouragement to us.

TOM PELTON

At the Feet of Jesus

*Then Mary took…an expensive perfume; she poured it on Jesus' feet and
wiped his feet with her hair…. The house was filled with the fragrance.*

JOHN 12:3

Scripture records three times that Mary found her way to the feet of
Jesus. She went there first to learn from Him. Obviously, she knew the
value of time. Like people today, Mary had only so much time, so she
spent it learning from Christ: "He came to a village where a woman
named Martha opened her home to him. She had a sister called Mary,
who sat at the Lord's feet listening to what he said" (Luke 10:38–39).

From a Christian perspective, time is an allotment of opportunities
from the Lord. Sitting at the feet of Jesus and learning from Him is the
wisest investment of that time. What we concentrate on during that
time will shape the rest of our lives.

Mary also brought her grief to Jesus' feet: "When Mary reached the
place where Jesus was and saw him, she fell at his feet and said, 'Lord,
if you had been here, my brother would not have died'" (John 11:32).
Mary understood something we need to understand: We all endure
grief at some point in our lives, but Jesus heals our broken hearts when
we bring them to Him.

Mary's third appearance at the feet of Jesus was to give Him her
best. Love never knows the cost of something, only the value. Mary's
love led her to give costly perfume, which she poured over His feet.
Jesus said that Mary's act that day would continue to live in the gospel
story as a memorial to her. Let it also encourage us to give Jesus our
best.

LIGHTHOUSE THOUGHT FOR THE DAY

At the feet of Jesus we will be taught His wisdom, comforted in grief,
and empowered to give Him our best.

JIM HYLTON

A Praying Lighthouse

"If my people…will humble themselves and pray and seek my face and
turn from their wicked ways, then will I hear from heaven
and will forgive their sin."

2 CHRONICLES 7:14

As people called by God's own name, we have the privilege of humbly approaching God and asking for revival and healing in our land. The Bible promises us that if we approach God with an attitude of humility and repentance, He will hear and answer our prayers.

Let's pray for a worldwide spiritual awakening—beginning with our families, our churches, and our communities, and us. As we pray, we should acknowledge God's mercy and forgiveness, confess our known sin, and seek His face for personal renewal (Psalm 66:18; 1 John 1:9).

We should also pray that our brothers and sisters in Christ realize God's love and draw upon His character and understanding (Psalm 1:1–3; Ephesians 3:13–19; 5:1–4; James 1:5) and that they become vital witnesses through their words and actions (2 Corinthians 5:17–20). Also, we need to pray for Christians to meet the conditions for revival set forth in 2 Chronicles 7:14, namely humbling themselves (1 Peter 5:6), praying effectually (Luke 18:1; James 5:16), seeking God's face (Jeremiah 29:13), and turning from sin (1 John 1:8–9).

We also need to pray that those in our circles of influence will be open to hearing the message of the gospel. We need to pray for wisdom in how to present the gospel to these people and follow up with those who have made decisions for Jesus Christ.

Finally, we need to put action behind our prayers as we reach out with God's love to those around us. We need to recognize God-provided opportunities to tell others about His great love and forgiveness, available to all people through our Lord Jesus Christ.

LIGHTHOUSE THOUGHT FOR THE DAY

Pray for spiritual renewal, starting with you. Pray for opportunities to share God's message through your words and your actions.

VONETTE Z. BRIGHT

Christ's Manifest Presence

"Stretch out your hand to heal and perform miraculous signs and wonders through the name of...Jesus."... Much grace was upon them all.

ACTS 4:30, 33

The Puritans called a God-initiated season of revival "the manifest presence of Christ."

The impact of such a gracious work as is recorded in Acts 4 touches people at every point of their need. Whenever Christ is manifested, His caring heart becomes very prominent. That is why praying for revival may be one of the most loving gifts you can give to your community.

During the Great Awakening in the 1700s, Jonathan Edwards wrote: "There scarcely was a single person in the town, old or young, left unconcerned about the great things of the eternal world. The work of conversion was carried out in a most astonishing manner and increased more and more. Soon it made a glorious alteration in the town, so that in 1735 the town seemed full of the presence of God: It was never so full of love, or of joy. The congregation was alive in God's service."

During the Hebrides Revival in 1949, Duncan Campbell confessed: "In that revival, the fear of God laid hold upon the community, moving men and women, who until then had no concern for spiritual things, to seek after God."

Such is the great need of this hour. What would happen to your neighborhood or city if true believers were activated to give loving ministry to unbelievers around them in the undeniable presence of the living Christ, poured out upon the whole place by the Holy Spirit Himself?

LIGHTHOUSE THOUGHT FOR THE DAY

Pray for revival in your community. When God grants revival, love for others flows with Christlike sweetness, healing, provision, and power.

DAVID BRYANT

Confessing Your Sin

I acknowledged my sin to you and did not cover up my iniquity. I said, "I will confess my transgressions to the LORD"—and you forgave the guilt of my sin.

PSALM 32:5

King David felt really bad! Why? Because he had sinned, and he felt guilty. I remember meeting someone who knew just how David felt.

As I walked along the beach at Daytona Beach, Florida, many years ago, I met a young man that I could see was deeply depressed. He was sitting in kind of a fetal position, and he had a scowl on his face.

"What's wrong?" I asked.

"I have just returned from the war in Vietnam, where I killed many people," he replied.

I could see that this young man's guilt was racking both his body and his mind. I told him that I knew what would free him from guilt; then I told him about Jesus Christ. He wasn't quick to believe this Good News, but finally, haltingly, he asked Jesus Christ to come into his life and forgive his sins.

What transpired in the next few moments was the most dramatic metamorphosis I have ever seen. This young man's countenance lifted, and his shoulders straightened. He stood, and the joy of Jesus radiated from his face. God had lifted the chains of guilt from his life and freed him!

One of the most common sources of anxiety—for believers and nonbelievers alike—is legitimate guilt for sins. The good news is that God has provided a remedy for our guilt: Jesus Christ's death on the cross. If we genuinely confess our sin and repent, Christ's blood sets us free.

LIGHTHOUSE THOUGHT FOR THE DAY

Christ's death on the cross has paid the price for our sins. We need to share this gift with our neighbors. By confessing and repenting, they too can receive forgiveness and freedom from guilt.

STEVE DOUGLASS

Exalting God

You are my God, and I will give you thanks;
you are my God, and I will exalt you.

PSALM 118:28

The Reverend A. J. Gordon wrote, "You can do more than pray after you have prayed, but you can never do more until you have prayed."

To keep our light for Jesus Christ shining brightly, we must keep our prayers rising fervently. That's why we need to look at how to exalt God through prayer. Just as any activity in life can be productive or unproductive, so it is with prayer. Productive prayer exalts God by placing the focus on who God is. The Lord's Prayer offers the model for us as we pray, and it begins with recognition of who the Father is. For our prayers to be productive, we, too, must recognize and exalt the Father.

Our lighthouses should also seek to exalt the Lord in our neighborhoods through focused times of praise and worship. This is the key to a successful lighthouse, because our ultimate goal is to shine forth the reality of who God is to our neighbors. The apostle Peter reminds us, "You are a chosen generation.... His own special people, that you may proclaim the praises of Him who called you out of darkness into His marvelous light" (1 Peter 2:9, NKJV). We're to do this because we are now children of the light.

If our goal is to proclaim God's praises, we must begin with productive prayer and then give of ourselves to the ministry of worship and praise to let the light of Jesus shine through us into our neighborhoods. Praise becomes vital to our lighthouse strategy because praise enthrones God and thereby dethrones Satan. The psalmist wrote that God is "enthroned in the praises of Israel" (Psalm 22:3, NKJV).

LIGHTHOUSE THOUGHT FOR THE DAY

Praise brings the glow of God's presence into all we do because it enthrones God as who He is: "the Father of the heavenly lights" (James 1:17).

DICK EASTMAN

Love or Offense?

*Love is patient, love is kind.... It is not rude, it is not self-seeking,
it is not easily angered, it keeps no record of wrongs.*

1 CORINTHIANS 13:4–5

Being relational has never been my strong suit. One of the first things I learned when I started praying for my neighbors was that as I pray, God grows a love for them within me. The exciting thing is that since I am incapable of loving my neighbors on my own, clearly God loves them through me.

One of the significant ways this God-given love shows itself is in how we respond when our neighbors offend us. First Corinthians 13 tells us that love is patient, not easily angered, and doesn't keep a record of wrongs. How often do we let petty things bring tension to our relationships with our neighbors?

If we want God's love to flow through us to our neighbors, we must not be offended by their actions, especially if we are praying for them. How Satan loves to drive a wedge between us and the people we are praying for and witnessing to!

We may need to be deliberate in not being offended by our neighbors. For example, when I walk my dog, I always carry a scoop and a bag so I can pick up my dog's messes. But I have a neighbor who continually lets his dog go in my front yard, and he never picks up the mess. At first, I felt I needed to talk to him about this, but my heart mellowed as I recalled these verses in Corinthians.

Although a secular thinker might say that we should, nowhere does Scripture tell us to confront a nonbeliever who has wronged us. In fact, Scripture tells us to turn the other cheek. We need to be obedient to the Word of God. In this case, it means not allowing our neighbors' offenses to harm our relationships with them.

LIGHTHOUSE THOUGHT FOR THE DAY

The next time you are offended by a neighbor's actions, ask God to remove it from your memory and fill you with love.

JONATHAN GRAF

Now's the Time!

> *"Behold, I say unto you, lift up your eyes, and look on the fields;*
> *for they are white already to harvest."*
>
> JOHN 4:35, KJV

Wouldn't it have been wonderful to have lived in the first century and heard Paul or Peter preach, perhaps, or maybe even followed in the very steps of Jesus? Or to have lived during Martin Luther's time and seen the changes in the church? Or to have lived in the days of Charles Spurgeon, Dwight Moody, or Billy Sunday and observed their work?

Those would have been exciting times to be a Christian, but I would assert that living right now is even better. Some studies indicate that as much as 80 percent of all that has been done to fulfill the great commission has been done in the twentieth century, and that over half has been in the past two decades.

The largest, fastest-growing churches in history exist right now, many of them overseas, but also many here in the United States. People are coming to Christ now more than ever before in history. Truly, the "fields are white *already* to harvest."

Not only are we living at the right time, but we are also in the right place to see the harvest. We tend to think of the mission field as somewhere else—maybe across the ocean or in another state, city, or community. We certainly don't think of the mission field as being our own neighborhoods.

Jesus strikes a deathblow to such muddled thinking when He exhorts, "Lift up your eyes! Look! Right there, under your noses, is a field white to harvest!" This is the time; right here is the place; and we are the people! Oh that we might say with Jesus, "My meat [food] is to do the will of him that sent me, and to finish his work" (John 4:34, KJV).

LIGHTHOUSE THOUGHT FOR THE DAY

The largest harvest ever can be reaped right in our neighborhoods! If we don't reap the harvest, who will?

LARRY LEWIS

Things That Last

*The present heavens and earth are reserved for fire.... Since everything will
be destroyed in this way, what kind of people ought you to be?*

2 PETER 3:7, 11

There is nothing like a natural disaster to remind us of what's really important.

I was with my wife and daughter near the epicenter of the 1994 Northridge, California, earthquake. When it was all over, we swept up glass and carried broken valuables to the backyard. Our things were destroyed. What had been collected for decades was gone in seconds.

We all have "things"—everyday, sentimental, and aesthetic—that we need and value. Some of these things are necessary for this temporal life. I want my life, however, to be centered on things that last eternally.

People will say, "Don't talk to me about eternity; I'm concerned about the here and now." But eternity deserves to be talked about. We are going to be there a long time—forever! I want lost and backslidden people to realize that Jesus is coming back and that the things they place so much value on will be burned up. I want to urge them not to live for what will become ashes.

There are big events ahead. Revelation speaks of natural disasters such as the world has never seen. It speaks of people hiding in caves, calling for the mountains to fall on them so that they can hide from God. It speaks of God's judgment, where everything that is not of eternal value will be burned up. But it also promises the redeemed a new heaven and new earth—a place where we will dwell with God forever.

LIGHTHOUSE THOUGHT FOR THE DAY

God challenges us to focus on what will last for eternity. Let's make sure the things we value will survive the fire.

BOB RICKER

Being a Light to the World

Is it not to share your food with the hungry and to provide the poor wanderer
with shelter—when you see the naked, to clothe him?...
Then your light will break forth like the dawn.

ISAIAH 58:7–8

There's a wonderful old chorus you may have sung as a child: "This little light of mine, I'm gonna let it shine...let it shine, let it shine, let it shine." But what, really, does that mean?

John reminds us that His *"life* was the light" (John 1:4, emphasis added). Wherever Jesus went, whatever He did, and whatever He said was a reflection of His glory. If we each wore a sign that read *I am a light to the world*, would those around us see the light? No. They would truly see light only in the way we live.

Jesus said, "Let your light shine before men, that they may see your good deeds and praise your Father in heaven" (Matthew 5:16). God communicates His message through His followers. *We are the message.* We are a living epistle, a shining star, a fragrant aroma, a beautiful bride, a wise fisherman, a patient farmer, good seed, salt and light.

Perhaps Isaiah can help us grasp what people really see when they see the light. Israel was upset because God did not seem to respond to her worship. Isaiah told Israel that when she fed the hungry, clothed the naked, visited the imprisoned, and cared for her senior citizens, *then* her light would break forth like the dawn...then her righteousness would go before her and the glory of the Lord be her rear guard.

It is interesting to note that you're never specifically told to "evangelize your neighbor"—you're told to "love your neighbor." When love is felt, the message comes through. Your home can be a center of light where needs are met and love is offered.

LIGHTHOUSE THOUGHT FOR THE DAY

May your home circle be an open one...and let it shine till Jesus comes.

JOE ALDRICH

Joy in the Name of Jesus

"Until now you have asked for nothing in My name; ask and you will receive, so that your joy may be made full."

JOHN 16:24, NASB

Christians have an incredible source of joy that people who lived before Jesus came to earth did not have—the name of the Lord Jesus Christ.

Do you realize the magnitude of His name? Philippians 2:9–11 tells us:

> God highly exalted Him, and bestowed on Him the name which is above every name, so that at the name of Jesus every knee will bow, of those who are in heaven and on earth and under the earth, and that every tongue will confess that Jesus Christ is Lord, to the glory of God the Father. (NASB)

This is the name He has freely offered us for our prayers.

It is Jesus' name that we extend to our friends, loved ones, neighbors, and colleagues when we reach out to them from our lighthouses. His is the only name by which any of us can be saved. "For there is no other name under heaven that has been given among men by which we must be saved" (Acts 4:12, NASB).

Jesus said that great joy comes into our hearts when we receive answers to our prayers in His name, and that joy is indescribable when one for whom we pray accepts Him as Lord and Savior. That same joy in the name of Jesus becomes the new convert's when he or she claims Him as his or her Lord and Savior.

That's the kind of joy there is in Jesus' name!

LIGHTHOUSE THOUGHT FOR THE DAY

Pray for all things in the name of the Lord Jesus Christ. There is great power and authority in that name!

EVELYN CHRISTENSON

Greater Than Our Hearts

Let us not love with words or tongue but with actions and in truth. This then is how we know that we belong to the truth, and how we set our hearts at rest in his presence whenever our hearts condemn us. For God is greater than our hearts, and he knows everything.

1 JOHN 3:18–20

I have a friend who feels unworthy of his salvation. He has struggled with doubt, wondering if he is right with God. I have told him that he can find assurance of his salvation in the Scriptures.

The apostle John tells us that our actions reveal whether we are truly saved. While our good works alone do not save us, John tells us that they are evidence of our relationship with God. "We know that we have passed from death to life, because we love our brothers. Anyone who does not love remains in death" (1 John 3:14).

One thing I do when I meet people who need assurance of their salvation is point to this verse and ask them if they love others, particularly their brothers and sisters in Christ. If they can honestly answer yes, then I tell them that that is evidence of their salvation.

My favorite part of this passage is, "God is greater than our hearts, and he knows everything" (v. 20). We should not let our desire for perfection or our oversensitivity rob us of peace with God. He knows everything—including our hearts.

Assurance is found in the Word of God, not in our emotions. The apostle Paul said, "I know that nothing good lives in me, that is, in my sinful nature" (Romans 7:18). This is at the heart of what the believing thief prayed as he hung dying beside Jesus: "'Jesus, remember me when you come into your kingdom.' Jesus answered him, 'I tell you the truth, today you will be with me in paradise'" (Luke 23:42–43).

LIGHTHOUSE THOUGHT FOR THE DAY

Rest in the knowledge that God is greater than your heart and that the assurance of your salvation is found in His Word.

LOWELL LUNDSTROM

Believing Is Receiving

To all who received him, to those who believed in his name,
he gave the right to become children of God.

JOHN 1:12

During an evangelistic meeting, I noticed a young man in a wheelchair. I later learned that he had leukemia. He looked thin, drawn, and pale. Though only in his early thirties, he was physically well on his way to eternity.

He had long ago turned against God, but he came that night with his Christian wife. To her surprise, he listened intently to the message. It seemed evident that the Spirit of God was working in his heart. When I gave the invitation, he was the first one to come forward.

After the meeting this young man said to me, "You know, Palau, all my life I've been blasting God. When I got leukemia, I became even more blasphemous. Tonight I realized that despite my antagonism, God loves me. I want eternal life. Do you think God will forgive me despite the awful things I've said about Him?"

I assured him that God would indeed forgive him, then opened my Bible to the promise from the Lord that "Their sins and lawless acts I will remember no more" (Hebrews 10:17).

No matter what our past has been like, we can receive forgiveness of sins and assurance of eternal life. Decision is the key. We can't wash our hands like Pilate did after Jesus was betrayed. We can't say, "I'll think about it sometime."

What must we do? To receive Jesus, we must make a simple decision: By faith we must accept Jesus' free gift of salvation offered to all of us through His death and resurrection. Believe and receive—it's as simple as that!

LIGHTHOUSE THOUGHT FOR THE DAY

As lighthouses for Jesus, we must share the good news of salvation with others: Receiving Jesus is as simple as accepting by faith His gift of salvation.

LUIS PALAU

Energized Living

But he said to me,…"My power is made perfect in [your] weakness."
2 CORINTHIANS 12:9

Remember the Energizer Bunny? That little pink critter that ran past every obstacle and kept going farther than any of its competitors? That rabbit just never ran out of energy!

Wouldn't it be great to be an Energizer Christian, a believer with all the energy necessary to do good works of God? We can be!

Jesus said that we are to let our light shine for Him (Matthew 5:14) and do the works of God (John 9:4). But producing spiritual light and supernatural works requires a power source. Like a flashlight needs batteries, we need "spiritual batteries." God came to live in us when we were born again, to save us and to energize and empower us. It is in and through us that He displays His strength.

Then why, compared with the early Christians, do we seem to possess so little of God's power? Too many of us don't know how to access it.

A flashlight, even one with good batteries, can't produce light unless it's turned on. As Spirit-filled Christians, we can be "switched on" when we learn to tune into God so closely that His thoughts are our thoughts and His heart our heart. When that happens, His power will be on in our lives.

There is another hindrance to our being light: unconfessed sin. If the electrical contacts in the flashlight become corroded, the current can't flow, and the light won't shine. Unconfessed sin in our lives is a corrosive that prohibits the flow of God's power through us. We must keep our spiritual contacts clean by confessing our sin regularly (1 John 1:9). When we live in this kind of communion with God, He can demonstrate His light and power through us as He chooses.

LIGHTHOUSE THOUGHT FOR THE DAY

Lighthouse Christians must stay in close communion with God, making sure that unconfessed sin doesn't hinder their relationship with Him.

EDDIE AND ALICE SMITH

The Key of Prayer

"O My Father…not as I will, but as You will."
MATTHEW 26:39, NKJV

No heart cry to our heavenly Father can equal Jesus' at Gethsemane. Neither has there been a prayer that has made such a difference in the lives of others, including our own, as the one He prayed at that moment.

It was the kind of prayer that makes a difference in the lives of people, the kind that brings the love of Christ to a dying world. We can pray this way, too.

God designed this kind of prayer to help His children know and do His will, which always involves the salvation of others. The Father's will, centered around the cross, where the redemption of the world was to be won, was the focus of Jesus' prayer at Gethsemane. Jesus knew God's will, and in prayer He submitted Himself to it. He arose from His knees at Gethsemane and followed the Father to the cross, where "God was in Christ reconciling the world to Himself" (2 Corinthians 5:19, NKJV).

There is always a redemptive dimension to prayer because the one who enters the "Most Holy Place" in prayer comes face-to-face with God and His heart for the lost (Hebrews 10:19–23). It is in prayer that God lays His heart over our hearts and waits to hear from us what He heard from His Son: "Not my will, but Yours be done!"

Prayer is often the place where we are moved to witness to specific people and where many of us yield our lives to ministry or missions. The change within us, as we submit our will to Christ, transforms our lives and our witness forever. This may be your experience—today.

LIGHTHOUSE THOUGHT FOR THE DAY

Lighthouses for Jesus Christ will find strength and purpose as they witness, when, in prayer, their own will has been conformed to that of Christ.

HENRY BLACKABY

The Free Gift of Life

"The thief comes only to steal and kill and destroy;
I have come that they may have life, and have it to the full."
JOHN 10:10

Everything God created in the Garden of Eden was accessible to Adam and Eve, save one. The first couple was told not to eat from one tree in the middle of the Garden, because to do so would be sin, and such willful disobedience would surely cause them to die.

Satan, however, questioned the word of God when he said to Eve, "Surely you won't die." Eve was deceived; Adam sinned when he ate from the tree; and together they died. Although physical death is one of the results of the Fall, Adam and Eve didn't immediately die physically. But they died spiritually at the moment they disobeyed, as sin separated them from God.

From that time on, every one of us is born dead in our trespasses and sins (Ephesians 2:1). We are born physically alive—our souls are in union with our bodies. But we are spiritually dead—our souls are separated from God. Only through Jesus Christ can we be made alive and be rejoined to God.

How would you make a dead person alive again? You'd have to remedy the condition that caused him to die. Because "the wages of sin is death" (Romans 6:23), someone had to pay that price: Jesus went to the cross and died for our sins. But that is only half the verse and half the gospel. The second half of the verse reads, "But the gift of God is eternal life." Because of the resurrection, we are made spiritually alive "in Christ" when we are born again. We have, as 2 Peter 1:4 puts it, become partakers of the divine nature because our souls are in union with Him and our bodies are now temples of the living God.

LIGHTHOUSE THOUGHT FOR THE DAY

To shine our lights for Christ, we need to present the message to our neighbors that Jesus came to earth to offer eternal life.

NEIL T. ANDERSON

Don't Give Up—Look Up

Create in me a pure heart, O God, and renew a steadfast spirit within me.
PSALM 51:10

My favorite chapter in the Bible is Psalm 51 because it gives me hope. This chapter assures me that no matter how much I have failed God and fallen short of my own expectations, He is willing to restore me to a position of righteousness.

God knows that we cannot live sinless lives and that we are prone to wander. Yet He welcomes us back with open arms (Luke 15:20). If you feel that your lighthouse witness could improve, Psalm 51 is for you.

As lighthouses for Christ, it is difficult to maintain the prayer-care-and-share model day in and day out. It is easy to get caught up in the daily grind of work and family and forget to pray for those in our neighborhood. A whole week can come and go without us sparing a minute to care for our own families, let alone our neighbors. This is when the tempter says, "Look! You have missed another week. You just don't have what it takes for this lighthouse stuff. Forget it! Leave it to someone who has more time."

But, like the psalmist, you can say, "Renew a steadfast spirit within me." It is not a question of you trying harder to do more. It is a question of God putting the right spirit within you, restoring to you the joy of your salvation, and giving you a willing spirit.

We must recognize that we cannot effectively evangelize in our own strength. Only by recognizing our own weakness and casting ourselves on the mercy of God can we hope to sustain a long-term evangelistic effort.

LIGHTHOUSE THOUGHT FOR THE DAY

Ask God to cleanse you and give you a pure heart. Read Psalm 51 as your own prayer to God. This will make your lighthouse witness effective.

ALI HANNA

Set Apart for a Purpose

But you are a chosen people, a royal priesthood, a holy nation,
a people belonging to God, that you may declare the praises of him who
called you out of darkness into his wonderful light.

1 PETER 2:9

The Bible says that Christians are a peculiar people. While we reside in this world, we are not *of* this world. Christ has chosen us out of the world for a specific purpose.

The great reformer Martin Luther rediscovered for believers what 1 Peter 2:9 points out—the God-given honor of priesthood. We all have the privilege and duty of priesthood in God's kingdom, which means that we have the duty of living exemplary lives and leading others to the Savior, Jesus Christ.

First Peter 2:9 also tells us that God has made us into a holy nation, meaning that He not only expects us to be an upright people, but also that He has set us apart for Himself. We are His sole possession because He purchased us and redeemed us through the atonement of His Son, Jesus Christ.

This is why Jesus declared in Caesarea Philippi, "I will build *my* church" (Matthew 16:18, emphasis added). The church is His. Christ is the head of the church, and the church is His body. The church is to be like Him, bear His image, and follow, love, and serve Him.

With all of this in mind, our task is twofold: evangelize nonbelievers *and* renew believers. We in the body of Christ should seek to bless our communities through praying and caring for and sharing the gospel with our neighbors as well as exhorting and encouraging fellow believers toward spiritual renewal.

LIGHTHOUSE THOUGHT FOR THE DAY

When you make your home or your church a lighthouse for Jesus Christ in your community, you join a nationwide network of people and churches that are committed to being conduits of God's blessing to people around them.

THOMAS WANG

Being Filled

Be filled with the Spirit.... always giving thanks to God the Father for everything, in the name of our Lord Jesus Christ.

EPHESIANS 5:18, 20

Some years ago, a couple traveled from their home in Chicago to Arrowhead Springs to talk to me about an idea they had.

"We heard your lecture on how to be filled with the Holy Spirit. Our lives have been dramatically changed as a result," they said enthusiastically. "We have come to encourage you to go on national television to tell Christians everywhere how they can know the Holy Spirit and experience His revolutionary impact in and through their lives."

I am humbly grateful to God for the privilege of teaching these great truths concerning the Holy Spirit to tens of millions of people throughout the world, often with the same dramatic results this couple enjoyed.

To be effective lighthouses for Jesus Christ, we must be empowered by the Holy Spirit. Without that filling, we will fail miserably in our spiritual lives and accomplish little to reach other people for Christ.

The disciples were good examples of this truth. They were with Jesus for more than three years. They heard Him teach and saw Him perform miracles such as no man had done before. But though they were exposed to the most godly life ever lived on earth, during Jesus' time of crisis, Judas betrayed Him, Peter denied Him, and all the others deserted Him.

Jesus knew His disciples were fruitless, quarreling, ambitious, self-centered men in need of the empowering Holy Spirit. So on the eve of His crucifixion, He told them, "It is to your advantage that I go away; for if I do not go away, the Helper [Holy Spirit] will not come to you; but if I depart, I will send Him to you" (John 16:7, NKJV). Jesus did. The rest is history.

LIGHTHOUSE THOUGHT FOR THE DAY

It is only through the empowering of the Holy Spirit that we can be effective witnesses for our Lord Jesus Christ.

BILL BRIGHT

Bold Believers

Now, Lord, consider their threats and enable your servants
to speak your word with great boldness.
ACTS 4:29

In Acts 4, Peter and John were arrested for standing up in the temple to tell crowds of Jewish people about Jesus. They were dragged before the Sanhedrin, the leadership of the political and religious ruling body. This assembly had the power to torture, imprison, and even execute. They demanded that the two men stop preaching. The intimidation level must have been pretty high! How did Peter and John respond? "Whether it is right in the sight of God to listen to you more than to God, you judge. For we cannot but speak the things which we have seen and heard" (Acts 4:19–20, NKJV).

Peter and John had a simple commitment—to tell others what they knew about Jesus. I believe that they felt fear in the pits of their stomachs as they heard the threats of those leaders, but God granted them the courage to carry on.

What do you need courage from the Lord to do? Perhaps you need holy boldness to speak of Christ to your friend or neighbor who doesn't know Him. Perhaps you need the courage to live for Christ despite the displeasure of an unbelieving spouse or parent. Maybe you need courage to refrain from joining the banter of office gossip. Whatever you need courage for, the Lord will give it.

Jonathan Edwards said, "True boldness for Christ transcends all; it is indifferent to the displeasure of either friends or foes. Boldness enables Christians to forsake all rather than Christ and to prefer to offend all rather than to offend Him." That kind of courage is based on commitment, but it is built by trust and endures through hope and love.

LIGHTHOUSE THOUGHT FOR THE DAY
As committed lighthouses for Jesus Christ, let's be profiles of godly courage so that we may do what He has called us for.

DAVID BRICKNER

Joy for Today

*"Today in the town of David a Savior
has been born to you; he is Christ the Lord."*
LUKE 2:11

Isn't it interesting that the first message from heaven accompanying the birth of the Savior was "good news of great joy"? The announcement was not "good news of great forgiveness," although Jesus came to provide forgiveness. I believe that the inherent message in this declaration is that God wants mankind to know the joy that is part of the salvation He offers through His Son.

This joy is not flimflam or a passing or transitory happiness. It is a deep, abiding, and flowing sense of confidence, certainty, and comfort that comes from knowing your life will realize its intended purpose.

The Savior, our Lord Jesus Christ, brings this joy about. The angel proclaimed this joy to the shepherds because the Savior had been given. And this message is also given specifically to you! As surely as the message came to the shepherds via an angelic voice, it is coming to you today.

Today a Savior has been given. The timing of today is important— this is not a distant or delayed promise. A Savior, a Rescuer, a Deliverer, a Healer has come *today,* and this is the basis for our joy.

The Christmas season is a wonderful time of celebration of the free gift of salvation through Jesus Christ. But we do not need to wait until December 25 to unwrap this gift. It is available for us each and every day!

LIGHTHOUSE THOUGHT FOR THE DAY

There is nothing our world needs more than to be touched by joy. As lighthouses for the Lord Jesus Christ, we can know this joy and pass it on to those around us every day.

JACK HAYFORD

Love in Action

Dear children, let us not love with words or tongue
but with actions and in truth.

1 JOHN 3:18

The poet Robert Burns said, "The heart that is benevolent and kind most resembles God." And so it is. Love (benevolence) is one of the fruits of the Spirit; kindness is another. Kindness is actually love—the kind of love that expresses itself not merely in words or with the tongue, but in action and in truth.

Henry Ward Beecher was an example of a kind person. It was once said that no one ever felt the full force of his kindness until that person did Beecher an injury. What a commentary of authentic love in action.

As children, many of us learned the verse of Scripture that says, "Be kind and compassionate to one another, forgiving each other, just as in Christ God forgave you" (Ephesians 4:32). That verse describes the very Spirit of Jesus, and it offers a model for us to follow as well.

Most of us have neighbors or associates at work or classmates at school who are special challenges. Some have hurt us or even made the effort to slander us or make our lives difficult. It is natural to want to retaliate or at least withdraw from them.

But those people that treat us unkindly or unfairly are the people who most desperately need our love and kindness. They need the love that flows from a Spirit-filled life—the unconditional love of Jesus. That is Christian caring at its very best. It is love in action.

LIGHTHOUSE THOUGHT FOR THE DAY

Caring for others as Jesus did includes reaching out from our homes with love and kindness to all those around us, even those who are critical or difficult.

PAUL CEDAR

"I Have Need"

My God will meet all your needs according to
his glorious riches in Christ Jesus.

PHILIPPIANS 4:19

If there is one qualification for being a light for Jesus, it's true discipleship. The first step toward true discipleship is humility, and the first step toward humility is admitting that we need more of God. Thus, honesty about our need for God is the beginning of true discipleship.

In our desire to know and serve almighty God, we must understand this: He resists the proud but showers His grace upon the humble (James 4:6). Grace is God's promise to do for us what we cannot do for ourselves, and humility brings His grace to us. Humility is the foundation of transformation, the essence of all other godly virtues.

At some phase in our Christian lives, the Holy Spirit will confront and expose the impurities of our hearts. The spirit of truth will reveal our sin, not to condemn us, but to establish humility and to show us our need for grace.

It is at this crossroads of self-discovery that both holy people and hypocrites are made. Those who become holy see their need for deliverance from sin and fall prostrate before God. Those who become hypocrites excuse their sin and thus remain unchanged. Though all humans eventually stand at this junction, few embrace the voice of truth and walk humbly toward true spiritual maturity.

Consider John the Baptist's revelation as he gazed at the purity of Christ. John humbly declared, "I have need to be baptized by You" (Matthew 3:14, NASB). Those who have not seen Jesus can't see how spiritually impoverished they are. But those who have truly beheld God's Son have but one reaction: "I have need."

LIGHTHOUSE THOUGHT FOR THE DAY

To be effective lighthouses for Jesus Christ, we must humbly recognize our need for His grace in our lives.

FRANCIS FRANGIPANE

Assurance of His Presence

"Do not fear, for I am with you; do not be dismayed, for I am your God.
I will strengthen you and help you."
ISAIAH 41:10

I was reaching up for bottom. It was my senior year at Baylor University, and a flu epidemic had hit the campus. I was one of many to attend class that day with a high fever. To make matters worse, a storm had drenched the area, and I had to wade through waist-deep floodwaters to get to class.

But that was not the worst of it. My wife had just undergone surgery for a terminal illness, but she was no better. She grew weaker daily.

About that time, my mother wrote me a tender, encouraging letter asking me to read Isaiah 41:10. I was caught in my own world of misery and grief, but somehow that verse penetrated my mind and became a treasure during the helpless months ahead as I watched Betty die.

"Fear not!" God said. *Why shouldn't I be afraid?* I thought. *My wife is dying, and my future is uncertain.*

"Fear not, for I am with you."

God, I don't feel like You are within a million miles of me!

Then God seemed to say, "I AM with you when you feel like it and when you don't. I am with you always. Do not be discouraged."

Why shouldn't I feel discouraged? I'm losing my wife! I have a little boy! You called me to preach. What church would want a single-parent pastor?

The answer came, "For I am your God. I will strengthen you and help you."

That is what I needed. Not for Him to fix every problem, but to assure me of His presence.

LIGHTHOUSE THOUGHT FOR THE DAY
When we know God is with us, His light shines brightly in us, no matter what our situation.

DARRELL ROBINSON

The Witness of the Bible

He chose to give us birth through the word of truth, that we might be a kind of firstfruits of all he created.

James 1:18

A certificate of ownership is a written document verifying that something of value belongs to its owner. It specifies what the item is and to whom it belongs.

God has given His children a certificate of ownership of sorts—the Bible. God's own written Word spells out for us in detail the assurance of salvation we have through the Lord Jesus Christ.

The apostle Paul wrote, "That if thou shalt confess with thy mouth the Lord Jesus, and shalt believe in thine heart that God hath raised him from the dead, thou shalt be saved" (Romans 10:9, KJV).

And Jesus said, "Behold, I stand at the door, and knock: if any man hear my voice, and open the door, I will come in to him, and will sup with him, and he with me" (Revelation 3:20, KJV). Our Lord also said, "Verily, verily, I say unto you, He that heareth my word, and believeth on him that sent me, hath everlasting life, and shall not come into condemnation; but is passed from death unto life" (John 5:24, KJV).

The witness of the Bible makes it clear that if you accept Jesus Christ as Lord and Savior, God will give you everlasting life. His promises are absolutely certain. What God asks of you is a positive act of your will, and if you have done what God asks, you have every right to believe that He has given you what He promised.

The promises of God are sure and eternal. The Word of God is forever settled in heaven. The reality of your salvation is recorded in God's Word.

LIGHTHOUSE THOUGHT FOR THE DAY

Our assurance of salvation is recorded for eternity in the Bible. We can say with confidence, as can those we lead to the Lord Jesus Christ, that we are His for eternity.

Pat Robertson

Giving Comfort

"'Love the Lord your God with all your heart...'
and, 'Love your neighbor as yourself.'"
LUKE 10:27

The organ burst forth with music, and the people filed out of the large church auditorium where I had just preached. As the sanctuary emptied, I began to think about the needs, hurts, and struggles of the people who had just listened to my message.

How many of those people were leaving with broken hearts? How many parents had unmanageable children? How many children had intolerable parents? Which of these couples was on the verge of divorce? Who among them was struggling with unconquerable addictions? How many had recently lost their jobs or suffered the death of a loved one? How many of them were enduring something grievous?

Sadly, there were many here today who are suffering, I thought.

Every Sunday morning thousands of people in our neighborhoods, cities, and nation come to church, where they sing, give their money, and listen to a sermon. Then they leave, bearing the same hurts and struggles they brought in with them. Where are they to receive ministry and comfort related to their felt needs?

From us, that's where!

Most adults in my congregation have been trained to minister in teams at the end of each service. At the conclusion of each service, people in need can come to be ministered to and prayed for that day and during the week. This is how the church should work—praying for and caring for those in need.

LIGHTHOUSE THOUGHT FOR THE DAY

The body of Christ should be a source of comfort and ministry to those within the church and to those outside its walls. This is at the heart of Christ's command that we "love our neighbors."

EDDIE SMITH

The Three Phases of Prayer

*"For everyone who asks receives; he who seeks finds; and
to him who knocks, the door will be opened."*

MATTHEW 7:8

At Oxford University three statues stand side by side. The first figure is seated with head in hands, thinking of things eternal. The second is kneeling with hands clasped and arms outstretched toward heaven. The third figure stands erect, with shield and sword, ready to do battle. They represent the three key aspects of prayer: solidarity, advocacy, and pursuit.

The seated statue demonstrates that part of intercession is coming into agreement with God, pondering what He wants, and then desiring it with Him—*solidarity* with God. The kneeling figure represents our pleading with the Father on behalf of situations or people where others will not or cannot pray—*advocating* for them to God. The third figure represents God calling us into battle to press His purposes forward with unflagging zeal until we see accomplished what He has burdened us to pray for. This is where *pursuing* prayer takes over.

Jesus highlights these intensifying paces of intercession when He talks about "asking," agreeing with God and wanting it with Him; "seeking," when, like a lawyer, we seek God's best on behalf of others; and "knocking"— clearly the most aggressive and the most demanding of the three—when we're in pursuit of answers.

As you pray daily for those around you, watch how the Spirit brings you into these different phases, tailoring your prayer to match the situations and people God has given you to care for in prayer.

LIGHTHOUSE THOUGHT FOR THE DAY

The Holy Spirit must design the prayer life of a Christian. Start with solidarity prayer, and let God take you on from there. No matter what the phase, the issue is to keep at it—asking, seeking, and knocking.

DAVID BRYANT

Keep Sowing

*Then he told them many things in parables, saying: "A farmer went out to
sow his seed. As he was scattering the seed, some fell along the path,
and the birds came and ate it up."*

MATTHEW 13:3–4

One of Jesus' favorite teaching tools was the parable. When He told the
Parable of the Sower, one of His most recognizable stories, His emphasis was on the seed, but let's take a moment and look at the sower.

In this parable the sower was doing what good farmers do; he was
scattering seeds. On the surface it appears that this sower wasn't very
careful where he scattered his seed. Some of the seed landed on the
path, and the birds came and ate it. That seed, apart from fattening our
feathered friends, didn't achieve much. Even more of the seed went to
waste: "Other seed fell among thorns, which grew up and choked the
plants" (Matthew 13:7).

Despite his failures, the sower was not disheartened. He didn't
measure his worth based on the results of his seed scattering. He knew
the seed was in God's hands. He just kept on sowing, right and left, letting the seed fall where it might. Finally there was success: "Still other
seed fell on good soil, where it produced a crop—a hundred, sixty or
thirty times what was sown" (Matthew 13: 8).

Remember that God is in control of everything, including the harvest. He works through His Spirit to bring people to Himself. All He
asks of us is to sow the seed of the gospel by sharing our faith with
those around us.

LIGHTHOUSE THOUGHT FOR THE DAY

As lighthouses for Jesus Christ, it is not our job to worry about the
fruits of our labor. Our job is to obediently sow the seeds of the gospel
of Jesus Christ and let God reap the harvest.

ALI HANNA

A Heart for the Harvest

*"Whoever serves me must follow me; and where I am,
my servant also will be. My Father will honor the one who serves me."*
JOHN 12:26

If the Holy Scriptures teach us anything about the Lord Jesus Christ, they teach us that His heart was always toward the harvest. He did not give His life on that terrible cross for fame, career, houses, cars, a better degree, or for sport. The Lord Jesus Christ poured Himself out completely at Calvary *for people.*

Jesus Christ lived and died to serve people, and as lights in the world for Him, we are to do the same. Being a lighthouse for Christ means having a passion for Jesus and compassion for those who have not yet come to know the wonder of a relationship with Him.

In his letters, the apostle Paul often called himself a "servant of Jesus Christ." Since I became a Christian, I have been convicted to use that very phrase to describe my relationship with the Lord.

The servant of Jesus Christ follows the Lord's example of love and compassion toward people by living a life that demonstrates practical and sacrificial ways to care for them. To serve Christ and others by being a culture-changing lighthouse for Jesus involves focusing on others and denying self (Matthew 16:24). That is Jesus' command, and it is the example He set for us in His every word and action.

Is that the kind of life you lead? Do your words and actions demonstrate a heart that is toward the harvest—toward people? Are you living to please and honor Christ in all you do and say?

So many people give themselves to acquiring possessions and power, but as lighthouses our lives should radiate the joy and love of Jesus Christ. We should have a heart for God's harvest!

LIGHTHOUSE THOUGHT FOR THE DAY

Our hearts need to be focused on the same thing Jesus' heart was focused on—seeing people come to the kingdom of God. That is what serving Christ is all about!

JARVIS WARD

Your First Love

> *"You have left your first love. Therefore remember from where you have fallen, and repent and do the deeds you did at first."*
>
> REVELATION 2:4–5, NASB

The ascended Jesus must have shocked the faithful, spiritually discerning, and hardworking church members at Ephesus when He sent word through the exiled John for them to repent. Why did He warn them to remember from where they had fallen and to do the deeds they did at first? Because they had left their first love.

What is this "first love" Jesus talked about? It's that love and zeal for Christ the Ephesians had felt when they first began following Him. It's that excitement, exuberance, and all-engulfing thrill we feel when we first fall in love with the Savior!

The Ephesian believers had not lost their first love by doing evil things. On the contrary, they were doing good things (Revelation 2:2–3). The problem was that they had substituted scripturally correct works for that first love that had initially motivated them to tell others about the Messiah.

Speaking on this passage in Brazil, I reminisced about my love and zeal for Jesus when I first accepted Him at age nine. I told about how I sat in a church pew every Sunday night—gritting my teeth and clenching my fists—praying for the unsaved loved ones and neighbors we had brought to the service. I prayed like that for weeks and months until they responded to the pastor's invitation to accept Jesus.

When I finished speaking, the Brazilian pastor gave an invitation to all who would pray and reach others for Jesus. As they surged forward, I began to weep. God was saying to me, "How long has it been since *you* have gritted your teeth and clenched your fists over a lost soul?"

LIGHTHOUSE THOUGHT FOR THE DAY

O Jesus, come! We remember our first love, and we repent. Please fill us anew with our first love and our zeal for You as we reach out from our lighthouses.

EVELYN CHRISTENSON

Cleaning Your Lens

"If therefore your eye is [clear], your whole body will be full of light."
MATTHEW 6:22, NKJV

For decades lighthouse keepers on the New England coast have had a wide variety of responsibilities, one of which is regularly cleaning the lenses of the lamps.

Dust, residue from candles, bugs, and assorted debris have a way of covering and dulling the clarity and brightness of the lenses. Even the slightest amount of dust on the lens can make a vast difference in what men several miles out at sea can view.

Likewise, Christians are urged to keep their spiritual eyes clear.

First of all, we are exhorted to be "made new in the attitude of [our] minds" (Ephesians 4:23). Living in a world so darkened by sin and selfishness has a way of affecting and infecting our minds and hearts. Our "lenses" get covered with spiritual debris, and this affects not only what we see in life, but also the *way* we see it. Reading the Bible daily renews our minds (Romans 12:1–2) and cleans the lenses of our hearts.

Secondly, we are exhorted to set no "vile thing" before our eyes (Psalm 101:3). In an age in which our lives are full of daily invitations to look at things God considers vile and corrupting, we need wisdom. A visual diet full of sinful images will dull our view of God. This will affect our behavior and, as a result, our witness for Him.

Finally, Paul says that the "eyes" of our hearts need to be opened up by God Himself: "I pray...that the eyes of your heart may be enlightened in order that you may know the hope to which he has called you...." (Ephesians 1:18) We must have a clear vision of God's will for our lives if we are to convey His love and light to a lost world.

LIGHTHOUSE THOUGHT FOR THE DAY

As your eyes are opened to see God more clearly, the eyes of others will be opened to see Him in you.

ROBERT C. CROSBY

For the Love of the Son

"If anyone loves Me, he will keep My word; and My Father will love him, and We will come to him and make Our abode with him."

JOHN 14:23, NASB

Our heavenly Father is absolutely passionate about our loving Jesus Christ and being wholly devoted to Him. Why is this?

The answer can be seen in the life that Jesus led. His heart was completely obedient and submissive to His Father's will, and he reveled in His dependence upon the Father. Jesus completely abandoned Himself to a singular objective: that His Father be glorified. To Him, the Cross was but one more way of expressing His love to His Father.

The Father's response to Jesus' life of obedience is the passion to see the Son loved. The Father is singularly devoted to His desire to see that every man and woman who has ever drawn breath honor His Son—indeed every knee shall bow and every tongue shall confess that Jesus Christ is Lord (Romans 14:11).

Laying hold of this truth should evoke in us not a sense of insignificance, but of privilege—the privilege of being a yielded vessel in league with Him for His divine purpose. This is not to say that the Father has no thought of us as individuals, or that He merely wants to use us for His pleasure. Jesus said that the Father loves those who are Christ's. In fact, the apostle John tells us that God is love and that everything He does is motivated by love (1 John 4:8–10).

In the same way, if we are completely sold out in our love for Jesus Christ, if this whole thing we call our existence is all about Him, then our every word and every action will be motivated by that love.

LIGHTHOUSE THOUGHT FOR THE DAY

As we endeavor to touch people for Christ, we must be motivated by our devotion and love for Him. If Christ is the singular focus, we will bear fruit for the kingdom.

STEVE FRY

Prayer for All People

"'My house will be called a house of prayer for all nations.'"
MARK 11:17

Have you ever wondered why Jesus became so violent when He cleared the temple? Why did He overturn tables? Why wouldn't He allow people to carry their goods through the temple courts?

Notice that Jesus quotes Isaiah as He clears the temple, "My house will be called a house of prayer for all nations" (Isaiah 56:7). We tend to emphasize the first part of the verse: "My house will be called a house of prayer," but the context of Isaiah 56 is that *outsiders* will be drawn to the Lord's house. Perhaps our emphasis should be on the second part: *all nations.*

Indeed, outsiders were coming to offer sacrifices of worship. But the religious establishment of Jesus' time declared their sacrifices unworthy and demanded that they exchange them for sacrifices the religious leaders provided.

Within a few days, Jesus went to the cross to lay down His life so that we can announce to a lost world, "The way to God is open!" Yet the house that bore His name had erected barriers to keep people away.

The same thing happens today. We in the modern-day church take part in religious practices that keep people away from church. Outsiders often feel unworthy or uncomfortable joining us in worship. However, Jesus' passion for all people to come to God is still the same. Prayer, worship, and God's Word must be available to *all* people.

Today, Jesus may not be overturning tables in the church, but He is certainly tearing down the walls that keep us isolated from our neighbors. He is mobilizing His church to take His Word to people who otherwise might not come to church.

LIGHTHOUSE THOUGHT FOR THE DAY

Your neighbors may be among those turned away from the house of prayer. Reassure them that they are of great value to God.

TOM PELTON

Called by God

"Come, follow me," Jesus said, "and I will make you fishers of men."
MATTHEW 4:19

I will never forget the sense of calling I felt during my devotions that first morning as a new pastor. I recognized that God had given me that mission field to labor in and that it was to be my place of service until He called me to move on. God gave me an understanding that my mission field was filled with needs and struggles and, more importantly, with souls He had died to save. From that morning on, I passionately served Him with that deep sense of calling.

Jesus called the disciples to be "fishers of men," and that calling applies to us, too. Today, He is calling each of us to a particular mission field. The people around us on a daily basis (our circle of influence) are not there by chance. God brings people into our lives so that we can shepherd them closer to eternal life through a personal relationship with Christ. We can do this by praying for them, caring for them in any way we can, and by verbally sharing the Good News of the gospel with them.

This is a wonderful privilege as well as an awesome responsibility. It is our calling from God, our purpose for being here on this earth, and the thing God promises to empower and equip us to do.

Let's recognize this calling; then let's serve passionately, knowing that we are doing the will of our heavenly Father.

LIGHTHOUSE THOUGHT FOR THE DAY

The people in our circle of influence are our "mission field." We are called to reach out to them. Let's approach our mission to bring Christ to them as not just an awesome responsibility, but an incredible privilege.

DALLAS ANDERSON

Lifestyle Evangelism

Whoever is thirsty…let him take the free gift of the water of life.
REVELATION 22:17

I like the term *lifestyle evangelism*. To me it means making my life—my words and my actions—a witness to those around me. I believe that if we truly love Christ and the lost souls around us, evangelism will come naturally. It won't be a duty, but something that flows out of us because of our relationship with Jesus.

The Bible tells us that when someone comes to Christ, it is because the Holy Spirit has drawn that person to Him. The Spirit of God works through our lives and our witness to bring people to an awareness of the Savior. What a privilege it is to be a part of that!

I grew up in a home and church where there was great emphasis on witnessing for Jesus. My parents lived with passion for the lost. Our church had evangelistic meetings in the spring and fall. I remember people walking the aisle to receive Christ. I remember the prayers, the tears, and the people repenting and being baptized and later bringing family members one by one to a saving knowledge of Christ.

I've never lost my desire to see people come to Jesus, starting with my neighbors. Our neighbors are important to my wife and me. We have a growing catalog of experiences together, some of which still touch our hearts today. By the power of the Holy Spirit, we do our best to let our words and actions show Jesus to our neighbors. In other words, we try to put lifestyle evangelism into practice.

Evangelism is one of the reasons we are here on earth. Christ expects that "you will be my witnesses" (Acts 1:8), and it is His commission to us to "go and make disciples" (Matthew 28:19). Let's do what we are here for.

LIGHTHOUSE THOUGHT FOR THE DAY

When we know Jesus, our lives have purpose, and that is to shine His light on those around us.

BOB RICKER

A Sense of Identity

For we are God's workmanship, created in Christ Jesus to do good works, which God prepared in advance for us to do.

EPHESIANS 2:10

Who are you? This sounds like a simple question, but the answers people give often reveal a very shallow perception of their existence. Some may give their names in response to the question, but names don't tell us who a person is. Other answers are "I'm an American" (one's nationality), "I'm an engineer" (one's occupation), or "I'm a Baptist" (one's church). Some may venture a little deeper and use their character traits (smart, personable, or honest) to tell us who they are.

Most people get at least some of their identity from their physical and cultural heritage or their vocation. But what happens to their identity when they leave home, change locations, or lose their job? They may feel as though they've lost who they are.

Christians find their identity in Christ. The Bible tells us, "You are all sons of God through faith in Christ Jesus" (Galatians 3:26) and "The Spirit Himself bears witness with our spirit that we are children of God" (Romans 8:16, NKJV).

According to the apostle John, knowing who we are affects how we live: "See how great a love the Father has bestowed on us, that we would be called children of God; and such we are. For this reason the world does not know us, because it did not know Him. Beloved, now we are children of God, and it has not appeared as yet what we will be. We know that when He appears, we will be like Him, because we will see Him just as He is. And everyone who has this hope fixed on Him purifies himself, just as He is pure" (1 John 3:1–3, NASB).

LIGHTHOUSE THOUGHT FOR THE DAY

As children of God, we know who we are. Share Jesus Christ and the peace and identity that come with belonging to Him with your neighbors today.

NEIL T. ANDERSON

If You Knew Him...

Jesus answered her, "If you knew the gift of God and who it is that asks you for a drink, you would have asked him and he would have given you living water."

JOHN 4:10

If you were a sailor severely afflicted with scurvy, and a generous man came aboard ship with his pockets bulging with vitamin C and asked you for an orange slice, you might give it to him. But if you knew he was generous, and that he carried all you needed to be well, you would turn the tables and ask him for help.

Jesus says to the woman, "If you just knew the gift of God and who I am, you would ask Me—you would pray to Me!" There is a direct correlation between not knowing Jesus well and not asking much from Him. A failure in our prayer life is generally a failure to know Jesus. "If you knew who was talking to you, you would ask Me!" A prayerless Christian is like a bus driver trying alone to push his bus out of a rut because he doesn't know Clark Kent is on board. "If you knew, you would ask." A prayerless Christian is like a person wallpapering his room with Sak's Fifth Avenue gift certificates but always shopping at Ragstock because he can't read. "If you knew the gift of God and who it is that speaks to you, you would ask—*you would ask!*"

And the implication is that those who do ask—Christians who spend time in prayer—do it because they see that God is the great Giver and that Christ is wise and merciful and powerful beyond measure. And therefore their prayer glorifies Christ and honors His Father. The chief end of man is to glorify God. Therefore, when we become what God created us to be, we become people of prayer.

LIGHTHOUSE THOUGHT FOR THE DAY

Since God is the great Giver and we are so needy, we should ask for what we need. He will get the glory, and we will get the joy.

JOHN PIPER, WITH JUSTIN TAYLOR

Modern Communication

Oh, the depth of the riches both of the wisdom and knowledge of God!
How unsearchable are His judgments and unfathomable His ways!
ROMANS 11:33, NASB

Are we in danger of replacing the most important method of communication in the universe?

My head whirls as I try to assimilate all the current methods of communication: the Internet, e-mail, chat rooms, cell phones. Faxes were supposed to be the answer to snail mail and even next-day mail. Now my computer can write out my words for me as I talk into it. By the time you read this, there will probably be several more communication innovations.

Yes, we have learned how to communicate. But because we receive from these sources only what others want us to receive, some of that communication might be truth, and some of it might be fiction.

There is a vastly more important—and more reliable—realm of information transfer that requires a different kind of communication skill: listening to God! He tells us those things no human being could ever know. He unerringly gives us the answers to life's problems, clearly shows us right from wrong, and safely guides us into our unknown future—which He alone knows. God is the only one who always speaks truth, always is honest, never is prejudiced, and never makes a mistake.

However, God speaking to us won't help if we don't listen. If our communication lines are jammed with an incessant flow of human input, we cannot hear God's voice. To hear God in prayer and in His Word takes quiet listening.

LIGHTHOUSE THOUGHT FOR THE DAY
What percentage of time do you think the average Christian spends listening to God through prayer and Bible study? What about you?

EVELYN CHRISTENSON

Moving Your Mountain

"Have faith in God."…"If anyone says to this mountain, 'Go, throw yourself into the sea,' and does not doubt in his heart…it will be done for him."

MARK 11:22–23

If you are facing a mountain of a problem—for example, something that hinders you from sharing the love of God with your neighbors—you can look to this passage, where Jesus gives three steps to removing that mountain. They are as follows:

1. *Have faith in God.* Energize your heart, mind, and soul with living confidence in God. Trust our heavenly Father.
2. *Speak to your mountain.* Tell your problem that God is greater than it is, that He has handled situations like this before, and that you will not be the victim, but the victor.
3. *Do not doubt.* Be on guard. Aggressively defend your faith. Don't allow fear to rush in and rob you of your faith in God. Declare aloud that God is faithful and that He knows what is best for you.

Hebrews 11 lists the heroes of faith who lived and died trusting God. Some were delivered from their troubles and persecutions, and others were not. But one thing is certain about these brave warriors of God: They were not passive. They stood firm in their faith, and they spoke boldly to their mountains. They refused to act cowardly in conflict, and they were rewarded for their courage. The Bible says of these heroes, "These were all commended for their faith" (v. 39).

These people should inspire us to be bold in our faith. They are examples to us of what it takes to move mountains for God.

LIGHTHOUSE THOUGHT FOR THE DAY

What kind of mountains do you face today? Prayerfully apply the principles our Lord spelled out in Mark 11, and watch those mountains move!

LOWELL LUNDSTROM

Spiritual Roots

> *Be wise in the way you act toward outsiders; make the most of*
> *every opportunity. Let your conversation be always full of grace,*
> *seasoned with salt, so that you may know how to answer everyone.*
>
> COLOSSIANS 4:5–6

In the highly acclaimed television miniseries *Roots*, there was a moving scene in which Kizzy explained to her son why she was not going to marry Sam. She said, "No one ever told Sam where he come from, so he never had a dream of where he ought to be going."

Some Christians seem to face that same challenge when it comes to sharing their faith with others. They live as though they have no concept of their spiritual roots.

It should not be so. All of us who have turned to Jesus as Savior and are seeking to follow Him as Lord should be able to articulate where we are coming from and where we are going. It can be a natural, wonderful thing to share simply and sincerely our own personal testimony of how we came to follow Jesus.

Explaining where we are going should be an exciting privilege, as we tell others about the wonderful gift of eternal life we have received through Jesus Christ—and that this invaluable gift is available to them. That is "Good News" in the best sense of the term.

Someone has said that such witnessing to others is simply like one beggar sharing a piece of bread with another. That's what we can do through our lighthouses. We can have the joy of sharing with our neighbors and friends, spontaneously and naturally, "What God has done for me, He can do for you!"

LIGHTHOUSE THOUGHT FOR THE DAY

Sharing our spiritual roots with others as the Lord gives us opportunity can be a wonderful gift of love and blessing.

PAUL CEDAR

The Key of Obedience

"If you love Me, keep My commandments."
JOHN 14:15, NKJV

Jesus told His disciples that obedience—practicing everything He commanded—would bring life-changing responses from both Him and the Father, namely that He would come and make His permanent home with them, that He would love them, and that He would manifest (show clearly) Himself to them.

Jesus insisted that the disciples "hear from Him" so they could know clearly what He commanded. This required that they be with Him and listen carefully to Him. His words were to be their very lives, and they were to diligently "keep"—obey, put into practice, and make a way of life—every word He spoke. Christ's response to the disciples rested on what they did with His words.

It is the same for us. Christ commands every disciple to spend time with Him and to hear and obey immediately and thoroughly all He tells us to do. Those who never take the time to know our Lord or what He is saying cannot obey Him and will miss out on the daily unfolding of God's love. On the other hand, those who hear the Lord but do not obey Him will likewise never know what God's love could bring them. Jesus said that the disobedient person does not love Him, and He added that this is how His Father sees it too (John 14:24).

As disciples and as lighthouses for Christ, we need to commit ourselves afresh to spending quality time in God's presence—in His Word and in prayer—and to being obedient to all He reveals to us during that time. Our lives and eternal destinies depend on it, as do the lives and eternal destinies of those around us.

LIGHTHOUSE THOUGHT FOR THE DAY

If we want to be lighthouses for Jesus Christ, we will seek out His commands and joyfully obey them, knowing that obedience is the key to doing anything for God.

HENRY BLACKABY

Caring Because He Cares

Cast all your anxiety on him because he cares for you.
1 PETER 5:7

A certain shoeshine boy worked in a train station in a large city. He would cry out to commuters as they disembarked, offering a quick shine. One cold day he was accidentally knocked over by the rush of the crowd. His polish and rags flew in all directions. Most of the people hurried past. But one gentleman stopped to help him pick things up. When he finished, he actually gave the boy a few dollars to help replenish the money that had been lost in the scuffle.

When he turned to leave, the boy called, "Sir, are you Jesus?"

"Of course not," the man said, embarrassed. "Why do you ask?"

"Well, sir," the response came, "Once I went to Sunday school and heard what Jesus was like. And I just thought maybe that's who you was."

"Praying, caring, and sharing" is the triad of the lighthouse lifestyle. All of these elements are vital to lighthouse ministry, but let's focus briefly on the middle of the three. Nothing will draw people's attention to Jesus more than caring for them freely.

Caring is a quality Jesus demonstrated beautifully in every way. No one has given more of himself than our Lord did. It was His caring that helped make Him so popular with the masses. Today, it is still His caring—through us—that will make Him attractive to the world.

Christians can rest confidently in the fact that God cares for us. That's why Peter could encourage his readers to cast all their anxieties on Him. He first cared for us, which marks us as His children. Christians should stand out to this world simply because we demonstrate a loving concern for those around us.

LIGHTHOUSE THOUGHT FOR THE DAY

Being compassionate toward people is a good way to acquaint others to our Lord and Savior. Prayer-care-and-share—it's at the core of the lighthouse lifestyle.

DAVID MAINS

The Big Choice

"Here I am! I stand at the door and knock. If you hear my voice and
open the door, I will come in and eat with you, and you will eat with me."
REVELATION 3:20, NCV

Jesus gives this invitation. To know God is to receive His invitation. Not just to hear it, not just to study it, not just to acknowledge it, but to receive it. It is possible to learn much about God's invitation and never respond to it personally.

Yet His invitation is clear and nonnegotiable. He gives all and we give Him all. Simple and absolute. He is clear in what He asks and clear in what He offers. The choice is up to us.

Isn't it incredible that God leaves the choice up to us? Think about it. There are many things in life we can't choose. We can't, for example, choose the weather. We can't control the economy.

We can't choose whether or not we are born with a big nose or blue eyes or a lot hair. We can't even choose how people respond to us.

But we can choose where we spend eternity. The big choice, God leaves to us. The critical decision is ours.

What are you doing with God's invitation? What are you doing with His personal request that you live with Him forever?

That is the only decision that really matters. Whether or not you take the job transfer is not critical. Whether or not you buy a new car is not crucial. What college you choose or what profession you select is important, but not compared to where you spend eternity. That is the decision you will remember.

What are you doing with His invitation?

LIGHTHOUSE THOUGHT FOR THE DAY

No decision we—or our neighbors—ever make will match the importance of what we do with God's invitation. That one decision determines where we spend eternity: in God's presence or separated from Him forever.

MAX LUCADO

Taking the Right Seat

*God, who is rich in mercy, made us alive with Christ even when we were
dead in transgressions—it is by grace you have been saved....
God raised us up with Christ and seated us with him
in the heavenly realms in Christ Jesus.*

EPHESIANS 2:4–6

"Will all passengers please take their seats!"

This is a frequently heard announcement on the intercom of commercial airline flights.

God makes a similar announcement to each of us because, as the Bible tells us, we have a reserved seat with Christ in the heavenly realm. Taking that seat is the key to our effectiveness in every form of ministry, particularly that of prayer.

The difference between the airline announcement and God's invitation is that He invites us to come to the cockpit and be seated *next to* the Captain. We are actually seated *with* Christ, who shares His position and authority with us. We actually join Him in what He is doing!

A seat in the heavenly realm is where the action is. It is where all spiritual battles are either won or lost. God tells us in Ephesians 6:12 that our battle is not with flesh and blood but with the spiritual forces of evil in the heavenly places.

The seat next to Christ is a place of rest. Resting in His completed victory is essential if we are to have strength to fight every battle. When we rest, we cease from our striving and allow God to do good works for and through us (Hebrews 4:10). We are also seated in a place of adequacy. God has made us able ministers. All things are already ours in Christ because we are joint heirs with Him.

LIGHTHOUSE THOUGHT FOR THE DAY

As a lighthouse for Jesus, Christ's authority is yours today, to wield in prayer and purposeful ministry. You have the power in Christ to fight the spiritual forces of evil.

JIM HYLTON

Prayer and Warfare

> *Through the gospel the Gentiles are heirs together with Israel, members together of one body, and sharers together in the promise in Christ Jesus.*
>
> EPHESIANS 3:6

We are living in a time of intense intercessory prayer and spiritual warfare within the body of Christ. As a result, the Holy Spirit is moving in our own lives and in our families, neighborhoods, and nations as God opens His arms wide to change hearts and welcome prodigals home.

Those involved in this explosion of prayer and warfare have seen a true merging of different streams in the body of Christ as God establishes His purposes and fulfills His promises. Our Father is the sovereign, holy God of Israel, and He keeps His covenants with His people. And, just as He promised, He is establishing and growing the body of Christ worldwide.

How is He doing these things? Through the obedience of His people, the church!

God has called us as lighthouses for Jesus Christ to go to spiritual battle on behalf of those within our spheres of influence. We should find joy in being called to take part in what God is doing today.

As Christians, the mainspring of our existence must be devotion to our precious Lord and Savior. From that devotion comes obedience to His calling to join the battle as prayer warriors for Him. When we do that, He will release all power from heaven so that we can carry out His plan by praying for the salvation of those around us, then personally sharing the Word of God with them.

LIGHTHOUSE THOUGHT FOR THE DAY

Lighthouses for Christ—*our* houses—are to be houses of intercessory prayer and spiritual warfare on behalf of those who need to know Jesus as their Lord and Savior.

BOBBYE BYERLY

Wearing the Uniform

He poured water into a basin and began to wash his disciples' feet,
drying them with the towel that was wrapped around him.

JOHN 13:5

God sends His children into the world to shine light on the kingdom of darkness. "You are my servant, Israel, in whom I will display my splendor.... I will also make you a light for the Gentiles, that you may bring my salvation to the ends of the earth" (Isaiah 49:3, 6).

Jesus incarnates Himself through His bride, the church. Peering down through the corridors of time, John describes the great wedding feast of the Lamb: "'Let us rejoice and be glad and give him the glory! For the wedding of the Lamb [Christ] has come, and his bride has made herself ready. Fine linen, bright and clean, was given her to wear.' (Fine linen stands for the righteous acts of the saints)" (Revelation 19:7–8). Jesus modeled the garment that brings blessings and fruitfulness to those who wear it. While His disciples were debating who was the greatest, the Greatest took off his robe, girded Himself with a towel, and got about the business of washing feet. The towel was there. The water was ready, the basin full. But there were no volunteers among the disciples. No servants. No one willing to perform "acts of righteousness."

None of us is wired to be a servant. Neither were the disciples. But Jesus told His followers that if they served others, God's blessing would be upon them. Paul links his success in ministry to his servant heart: "For though I am free from all men, I have made myself a servant to all, that I might win the more. (1 Corinthians 9:19, NKJV).

LIGHTHOUSE THOUGHT FOR THE DAY

How can you be a "basin bearer and a towel wearer" on your street or in your cul-de-sac? Can you let Jesus' light shine by being a servant among your neighbors?

JOE ALDRICH

The Relationship Key

*"If you abide in My word…you shall know the truth, and
the truth shall make you free."*

JOHN 8:31–32, NKJV

Jesus spoke often about "abiding," which means taking up permanent residence in a relationship with Him. This is more than a religious exercise: It is a vital way of life, an unceasing and unbroken relationship with Him. It is consciously choosing to spend personal time with Jesus and remaining with Him.

In order to grow in our faith, we must hear from God, and we cannot hear from Him unless we spend time in His presence. Jesus said, "It is the Spirit who gives life; the flesh profits nothing. The words that I speak to you are spirit, and they are life" (John 6:63, NKJV). God's words are life to us, and we hear those words when we study the written Word, the Bible, and when we fellowship with Him through prayer.

God remains with us all day long, reminding us of the things He has taught or commanded us. When we abide in a relationship with Christ, we can hear from Him and obey Him, and that allows us to live in freedom and joy in every situation, decision, and relationship.

There is much at stake—in your own life and in the lives of those around you—when it comes to the depth and quality of your relationship with Jesus Christ. Make a decision to strengthen that relationship. Vow to spend more quality time with God, and then live in awareness of His Word and presence. Be ready to walk in truth and freedom in a newer, fuller way. As you do, others will want to know Christ as you know Him.

LIGHTHOUSE THOUGHT FOR THE DAY

As a lighthouse for Jesus Christ, you should choose to make your relationship with Christ your top priority.

HENRY BLACKABY

Knowing the Holy Spirit

"You will receive power when the Holy Spirit comes on you; and you will be my witnesses...to the ends of the earth."

ACTS 1:8

Thousands of evangelists from more than 130 countries have attended the International Conference for Itinerant Evangelists, sponsored by the Billy Graham Evangelistic Association. One year, I was asked to speak on how to be filled with the Holy Spirit. Just before I was to speak, I received a note from Billy Graham that read, "I consider this one of the most important addresses of the entire conference."

Acts 1:8 addresses this subject, which is vital to every lighthouse for Jesus Christ. Unfortunately, according to our worldwide surveys, 95 percent of professing believers do not understand the ministry of the Holy Spirit. This includes pastors, evangelists, and missionaries.

If I were allowed to bring only one message to the Christian world, it would be on how to be filled with the Holy Spirit and walk moment by moment in the fullness of His power. I would even choose helping a defeated Christian understand the Holy Spirit over introducing a non-believer to Christ, because helping a believer understand the Holy Spirit would inevitably result in far more people receiving and following Christ.

Today the body of Christ needs to be awakened to the person and ministry of the Holy Spirit. We need Him to empower and control us, and we need to invite Him to exalt and honor our Lord Jesus Christ in and through us (John 16:14).

You can receive the fullness of the Holy Spirit by faith right now. Simply claim God's command to be filled (Ephesians 5:18) and His promise that He will release the Spirit's power in and through you to make you an effective witness for the Lord (1 John 5:14–15).

LIGHTHOUSE THOUGHT FOR THE DAY

Without the Holy Spirit we can do nothing. With Him, we can do great and mighty things for His glory.

BILL BRIGHT

A Worshipful Attitude

"God is spirit, and his worshipers must worship in spirit and in truth."
JOHN 4:24

As the spiritual leader of his family, a man must set the tone as he lights up his home for Christ. Just as we men like to control the physical temperature of the house, we also need to set the spiritual heat level. A man of God establishes the right spiritual climate in his home by modeling a worshipful attitude.

A worshipful attitude is a matter of the heart. It begins in our hearts—from spirits that have been born again of the Spirit of God—but also includes our minds. It is worshiping the Lord "in spirit and in truth." True worship is passionate, borne of deep love for God and all He has done for us, but it is also intellectual, including sound biblical knowledge and the truths established therein. It's humble, like the woman at the well. It recognizes Jesus for who He is: Lord. It's sincere; it's genuine; there's nothing phony or forced about it. It's constant—daily, hourly, minute-by-minute.

The religious leaders of Jesus' day did and said all the correct things, particularly regarding worship, but they lacked the right attitude. Speaking to the Pharisees, Jesus said, "You hypocrites! Isaiah was right when he prophesied... 'These people honor me with their lips, but their hearts are far from me'" (Matthew 15:7–8). In dramatic contrast, Christ explained the secret of genuine worship to a sinful Samaritan woman, who worshiped God in all the "wrong" ways. Why? Because she was open. She was humble and teachable. She had the right attitude.

LIGHTHOUSE THOUGHT FOR THE DAY

Set the spiritual temperature of your lighthouse on high. Play worshipful music in your home and have times of family worship when you humbly bow before almighty God.

BILL MCCARTNEY

Exercising Authority

He called his twelve disciples to him and gave them authority
to drive out evil spirits and to heal every disease and sickness.
MATTHEW 10:1

"To adequately define prayer, one must use the language of war," declared S. D. Gordon. "Peace language is not equal to the situation. The earth is in a state of war and is being hotly besieged. Thus, one must use war talk to grasp the fact with which prayer is concerned. Prayer from God's side is communication between Himself and His allies in the enemy country."

Productive prayer exercises authority. Jesus told His disciples, "I have given you authority...to overcome all the power of the enemy; nothing will harm you" (Luke 10:19). Elsewhere Christ asserted, "Have faith in God.... If anyone says to this mountain, 'Go, throw yourself into the sea,' and does not doubt in his heart,...it will be done for him" (Mark 11:22–23).

Prayer that seeks to shine Christ's light into our neighborhoods requires a holy boldness. It's a boldness that begins with speaking to the mountains and ends with speaking to our neighbors.

The late Paul E. Billheimer, in his classic work *Destined for the Throne*, describes this spiritual authority: "Through the use of Christ's weapons of prayer and faith the Church holds in this present throbbing moment the balance of power in world affairs." He concludes, "In spite of all her lamentable weaknesses...the Church is the mightiest force for civilization and enlightened social consciousness in the world today."

It is indeed! And we, the church in our neighborhoods, must help bring that enlightenment to every person in our sphere of influence by exercising our authority in Christ.

LIGHTHOUSE THOUGHT FOR THE DAY

We have been given power through Christ Jesus to boldly share His message with our neighbors.

DICK EASTMAN

Prayer Is the Key!

*I urge, then, first of all, that requests, prayers, intercession and thanksgiving
be made for everyone.... This is good, and pleases God our Savior, who
wants all men to be saved and to come to a knowledge of the truth.*

1 TIMOTHY 2:1, 3–4

"Satan laughs at our toils and mocks our efforts, but he trembles when
he sees the weakest saints of God on their knees."

This is an important insight for us as lighthouse keepers to grasp. It
is natural for us to try and toil and plot as we attempt to reach out to
our neighbors. Our first reaction to a challenge is to formulate a plan.
Although planning can be very valuable, it will not be enough when
witnessing.

The first thing we need to do as we reach out to our neighbors,
classmates, and friends is to pray for them by name. In fact, only as we
pray specifically and fervently for the Holy Spirit to move in their
hearts will we begin to see special opportunities for caring and sharing.

Amazing things will happen when we pray specifically and regularly for others. The Holy Spirit will begin to work in their lives: woo-
ing them, drawing them near, and even convicting them. Only the
Spirit of God can effectively prepare hearts to receive Jesus.

That should not be surprising. It happened to you, and it happened to me. Someone who cared about you, or several such people,
began praying for you. That eventually resulted in you coming to
Christ. When we pray, our Lord will bring opportunities for us to care
and then share the love of Christ in natural ways.

LIGHTHOUSE THOUGHT FOR THE DAY

Prayer is not the only thing we can do for our neighbors—but it is the
foundation for all our caring and sharing. It shakes the gates of hell and
opens the gates of heaven.

PAUL CEDAR

Letting the Light Shine

"Let your light shine before men, that they may see your good deeds and praise your Father in heaven."

MATTHEW 5:16

"The tallest candlestick ain't much good without a wick. You gotta live right to be the light of the world."

These lines from a popular song are from the musical *Godspell*. The production was based on the life of Christ as recorded in the Gospel of Matthew. The writers weren't Christians, but they certainly understood what our Lord's words meant. If you're not a shining example of what you believe, who's going to be interested in what you say?

Godspell made it clear that Christ's early disciples weren't perfect. Audiences laughed as they watched the disciples wrestle with their Lord's ideas, struggling to pick a speck out of a brother's eye when they had a plank in their own. Over time the twelve started to get it right. They changed. That was the theme of another of the songs: "Day by day, day by day, O dear Lord three things I pray: to see Thee more clearly, to love Thee more dearly, to follow Thee more nearly, day by day."

Lighthouse Christians aren't perfect and never will be in this life. But we need to be learners. And that's really all our audience expects. They expect some light—light that brightens the dark world they know, light that sheds illumination in areas where they're not used to having any.

We will never be perfect in this life, but we've got to live right to be the light of the world.

LIGHTHOUSE THOUGHT FOR THE DAY

Jesus' words and actions were perfect examples of how to be lights in this dark world.

DAVID MAINS

People of the Resurrection

Christ has indeed been raised from the dead.
1 CORINTHIANS 15:20

French thinker Auguste Comte once told Thomas Carlyle that he was going to start a new religion to replace Christianity. "Very good," replied Carlyle. "All you will have to do is to be crucified, rise again the third day, and get the world to believe you are still alive. Then your new religion will have a chance."

Christianity is a religion of resurrection. But what about the historical certainty of the resurrection? Have you ever thought about how the apostles could have proclaimed the risen Christ if they didn't really believe it? Would they have risked or even forfeited their lives if they didn't believe? Of course not! They knew the resurrection was a real event, not some fabrication of their corporate imagination. They not only saw an empty tomb but also repeatedly saw the risen Lord.

Mary Magdalene shouted for joy to the disciples, "I have seen the Lord!" Before she saw Christ she was convinced someone had stolen His body. Seeing Jesus alive must have taken her breath away. What about Thomas, the first skeptic? Christ certainly took care of his doubt.

Our faith is based on belief in the resurrected Christ. As Paul wrote, "If Christ has not been raised, our preaching is useless and so is your faith" (1 Corinthians 15:14). Without a raised Jesus, we are without hope; with a resurrected Christ, we have the assurance of eternal life. I like what one man had engraved on his wife's tombstone concerning this assurance: "Till death us unite."

We are to be people of the resurrection. May the meaning of the resurrection fill us with such intensity and joy that it permeates our lives.

LIGHTHOUSE THOUGHT FOR THE DAY

As we share the gospel of Jesus, let's not leave Him on the cross or in the tomb. Let's proclaim a risen Lord!

BOB RICKER

Knowing Our Limitations

"Without Me you can do nothing."
JOHN 15:5, NKJV

In this verse, Jesus was stating the most basic truth of the Christian life.

Now what does this really mean in a practical way? Obviously there are a great many people across our world who have no time for Jesus Christ and yet accomplish many amazing and wonderful things. When Jesus said, "Without Me you can do nothing," does that mean I can't get a job? No, I can get a job. Does that mean I can't marry a wife and have a family? No, I can get married and have a family. Does that mean I can't buy a house? No, I can buy a house. Does that mean I can't put together a budget or write a novel or design a skyscraper or win the Nobel Prize for physics? No, I could accomplish any or all of those things if I had the opportunities and training and natural ability.

You can do a lot of things without the Lord, but there's one thing you can't do: *You can't be like Him.*

You can sail a dinghy across the Pacific; you can complete the Boston Marathon in a wheelchair; you can sit on the Supreme Court and wrestle with great constitutional questions; you can write a piece of music that will make grown men weak; and you can create a two-story, stained-glass window that people from all over the world will come to applaud and admire. But you can't be what God wants you to be, and you can't do what God wants you to do without the specific, daily empowering of His Spirit. You can't bear spiritual fruit—not so much as a spiritual crab apple—unless the life of Christ is flowing in you and through you.

LIGHTHOUSE THOUGHT FOR THE DAY

We can't accomplish anything for Christ and His kingdom unless He does it in us and through us. That will only happen when we are daily filled with and empowered by the Spirit of God.

RON MEHL

The Worship of Praise

*Through Jesus, therefore, let us continually offer to God a sacrifice
of praise—the fruit of lips that confess his name.*

HEBREWS 13:15

A worshipful attitude in the home should lead naturally to an atmosphere of constant praise to almighty God. In the Old Testament, worshipers were required to bring many types of sacrifices, including animals, fruits, and grains. In the New Covenant, however, we are told to offer the Lord "a sacrifice of praise."

The Bible, especially in the psalms, is full of admonitions to "Praise the Lord!" It's not a bad practice to get into the habit of saying "Praise the Lord" out loud when something good happens. In addition, while maintaining a worshipful attitude doesn't necessarily involve singing, the praise of God often does. In Psalm 146:2, King David states, "I will praise the LORD all my life; I will sing praise to my God as long as I live."

Other psalms indicate that praise also involves music and even dancing. The apostle Paul echoes David when he says, "Be filled with the Spirit. Speak to one another with psalms, hymns and spiritual songs. Sing and make music in your heart to the Lord" (Ephesians 5:18–19). We are to praise God in word, in song, and in deed. In a sense, everything we do should praise the Lord!

Our praise is especially meaningful to God when our circumstances are difficult. When everything seems dark and hopeless and there appears to be no reason to praise God—that's when we need to praise Him the most! Times like that test our faith, but praising the Lord for who He is, for His great works, for His past blessings, and for His faithfulness exerts power in the spiritual realm.

LIGHTHOUSE THOUGHT FOR THE DAY

A family lights up its home for Christ by praising God continually. Be the first one in your home to sing God's praises, whether in word or song. Boast to your family about the great things He has done for you.

BILL MCCARTNEY

About Simplicity

I consider everything a loss compared to the surpassing greatness of knowing Christ Jesus my Lord, for whose sake I have lost all things.

PHILIPPIANS 3:8

In *My Utmost for His Highest,* Oswald Chambers wrote, "If we have a purpose of our own, it destroys the simplicity and the leisureliness which ought to characterize the children of God" (August 5).

In Philippians 3, we read how the apostle Paul changed his focus from his own purposes to those of God. His purpose was then to lay aside all things and simply know and serve God. This kind of singular focus simplifies life. When Christ is our life and our goal, many things that were points of anxiety and longing fall away. The lesser is replaced by the greater. We experience what the title of a classic sermon describes: "The Expulsive Power of a New Affection."

Faith is alive in this kind of life. It is natural to trust Christ with all of life when all of life is lived for Him. Chambers writes about how far faith can take us: "The saint is hilarious when he is crushed with difficulties because the thing is so ludicrously impossible to anyone but God" (August 2).

Do we believe? Can we trust the One who "works out everything in conformity with the purpose of his will"? (Ephesians 1:11). Mrs. Cowman included this thought in *Streams in the Desert*: "There is nothing in life which harasses and annoys that may not be subservient to the highest ends. They are His mountains. He puts them there."

Think of how far Joseph's growing faith had taken him when he was able to say to his brothers, "It was not you who sent me here, but God" (Genesis 45:8). He believed that God could draw straight lines with crooked sticks. We should believe that, too.

LIGHTHOUSE THOUGHT FOR THE DAY

As lighthouses for Jesus Christ, our focus should be first on knowing and serving God. When we put Him first, other things fall into their rightful places.

BOB RICKER

Strength to Persevere

I pray that out of his glorious riches he may strengthen you with power through his Spirit in your inner being.

EPHESIANS 3:16

The apostle Paul knew a lot about persevering in prayer. Most of us have a good deal to learn in that area, and that's why Paul's prayer for the Ephesian church is one we need to pray for ourselves and for others. We need the inner strength given through the power of the Holy Spirit in order to persevere in our prayers for our neighbors.

Many of us probably have not seen the large numbers of people coming to Christ through our lighthouse ministry that we have heard about from others in the Lighthouse Movement. Those "success" stories are not the typical experiences of most lighthouses. Most lighthouses make progress one small step at a time, and many don't see tangible results for several months or longer.

We need the strength to persevere over the long haul. We need God to well up within us such a love for our neighbors that we will not give up in a month, or six months, or a year, if we don't see results.

Paul's prayer for the Ephesian church continues, showing us his reason for praying for inner strength: "So that Christ may dwell in your hearts through faith. And I pray that you, being rooted and established in love, may have power…to grasp how wide and long and high and deep is the love of Christ" (Ephesians 3:17–18). Christ's love doesn't die, and it doesn't fade. He patiently perseveres in His love for people. He continually intercedes on our behalf.

LIGHTHOUSE THOUGHT FOR THE DAY

Pray that Christ's love might dwell richly in you. Jesus Christ is "able to do immeasurably more than all we ask or imagine, according to his power that is at work within us" (Ephesians 3:20). He will give you the strength to persevere.

JONATHAN GRAF

Real Wisdom

The fruit of the righteous is a tree of life; and he that winneth souls is wise.
PROVERBS 11:30, KJV

I've heard it said that Christians should not use the term *soul-winning*. Rather, we should talk of *sharing our faith, leading others to Jesus, personal witnessing*, or some other less confrontational term.

I suppose objections to the term are for the obvious reason that none of us, in the strictest sense and by ourselves, wins anyone to Christ. We cannot convict anybody of his sins nor convince anyone of her need. Certainly we can't convert anybody, against his or her will, to faith in God. This is a work of the Holy Spirit, as He alone can convict, convince, and convert.

Scripture is clear: "Faith comes by hearing, and hearing by the word of God" (Romans 10:17, NKJV). Through the power of the Word, the Holy Spirit flows to do His converting work and draw people to the Savior. As believers, we are privileged to be instruments in God's hand—sowing the precious seed of the gospel—knowing that "My word...shall not return to Me void" (Isaiah 55:11, NKJV).

For this reason, the writer of Proverbs could boldly assert that "he who wins souls is wise" (Proverbs 11:30, NKJV). This declaration assures us that it is not only possible to be a soul-winner—one whom God uses effectively through the power of His Spirit to bring people to Jesus—but that it is wise to win souls. And if winning souls is wise, surely it is foolish not to make this Christian discipline a priority.

What could be wiser than obeying our Lord's command to "go ye into all the world, and preach the gospel to every creature" (Mark 16:15, KJV)?

We should take to heart the words of the old hymn: "Rescue the perishing, care for the dying. Snatch them in pity from sin and the grave; Weep o'er the erring one, lift up the fallen.... Jesus is merciful, Jesus will save!"

LIGHTHOUSE THOUGHT FOR THE DAY

Winning souls is wise. We would do well to make this a higher priority in our lives.

LARRY LEWIS

Ah, Stop Complaining!

Do everything without complaining or arguing.
PHILIPPIANS 2:14

There aren't many—if any—areas of life that God won't use to teach us. During my time in the corporate world, I learned a very valuable and humbling lesson about what it means to be a lighthouse for Jesus.

Early in my career, I worked in a department with many employees who professed to be Christians. On several occasions, we received memos about some change in how we were to do our jobs. Many times we concluded that the changes would complicate our jobs.

One day the director communicated a change that sent the entire department into an uproar. The change wasn't wrong, but it could have made our jobs more difficult. Sadly, the Christians complained and murmured as much as the non-Christians. I was caught up in this complaining myself.

Yet one Christian woman never joined in the chorus of complaining, but faithfully and earnestly fulfilled her duties. Many of her coworkers noticed and commented on how differently she acted. They were attracted to her character, and she was able to share her faith with many of the employees. It was clear to me that God provided this opening to share her faith simply because she waited on Him.

As for me, a short time later the Lord brought Philippians 2:14 to my memory, and I repented of my shameful attitudes and actions.

When we serve Jesus Christ by serving others, we avoid the devil's trap of murmuring and complaining. Then we follow the example Christ set when He went to the cross for us without one word of complaint.

LIGHTHOUSE THOUGHT FOR THE DAY

We should never let grumbling dim or darken our light for Jesus Christ; rather we should do everything with a humble, cheerful attitude.

JARVIS WARD

Cast Your Cares

Cast all your anxiety on him because he cares for you.
1 PETER 5:7

Years ago, when I was a college student, I had a summer job in a factory. One of my assignments was to degrease fifty-pound metal parts. I did that by lowering the parts into a vat of a strong chemical solution, then lifting them back out.

As you might imagine, after several hours of lifting and lowering and lowering and lifting those fifty-pound weights, my back became quite tired and sore. Just then the foreman came by. He was horrified at what I was doing. He pointed up over the vat to a large metal hook connected to a chain and motor and said, "Why aren't you using the power lift?" No wonder I was so tired and sore! I had been bearing those heavy burdens all morning, when I should have been letting the power lift bear the burdens for me.

It's like that with our concerns in life. So often we bear the heavy burdens ourselves and develop very sore hearts, when all along God wanted to carry the load for us. We simply needed to cast our anxieties, cares, and burdens on Him.

Are you carrying heavy burdens by your own strength and becoming discouraged as a result? Then hold to the truth that God is available to bear your burdens. Are you praying for people who are carrying heavy loads and becoming weary and disheartened? Tell them today the powerful truth that God is available to be their "power lift." Pray with them that they will be able to entrust their loads to Him.

LIGHTHOUSE THOUGHT FOR THE DAY

As lighthouses for Jesus Christ, we know the One who wants to bear our burdens and those of our friends and neighbors. Let's start by casting our own cares on Him.

STEVE DOUGLASS

Free to Share Our Faith

Salvation is found in no one else, for there is no other name under heaven given to men by which we must be saved.

ACTS 4:12

"Evangelism is not the imposition of a point of view," Donald Bloesch writes, "but the overflow of a thankful heart."

Christians sometimes try to communicate their faith as if they were salespeople trying to sell a product. But evangelism is not the employing of a super sales strategy. Why? Because the gospel is not for sale! It is the free gift of grace for those who will accept it. We are called to *expose* our faith in the most winsome way possible—not *impose* it.

How are we to expose our faith? By realizing that God has already provided everything we need to be effective witnesses: His truth, His love, and His power. Think of it! It is not a story of human invention we offer, but a God-authored gospel that has the power to save. It's not merely our love we give our neighbors, but Christ's love mediated through us by the presence of the Spirit. It is not through our persuasive powers that anyone comes to Christ—it's the Spirit of God who convicts and converts others.

Evangelism, then, is most effective when it declares God's truth, displays Christ's love, depends on God's Spirit, and points to God's power. Let us remember that evangelism is something *God* does in people's lives; we are only the instruments He uses.

It is so liberating to realize that God's initiative precedes our response. God is always there before us. Once we understand what evangelism entails and see that God has provided all we need to accomplish the task, it frees us to share the Good News with joy.

LIGHTHOUSE THOUGHT FOR THE DAY

Thank the Lord for giving you everything you need to share His glorious gospel. Ask Him to show you what His Spirit is already doing in the lives of your friends who do not know Him.

REBECCA MANLEY PIPPERT

Arise! Shine!

Arise, shine; for thy light is come,
and the glory of the LORD is risen upon thee.

Isaiah 60:1, kjv

I once witnessed a sunrise at the summit of Tai Mountain in northern China. It was unforgettable. Into the silent gloom, a faint flush of pink appeared in the eastern sky. The rosy glow bashfully intensified into orange, brighter and still brighter. Suddenly the giant fireball seemed to leap into the sky, full of brilliance and glory, as if announcing to the world, "Arise and shine, for thy light is come!"

God spoke these words through His prophet Isaiah to awaken and encourage people who, because of His judgment, had been stricken down and were depleted in strength, confidence, and hope. At precisely this hour of gloom and darkness, God's life-giving word thundered forth: "Arise and shine!"

God has often encouraged His people to rise to the occasion, to the need, and to the task. Through David, He bade the Israelites, "*Arise* and build the sanctuary of the Lord God." Through Nehemiah, He urged the people to "*Arise* and build" Jerusalem's city wall. He commanded the reluctant Jonah for the second time to "*Arise,* go to Nineveh." He instructed the repentant Saul to "*Arise* and go into the city." And He instructed the not-yet-enlightened Peter to "*Arise,* slay and eat."

I firmly believe that God is saying the same thing to His church in America today: "*Arise* and shine into your neighborhoods, your nation, and the world!" He is calling all of us who are called by His wonderful name to be lighthouses in our neighborhoods and our cities for the Lord Jesus Christ. May we heed that call and witness a tremendous move of God!

Lighthouse Thought for the Day

It is an immense privilege and calling for us to "Arise, shine" for the Lord Jesus Christ before our neighbors. We should not just obey that call—we should *joyfully* obey it!

Thomas Wang

Prayer Journaling

They raised their voices together in prayer to God....
All the believers were one in heart and mind.

ACTS 4:24, 32

Developing a consistent and effective prayer life means learning to talk to God, listen to God, and pray from His heart. It also involves praying in a spirit of unity with other believers. A personal prayer journal can be helpful as you learn to do this. It can assist you as you pray for people, circumstances, and events.

A prayer journal can help you organize your prayer requests, including the date you began praying for someone or something and the date you recognized an answer to that prayer. It can also help you more effectively pray in unity with other believers. You can find professionally prepared prayer journals at your local Christian bookstore, or you can use a simple notebook.

My prayer concerns fall into several categories, such as development of personal ministry; my family members and Christian friends; those who need Christ, need encouragement, or are ill; those in authority; laborers for the harvest; and for spiritual and moral awakening. Some of these may be short-term prayer concerns, while others will be long-term.

I have found it helpful to designate days of the week to pray for different concerns. For example, I can pick one day of the week to pray for my neighbors who need Christ and another to pray for family members who have not yet received Him. I can pick another day to pray for government bodies and leaders (local, national, and global)—such as the president and vice president, cabinet members, members of congress or parliament, members of the judicial system, military officers, ambassadors, and others in positions of authority at home and abroad.

LIGHTHOUSE THOUGHT FOR THE DAY

By using a prayer journal, you can pray specifically and strategically every day of the week

VONETTE Z. BRIGHT

Blessed to Be a Blessing

*"I will make you into a great nation and I will bless you;
I will make your name great, and you will be a blessing."*

GENESIS 12:2

For many years I carried a little card in my wallet that read, "Love isn't love until you give it away." How true that is! Love isn't something we can keep or hoard as if it were a possession to collect. The only time we can truly enjoy love is when we pour it on those around us.

God's love was never meant to stop with us, but instead to flow through us to others in our spheres of influence. In that respect, we should be like free-flowing rivers of God's love and not like reservoirs whose water is held back by a dam.

How do we love those around us? By living the way Jesus lived. By doing for those around us the same things Jesus would have done. Jesus prayed regularly for the people God placed in His path, and He lovingly cared for them in large and small ways, depending on their needs.

Expressing our love for people around us can mean a lot of things. Certainly, it means praying for them. At times, it might mean something as simple as a smile or a hug, but it could also mean a sacrifice on our part.

We live in a world that desperately needs to see demonstrations of the heavenly Father's love. Let's make sure we are an open, flowing channel of His blessings to those we come into contact with on a daily basis.

LIGHTHOUSE THOUGHT FOR THE DAY

God didn't give us His love so we could keep it to ourselves. He showers us with His love so that we can shower it on those around us. We should always be on the lookout for ways to express God's love to our neighbors.

DALLAS ANDERSON

Esteem vs. Denial

*"Foxes have holes and birds of the air have nests,
but the Son of Man has no place to lay his head."*

LUKE 9:58

Someone asked missionary Hudson Taylor why God chose him to help usher in the Chinese revival. He thought for a moment and said, "I suppose God looked around until he found someone weak enough."

The false gospel of self-esteem that many Christian psychologists and even pastors are guilty of preaching is crippling the American church. A self-filled person cannot be a Spirit-filled Christian. The two are mutually exclusive.

The gospel of Christ is the gospel of self-denial, not self-esteem (Matthew 16:24). God used forty years of desert life to rid Moses of his overinflated self-esteem. God had to cripple Jacob before He could use him. Before God could bless Job, He had to reduce him to nothing. God stripped the apostle Paul of all self-worthiness (Philippians 3:8).

Jesus, our example of self-denial, humbled Himself, took the form of a servant, and came to earth as a man to die for us (Philippians 2:5–8). But the self-filled American church, like the Laodician church, sees itself as needing nothing. Christ, however, sees us as "wretched, pitiful, poor, blind and naked" (Revelation 3:16–17).

There is a difference between self-acceptance and self-esteem. We are to *accept* ourselves and take the responsibility of stewardship over ourselves for Christ's sake seriously, but we are not to *esteem* ourselves (Romans 12:3). In fact, Scripture teaches us that there are only three things to esteem: God's Word (Psalm 119:128), God's Son (Isaiah 53:4), and others over ourselves (Philippians 2:3). Let us repent of trying to find value in ourselves rather than valuing our great God's Word, His Son, and others.

LIGHTHOUSE THOUGHT FOR THE DAY

We need to learn what it means to "deny ourselves." Then we will make a difference in the lives of others.

EDDIE AND ALICE SMITH

Crossing the Finish Line

*"As long as it is day, we must do the work of him who sent me.
Night is coming, when no one can work."*

JOHN 9:4

In spring 2000, I was blessed to visit a literacy project among an unreached group of Muslims in southern Asia. Along with teaching them to read and write, the thirty young, enthusiastic workers also shared the gospel with them. In less than six months, three families had come to accept Jesus Christ as Savior.

While talking with one of the converts, I reiterated the danger of persecution for proclaiming his faith. He responded: "I will continue to share my newfound faith. The worst thing they can do is to cut my neck. If that happens, I will go to meet the Lord Jesus Christ, who revealed Himself to me." That is the kind of spirit and determination that is needed to fulfill the great commission.

In John 9:4, Jesus told the disciples three things concerning the fast move toward the finish line: First is the issue of *diligence*. For the Christian, this means diligence in prayer, planning, and action. We are all called to fulfill the great commission and give it our best effort.

Second is *direction*. God-given direction is rooted in Scripture; it utilizes the talents the Lord has given us. It is very specific to our personal gifts and calling. The direction is confirmed by God's open doors and is made possible by His wisdom, anointing, and strength.

Third is the *deadline*. We do not have forever to get the job done. One day the last song will be sung, the last sermon delivered, and the last prayer offered. Then we will see the Master face-to-face. In the realm of eternity, there will be a vital place for worship and learning in His presence, but it will be too late to win lost souls.

LIGHTHOUSE THOUGHT FOR THE DAY

We are living in a soul-winning age. Let's use our time to bring others with us into the kingdom!

DR. DOUGLAS SHAW

A Way of Life

> *"You are the salt of the earth. But if the salt loses its saltiness, how*
> *can it be made salty again? It is no longer good for anything."*
> MATTHEW 5:13

Consistency is a must if you want your light to shine for the Lord Jesus Christ. You've got to let the light of God shine every day. You can't say, "I'll shine for a while, but after next month another arrangement needs to be worked out." Consistency is vital because you never know when someone will need the light of Jesus to shine into his or her life. A prayer-care-and-share lifestyle has to become as much a part of your Christian life as attending worship services. It has to become a basic component of your identity.

This is not a new concept. In the Old Testament, Isaiah says, "I will also make you a light for the Gentiles, that you may bring my salvation to the ends of the earth" (49:6). In the New Testament, Paul writes, "Become blameless and pure, children of God without fault in a crooked and depraved generation, in which you shine like stars in the universe as you hold out the word of life" (Philippians 2:15–16).

In good times as well as bad, your lighthouse needs to be shining for those around you. People might not appreciate what you're doing when times are good for them. They may dismiss you as a relic from a past generation. But when bad times hit, people will be grateful that your lighthouse is there. Their appreciation will be immediate; words of commendation will be quick to come. Suddenly your lighthouse will be as relevant as life itself.

LIGHTHOUSE THOUGHT FOR THE DAY

Your friends, family, and coworkers need to see consistency in your lighthouse ministry. You have to be there over the long haul—consistently praying, caring, and sharing!

DAVID MAINS

The Thirsting Soul

As the deer pants for streams of water, so my soul pants for you, O God. My soul thirsts for God, for the living God. When can I go and meet with God?
PSALM 42:1–2

The picture of the soul thirsting after God to the point of panting fits neatly into our image of what is truly spiritual. Many of us see this thirst for God as the domain of those much further on the road to true spirituality—the "spiritual giants" whose inner sensitivities are pitched to a much higher degree than ours. We, on the other hand, seem earthbound, weighted down with everyday concerns.

But perhaps we have romanticized this picture of the thirsting soul and, in so doing, unintentionally distanced ourselves from true spirituality and left intimacy with God to the select few who have been called. After all, we reason, only the holy are thirsty for God.

I believe we have misread what the psalmist is expressing, for in this passage he is drawing a simple comparison between a deer in need of life-sustaining water and a soul in need of the presence of God.

Is the panting deer a picture of higher development or maturity? Of superior animal intelligence? Of course not! It is simply a picture of a basic survival instinct, of a thirsty deer doing what a thirsty deer does: panting for water when it needs to replenish its fluids. There's nothing amazing about that!

The same holds true for us when our emotions are pinched by discouragement, despair, or anxiety. Just as a deer pants when it does not have enough water, we "pant"—become discouraged and anxious or just feel far away from our Lord—when we don't have enough God! Then, it's time for some water. There's nothing superspiritual about that; it's just a basic survival instinct.

LIGHTHOUSE THOUGHT FOR THE DAY

We will be more effective for Jesus Christ when we learn to recognize our thirst for God and what to do about it: drink!

STEVE FRY

Solidarity Prayer

He who searches our hearts knows the mind of the Spirit, because
the Spirit intercedes for the saints in accordance with God's will.

ROMANS 8:27

To Martin Luther is attributed this definition of prayer: "Prayer is not the overcoming of God's reluctance; it is laying hold of His highest willingness." A friend of mine calls it "jumping on God's bandwagon." I call it "solidarity prayer." In it we align ourselves with God's purposes and promises, agreeing with them and saying, "Father, I want what you want—for my family, my neighbors, my church, my generation."

Here is where praying "in Jesus' name" finds its true meaning. This is not a phrase to be tacked on to a prayer to indicate that our prayer is finished. Jesus meant for us to pray with the authority that comes from linking our desires with His desires. In essence, we're saying, "Father, Your Son's life perspective, life direction, and life mission are mine too. They shape everything I am asking You to do."

In solidarity prayer we align ourselves, not first of all with the needs and problems of the world around us, but with God's kingdom advance. According to Romans 8, the Spirit who prays with us and helps us to pray intercedes in the very same way. The kingship of Christ must control our agenda in prayer and, in turn, shape how we pray for our neighbors and beyond. In our prayers we link up with the ongoing intercession of the King, making His prayers our prayers. In fact, we should regularly incorporate the words of Scripture itself into our praying. There is great confidence and hope when we learn to pray like that.

LIGHTHOUSE THOUGHT FOR THE DAY

Prayer is not about our desires, but about God's desires. Based on God's promises in Christ, what does He desire for those for whom I am praying today? Does one specific promise come to mind? How will that change the very content of my praying?

DAVID BRYANT

Confidence to Share Jesus

After they prayed, the place where they were meeting was shaken.
And they were all filled with the Holy Spirit and
spoke the word of God boldly.

ACTS 4:31

God has a power team of three that He uses to bring people to Christ: the Word of God, the work of the Spirit, and the witness of the believer.

There is power in the Word of God. Romans 10:17 tells us, "Faith comes from hearing, and hearing by the word of God" (NKJV). The Word of God is the sword of the Spirit He uses to pierce deeply into the heart and mind of the nonbeliever.

The Holy Spirit is the ultimate soul-winner. Jesus said, "No one can come to me unless the Father who sent me draws him" (John 6:44). God draws the nonbeliever through the enlightenment, revelation, and conviction of the Spirit.

Finally, God uses the witness of the believer to bring people to Christ. As the believer faithfully shares the Word of God, the Holy Spirit uses the Word to convince and draw unbelievers to Christ. God uses the believer to guide those the Holy Spirit is drawing to Christ through the conversion experience.

Acts 3–4 record how God did a mighty work through the witness of the church. Multitudes were coming to Christ and being saved, and opposition arose. The Bible tells us that the believers in Acts went to God in prayer, asking God for boldness to proclaim the gospel. They were filled with the Holy Spirit and spoke the word of God with boldness.

You and I can have that same boldness to share Christ because we know that God wants to use us to bring the lost to Christ.

LIGHTHOUSE THOUGHT FOR THE DAY

Because our confidence is in Jesus Christ, we can confidently shine like stars in the universe as we "hold out the word of life" (Philippians 2:16).

DARRELL ROBINSON

Not Ashamed

I am not ashamed of the gospel, because it is the power of God.
ROMANS 1:16

I was shopping one day at the grocery store when I noticed a strapping young man wearing a necklace bearing the letters *WWJD*. After eyeing it for a few seconds, I decided to ask him the obvious question: "What does *WWJD* stand for?"

His face changed color, and he looked shocked. Then he softly whispered to me, "What would Jesus do?"

"You really believe that stuff?" I asked. Again, he almost looked frightened—of puny little me.

Then, in slightly louder than a whisper, he said, "Yes."

"I do too," I replied. He looked very relieved.

My encounter with this nervous young man reminded me of Romans 1:16, where the apostle Paul affirms three things.

First, Paul affirms his *confidence* in the gospel. Christians who are not confident that they possess the only message of hope and eternal salvation will project a tone of uncertainty in their personal witness, just like the young man at the grocery store.

Second, Paul affirms the *core issue* when we witness, which is the power in the gospel. We must never forget the power of the message of Jesus Christ. This power is not in our self-confidence or in any "system"; it is in the gospel.

Third, Paul affirms *conversion*. Only the gospel of Jesus Christ can convert the sinner and make that person a saint. Only the Holy Spirit has the power to convict the world of sin and judgment and draw people to God.

This is why we have no reason to be ashamed of the gospel.

LIGHTHOUSE THOUGHT FOR THE DAY

What would happen to our witness if we truly understood the power of the gospel we are called to preach? I'm guessing our timidity would be replaced with boldness!

DR. DOUGLAS SHAW

What's a Lighthouse?

*"I am the Light of the world; he who follows Me will not walk in
the darkness, but will have the Light of life."*

JOHN 8:12, NASB

For fifty summers we have deep-sea fished in Lake Michigan. Many
times when we were out on that enormous body of water and a sud-
den storm or night's blackness descended, we found ourselves anxiously scanning the horizon for a lighthouse.

Nautical lighthouses are needed when people are lost in darkness
and scrambling for safety. Christian lighthouses are needed for the
same reason. People all around us are lost in spiritual darkness, and the
Light of the World, Jesus Christ, is their only hope for finding safety.

What exactly are Christian lighthouses? They are not just decals or
light bulbs shining out a window, but people who have Jesus living *in*
them, shining the light of Christ *out* from the house and *into* the world.
True lighthouses share Jesus with those around them. Then, as others
accept Him, lighthouses multiply—radiating Jesus to a lost world.

When John Glenn first orbited the earth on February 20, 1962, the
people of Perth, Australia, turned on their lights for him. From his
space pod, he saw a very bright light. October 31, 1998, when he
orbited the earth again, the residents of Perth honored him by lighting
their city office towers, stadiums, and backyards. That time he saw an
absolutely brilliant light.

When Jesus ascended back to heaven, He entrusted us to be the
lights of the world (Matthew 45:14). Looking from heaven, Jesus has
been waiting two millennia to see earth ablaze with His light. How
long will Jesus have to wait until the light is a brilliant blaze?

LIGHTHOUSE THOUGHT FOR THE DAY

We need to make our homes lighthouses for Christ, until Jesus can
look down and see our whole nation ablaze with His light.

EVELYN CHRISTENSON

Hearing and Doing

"But why do you call Me 'Lord, Lord,' and not do the things which I say?"
LUKE 6:46, NKJV

Do you want to have a strong, mature walk with the Lord Jesus Christ? Do you desire to be an effective witness for Him? The Word of God gives simple steps to having these things.

The first step toward a mature walk with and effective witness for Christ is simply coming to Him—that is, taking time to be with Him through reading His Word, the Bible, and spending personal time with Him through prayer.

The next step is to hear what He is saying to you through your Bible study and prayer. It is not enough just to read God's Word. It is also important to allow God to speak to you through it and to listen for instruction.

The final step is simply doing what Jesus says. As Lord of all aspects of our lives, Jesus is not a silent partner. He actively speaks to us and guides us. He does so to ensure that we are secure during stormy times and to make sure that we pass the tests we will most certainly encounter. But all the guidance and help He provides will not make a difference unless we obey immediately when He speaks.

Jesus sought to impress on His disciples that if they did not obey when He spoke, life's circumstances would bring great ruin to that house [life] (Luke 6:49). Your continued safety and growth as a Christian depends on the lordship of Jesus Christ. He is Savior, but your daily life in Him depends on His lordship.

Today, reaffirm to Christ and yourself your readiness to come to Him daily, listen to Him, and obey Him fully. In short, make Him Lord of all!

LIGHTHOUSE THOUGHT FOR THE DAY

As lighthouses for Jesus Christ, it is vital that we learn to hear Jesus' words and obey them fully. We need to affirm and reaffirm His lordship.

HENRY BLACKABY

Back to Basics

All Scripture is God-breathed and is useful for teaching, rebuking, correcting and training in righteousness, so that the man of God may be thoroughly equipped for every good work.

2 TIMOTHY 3:16–17

Dr. Howard Hendricks, professor at Dallas Theological Seminary, is a big fan of the famous pianist Van Cliburn. On one occasion, a friend arranged for Dr. Hendricks to meet Mr. Cliburn after attending a concert. Dr. Hendricks expressed great admiration for the pianist's remarkable musical abilities and then asked how much time he spent practicing.

With a smile, Van Cliburn replied, "I practice about eight to nine hours a day." He went on to note that two of those hours were invested in nothing more than running scales and finger exercises—doing the basics.

It is amazing, isn't it, how even the most accomplished among us in their chosen fields—in music, athletics, or public speaking, to name a few—still have to practice the basics.

Likewise, the church, God's family, is made strong by practicing the basics. God loved us enough to give us an owner's manual called the Bible. Second Timothy 3:16–17 assures us that the Word is more than adequate to prepare us to do good works for God. If we will simply live out the basics found in Scripture, God will thoroughly equip us for every good work. And there is no better place to practice the basics than among the people of God.

LIGHTHOUSE THOUGHT FOR THE DAY

We need look no further for the basics of the faith than to the written Word of God, the Bible.

ROBERT E. RECCORD

Time to Pray!

"The harvest is plentiful, but the workers are few. Ask the Lord of the harvest, therefore, to send out workers into his harvest field."

LUKE 10:2

It's a farmer's worst nightmare: time for the harvest but no one to do the harvesting. He has trees loaded with ripe fruit, but no laborers; grape arbors bent to the earth with grapes, but only a few workers.

It's something like that in our neighborhoods today. They are packed with disillusioned, broken individuals and families—some of them seeking, some indifferent—in close proximity to homes where the light shines, where hope is observed, where acts of righteousness take place, and where the music of the gospel sounds.

Before sending the seventy-two on their missionary journey, Jesus raised their expectations. "The harvest is plentiful," He taught, "but the laborers are few." Jesus knew there were multitudes ready to hear and respond to the gospel. He is saying the same thing now. The harvest is plentiful—in our own neighborhoods!

How should we respond? First of all, pray! We must bathe our desire and effort to reach out to others in prayer. Prayer enables the mission. Prayer reminds us of our total dependence upon the Lord of the harvest. It releases the nonbeliever from the entrapment of the forces of evil and increases our burden for the lost. Prayer focuses our priorities and results in a call to be a light in our area of influence.

Jesus told His trainees, "I am sending you out like lambs among wolves" (Luke 10:3). Lambs among wolves are totally helpless. We need to be loaded up with the full armor of God and become attack lambs—lambs with steel wool, lambs who aggressively do battle for the kingdom of God.

LIGHTHOUSE THOUGHT FOR THE DAY

Prayer—for ourselves, for fellow believers, and for our neighbors—is a must if we are to see people come to Christ through our lighthouse ministries.

JOE ALDRICH

Displays of Compassion

"This is what the LORD Almighty says: 'Administer true justice;
show mercy and compassion to one another.'"
ZECHARIAH 7:9

For a couple of years, our friend Ben came to the church pantry every Thursday to get food for his family. He was, as they say, "down on his luck."

God's people ministered to Ben's family during those dark days—in both word and deed. The people in our church responded to Ben's needs out of true godly compassion.

Before long, God blessed Ben financially, giving him a vision for his own business, then miraculously providing the money for him to get it started. Ben ran his business in a way that pleased God, and the Lord blessed him. Within a year, Ben was investing thousands of dollars each month into Christian ministries around the world.

Ben's family understands well the value of compassion during life's valleys. Life is not lived entirely on a mountaintop. At some point, each of us will know heartache and loss, and when bad things happen to us, we need the compassion and encouragement of Christian brothers and sisters.

Can you think of people in your church who need your compassion and encouragement today? How about in your neighborhood? Can you think of specific acts of compassion you can perform for them? Compassion is more than concern for someone. It's more than a simple pledge of "I'll pray for you." Real compassion finds work to do, then does it with a glad heart. Compassion identifies and ministers to the Bens of this world. They are living around you—so go to work!

LIGHTHOUSE THOUGHT FOR THE DAY

Caring for hurting and needy people is what being a light for Christ is all about. Ask God who around you could benefit from an act of compassion; then go do it!

EDDIE AND ALICE SMITH

Seeking the One True King

He had a choice and handsome son whose name was Saul.
There was not a more handsome person than he among the children of Israel.
From his shoulders upward he was taller than any of the people.
1 SAMUEL 9:2, NKJV

In this passage we read of Israel's desire for a king and how Saul fit the bill. Saul was a handsome man. He stood head and shoulders above the crowd. He was young, energetic, and charismatic.

It grieved God that Israel wanted a king of flesh and blood because He alone was to be King of Israel (1 Samuel 10:19). Nevertheless, the people wanted a leader who was like them but who appeared better than they. God, knowing the fickleness of the Israelites, sent them exactly what they wanted.

The Israelites were like a certain little boy who lay in bed frightened of the dark. "Daddy! Daddy!" he cried out. When Daddy came, he tried to reassure his son by saying, "God is always here with you, and He is your heavenly Father who takes care of you." The boy answered, "But I need a daddy that has skin."

The Israelites wanted a flesh-and-blood ruler. In many ways we are no different from them. We clamor for human heroes. We want the handsome, smart, strong people to bear our burdens.

Jesus, the true King, did not stand head and shoulders above the crowd in any physical sense. The prophecy from Isaiah is succinct. "There is no beauty that we should desire Him" (Isaiah 53:2, NKJV). Christ's authority did not come from His looks or fame. He just spoke the Word of God with ringing conviction and authority. The authority with which Jesus spoke came from who He was: the Chosen One, the King of kings.

LIGHTHOUSE THOUGHT FOR THE DAY

Are we still seeking worldly heroes like Saul when we should be seeking the Savior? Let us look to Jesus Christ as the bearer of our burdens.

MOISHE ROSEN

This "Spiritual" Age

"The Counselor, the Holy Spirit,...will teach you all things and will remind you of everything I have said to you."
JOHN 14:26

It is astonishing to reflect on the rise of spirituality in recent years. Twenty years ago we didn't even have names for spiritual practices that today are commonplace. Yet not all that is spiritual is Christian. *Spiritual* can mean anything from doing crystal therapy to meditating oneself through the millennium with zither music and Tibetan bells.

How then do we share Christ in our present "spiritual" age? How do we communicate Jesus at this moment in our history when pop spirituality is eroding what is distinctive about the Christian message?

There is no greater power than the Holy Spirit. We don't just impart information when we share the gospel; the Spirit gives our words meaning and effectiveness. Evangelization is not merely communication skills. It's a spiritual activity that is based on the supernatural power of God.

In our age people are hungering to reconnect with God. That's why there is this rise in spiritual interest. But for lack of truth, people are settling for lies. Christians must realize that what we have to offer is the very presence of God in our midst. Let them see God through you.

I have seen seekers won to Christ because they saw the unmistakable power of God's presence through the love, joy, and peace of the lives of the Christians who witnessed to them. I have seen people converted because they heard the Word of truth and experienced God's Spirit as they saw Christians at worship. God's invisible qualities can be seen in the lives of His children, and this draws seekers to Him.

LIGHTHOUSE THOUGHT FOR THE DAY

The transformational power of Jesus comes to us and reaches out to others through His Word, through worship, through the sacraments, and through our lives.

REBECCA MANLEY PIPPERT

Peace in God's Presence

*Let us draw near to God...in full assurance of faith.... Let us
hold unswervingly to the hope we profess, for he who promised is faithful.*

HEBREWS 10:22–23

The early Jewish Christians suffered persecution so great that many were tempted to turn away from their faith in Jesus. The writer of the book of Hebrews encouraged them to stand fast in their faith and not doubt. One of his key points was that Jesus is our high priest and that we should enter boldly into God's presence with our prayer requests, for this will bring us peace and assurance.

When Moses was doubting his ability to lead the children of Israel through the wilderness to the Promised Land, God said, "My Presence will go with you, and I will give you rest" (Exodus 33:14).

The key to assurance is God's presence. Paul wrote to the Roman believers saying, "The Spirit himself testifies with our spirit that we are God's children" (Romans 8:16). Another translation reads, "His Holy Spirit speaks to us deep in our hearts and tells us that we are God's children" (NLT).

If you are seeking strength and peace in a troubling time, you need to get into God's presence. Two key ways to doing that are:

- *Read the promises in God's Word.* When a passage of Scripture is made real to your heart, write the date in the margin of your Bible next to that passage.
- *Listen to faith-inspiring praise and worship music.* Lift your voice in praise and worship to the Lord. Thank God for His faithfulness and steadfast character and for keeping His promises.

LIGHTHOUSE THOUGHT FOR THE DAY

As God's promises fill your mind and as your praise and worship fill the room, the Holy Spirit will fill your heart with God's presence, and doubts will vanish.

LOWELL LUNDSTROM

Play to Their Strength

Jesus, tired as he was from the journey, sat down by the well.... When a Samaritan woman came to draw water, Jesus said to her, "Will you give me a drink?"

JOHN 4:6–7

Jesus knew something about the value of meeting people where they are. In John 4 we read the account of the Lord stopping at a small Samaritan town on His way to Galilee. He could have stopped anywhere, but he chose to sit by Jacob's well. It was about noon when Jesus arrived, and it was probably boiling hot in the sun. Anyone coming to the well would likely be in need of water.

Jesus seated Himself at a seeker-sensitive spot—one a needy person, alone and with a little time on her hands, would likely pass. When the Samaritan woman came along, He was ready with a very natural request: "Will you give me a drink?" Jesus put Himself into the woman's world. He was thirsty and so was she, but He took a risk by placing Himself in her hands because she could have snubbed Him.

We should follow Jesus' example of evangelization. We should observe our neighbors and find out what we can about them. Are they commuters, parents of small children, sports fans, car enthusiasts, couch potatoes, or party animals?

It is helpful to know what you have in common with your neighbors and what they may have to offer you. People open up naturally to those who are interested in areas where they excel. Ask them the secret to their success. Let them talk about what they do well. Genuinely enter their world. Take a risk. Play to their strengths, and see how God can work through you as your neighbors open up to you.

LIGHTHOUSE THOUGHT FOR THE DAY

As lighthouses for Jesus Christ, we need to be willing to be vulnerable and take risks when we approach our neighbors.

ALI HANNA

Praying Locally

Unless the LORD watches over the city, the watchmen stand guard in vain.
PSALM 127:1

Your local newspaper and other news outlets can be more than just sources of information, entertainment, and advertising. They can also help you pray more effectively as you search these sources for specific individuals and local concerns for which to pray.

Keep your lighthouse shining brightly for Jesus by uniting in prayer for local leaders and concerns. List the leaders—governors, legislators, provincial administrators, county officials, courts, district administrators, city officials, law enforcement officials, school authorities—by name in your prayer journal. Pray that God will give Christian leaders knowledge and discernment so that they may be able to distinguish right from wrong (Philippians 1:9–10).

Pray about local concerns, asking God to give your leaders wisdom. Pray that God will expose unrighteousness in high places. Ask Him to grant repentance to unbelievers, leading them to knowledge of the truth, and pray that those who are sensitive to His Spirit will remain in their positions of authority (Proverbs 10:9; Daniel 2:21; 2 Timothy 2:25).

When you pray about these things, be specific with names and issues. Read the Scriptures I've listed for each request, and pray them back to God, adapting them as worship, praise, and request. When you pray in accordance with God's Word, you are praying according to God's will, and He will answer those prayers.

As with all your prayers, when you pray for your state and local governments, remember to worship God for who He is (Psalm 103–104). Praise Him for His attributes (Psalm 145–150). Rejoice in your fellowship with Him, just as He delights in you (Proverbs 15:8).

LIGHTHOUSE THOUGHT FOR THE DAY
Believe, claim, and act as though the fervent prayers of your lighthouse will change your state and city. They will! (1 John 5:14–15).

VONETTE Z. BRIGHT

Why Are You So Happy?

*For the kingdom of God is not a matter of eating and drinking, but
of righteousness, peace and joy in the Holy Spirit.*

ROMANS 14:17

Alex worked in a print shop to put himself through college. He didn't often work directly with customers; usually, he worked in the back, folding, collating, or stapling some last-minute project.

One day, when the customer service staff was shorthanded, Alex found himself behind the cash register interacting with the walk-in customers. In the middle of one transaction the customer stopped what he was doing and asked, "Why are you so happy?"

Taken aback at such an unusually direct question, Alex mumbled, "I don't know."

The customer, sensing the truth and perhaps spurred on by the Holy Spirit, gave him one more chance: "No, really. Why are you so happy?"

Sensing the Spirit's conviction at missing the previous opportunity, Alex answered boldly, "God makes me happy!"

"I thought so," the intrigued customer answered.

As Christians, we are to be different in our behavior, our attitudes, and our demeanor. We are to demonstrate to the world around us the joy within us that comes from knowing Jesus Christ, and we are to be ready with an answer when someone asks us about it.

That day, Alex missed an opportunity to proclaim the love of God, but he was blessed with a second chance. He seized the moment, and as a result, he blessed someone who may have needed to hear about God.

We need to be ready when God gives us the opportunity to glorify His name, and we need to seize those moments. We may not always get a second chance!

LIGHTHOUSE THOUGHT FOR THE DAY

When you demonstrate the joy of the Lord, He will be faithful in providing opportunities to tell others of His love.

MARY L. MARR

Sacrificial Strength

"My grace is sufficient for you, for my power is made perfect in weakness."
Therefore I will boast…about my weaknesses,
so that Christ's power may rest on me.

2 CORINTHIANS 12:9

Is there strength in sacrifice? This appears to be a paradox. Today sacrifice is often viewed as weakness rather than strength. We perceive strength in terms of independence, self-sufficiency, boldness, and fearlessness. We honor those who can "gut it out" or "pull themselves up by their bootstraps."

Yet our model for sacrifice is Jesus Christ, who displayed His strength through His faithfulness, obedience, humility, and dependence upon the Father. He found strength from God in sacrificing His heavenly home to come to earth. As Jesus focused on bringing salvation to all, he endured great trials and eventually sacrificed His own life on the cross. Jesus' focus was not on bringing glory to Himself. It didn't matter if others thought He was strong or weak. His strength was in the Father, just as our strength should be. And though He failed the world's test of strength, His sacrificial strength was enough to raise Him from the dead and save the world from eternal hell.

Christ's sacrificial strength is the model for His followers today. While we seek glory, He calls us to humility. While we strive for independence, He calls us to dependence upon Him. While we desire earthly wealth, He offers heavenly riches. Temporal versus eternal. Our weakness is His strength.

As lighthouses, we are called to be sacrificial. We sacrifice our time for prayer and for nurturing relationships. We sacrifice our desire for privacy by letting others into our lives so that they might see Christ. Our sacrificial actions may sometimes appear to be weaknesses, but in those actions, Christ is strong.

LIGHTHOUSE THOUGHT FOR THE DAY

Where can you make sacrifices in your own life so that Christ's strength can flow in and through you?

TOM PHILLIPS

Witness of the Spirit

The Spirit himself testifies with our spirit that we are God's children.
ROMANS 8:16

In a courtroom there is nothing more valuable to an attorney's case than an eyewitness. This is the witness who can look a jury in the eye and say, "I was there, and I can tell you what happened."

God has provided something even better than an eyewitness, and He will assure you that your experience with Jesus is real. That witness is God's own Spirit. Romans 8:16 tells us that the Holy Spirit testifies *with our spirits* that we are, in fact, God's children.

What does this mean? It means that when you accepted Jesus Christ as your Lord and Savior, His Spirit actually entered into your being. When we use the phrase, "I have Christ in my heart," we mean that we have His Spirit within us. The Holy Spirit makes Jesus a living reality to us. He prays through us, leads us, tells us when we are going the wrong way, and reassures us with a deep sense of peace. His peace is so real in our inner being that we can let it become the umpire of all our thoughts and actions, ruling on whether they are right or wrong.

This assurance is not an emotion; it is much deeper than that. It is a peace that surpasses our human understanding, an all-encompassing peace that rests in our deepest being, allowing us to know beyond any doubt that we belong to the Lord Jesus Christ and that He belongs to us. It is that peace that frees us to live as God wants us to live and to make His love known to those around us.

Deep calls to deep. Through the witness of God's Spirit, children of God can say from deep within: "I know that I know that I know."

LIGHTHOUSE THOUGHT FOR THE DAY

The world longs for peace. Christians have it. The Holy Spirit's witness of the reality of our standing with God is all the assurance we need. Let's make that fact part of our personal evangelism.

PAT ROBERTSON

Tearing Down Strongholds

Bless those who persecute you; bless and do not curse.

ROMANS 12:14

Strongholds often exist in people's hearts and minds because they have been wounded in the past. Our earliest experiences can condition our minds as to what to expect in relationships.

God's plan is that the nurture and care of loving parents introduce us to His love and prepare us for life in His family. Sadly, that does not always occur. Many people have a hard time believing in anything, much less a loving God, because they've been wounded by someone they trusted in the past. For this reason, even believers may have a hard time giving and receiving unconditional love.

Some of your neighbors may have strongholds that blind them from seeing the truth of God's love. Reaching these people will be a spiritual battle, one that will bring you to the essence of what it is to live as a follower of Jesus. It may be especially difficult because those who are wounded will expect you to treat them the way they are used to being treated. Wounded people wound people, and the bondage continues. Your challenge is more than just communicating information; you have to demonstrate the kingdom so that others can experience God's unconditional love and acceptance.

Breaking a spiritual stronghold may require a dramatic event in the person's life—one that shatters stereotypes by the display of new truth. It often involves treating people (even difficult ones) the opposite of the way they expect to be treated, as well as the opposite of how we may *want* to treat them. Jesus talked about this when He commanded us to love our enemies, bless those who curse us, and pray for those who spitefully use us (Matthew 5:44).

LIGHTHOUSE THOUGHT FOR THE DAY

You hold the keys to liberation from darkness. As you live out the kingdom, you can shatter spiritual strongholds in your life and in the lives of your neighbors.

TOM PELTON

Fruit-Bearing Christians

This is to my Father's glory, that you bear much fruit,
showing yourselves to be my disciples.

JOHN 15:8

Can you imagine the fruit of six million lighthouses across America praying for, caring for, and sharing Jesus Christ with their neighbors, friends, and family?

I can imagine it, but there was a time when I couldn't have.

Early in my Christian life, I had little faith as I prayed for one particular person. But, by God's grace, this person received Christ. Then my faith grew, and I could pray for two who received Christ. The more I understood the attributes of God and recognized His blessing on my witness for Him, the more I could trust Him for greater fruit.

Later, as our Campus Crusade for Christ staff grew in number and as we trained more students and laymen, we began to pray for millions to receive Christ. God honored our faith and prayers with many millions of recorded decisions for our Savior in more than 182 countries.

Now we are helping to train millions of Christians on every continent. We are associated with thousands of Christian organizations and churches of all denominations. Now I have the faith to pray for a *billion* souls to receive Christ. As I have come to know our Lord better, I have learned to trust Him more.

Faith is like a muscle—it grows with exercise. The more we see God do in the lives of His children, the more we expect Him to do.

We glorify God when we bear much fruit. Too many Christians are satisfied with modest efforts and modest results. Yet the better we know God and His Word, the more we grasp His vision and His burden for all people throughout the world.

LIGHTHOUSE THOUGHT FOR THE DAY

As lighthouses for Christ, there is no greater privilege than bearing fruit for God our Savior. The truly Spirit-filled believer has faith that God will provide the opportunities and draw others to Christ.

BILL BRIGHT

Light in the Darkness

"You are the salt of the earth. But if the salt loses its saltiness, how can it be made salty again? It is no longer good for anything....
You are the light of the world. A city on a hill cannot be hidden."

MATTHEW 5:13–14

As the female cab driver drove me to the airport, I thought about sharing my faith; but it was 6:00 A.M., I was half asleep, and the cab driver had a speech impediment, making her hard to understand. The circumstances just didn't seem right.

Then this woman started talking about how much she and her husband loved their little children and how they hoped they would grow up to be "good kids." Then she asked me about my family. Soon my part in the conversation came to the importance of biblical training and involvement in a good church youth group. At that point she said, "I used to go to church when I was a little girl, but then we stopped going. We felt unaccepted, I guess because we were too poor." Her voice cracked, as if she might cry.

It was not the first time I have apologized for the way Christians sometimes misrepresent Jesus Christ. But it was also a perfect opportunity for me to point her back to the Shepherd. It turned out to be a spiritually valuable conversation. By the time she dropped me off at the airport, I was able to help her take the first steps back to Jesus.

Jesus didn't ask us to be the lights of the world; He *declared* us the lights (Matthew 5:14). We can be hidden or openly shining lights, but we are still His lights. We are not called to conjure up light on our own; we are to be filled with His light, which will make us shine in this world. The power of His light is ours to receive, as is the privilege to shine His light into this dark world.

LIGHTHOUSE THOUGHT FOR THE DAY

We are the lights of the world. Let us pray for and look for ways to let that light shine.

DR. DOUGLAS SHAW

Hospitable Christianity

*"The wedding of the Lamb has come, and his bride has made herself ready.
Fine linen, bright and clean, was given her to wear."
(Fine linen stands for the righteous acts of the saints.)*
REVELATION 19:7–8

Revelation tells us that the wedding gown adorning the bride is her
righteous acts—acts such feeding the hungry, protecting the weak, or
visiting those in prison. Today we might add acts like taking a fresh-
baked cherry pie to a neighbor, hosting block parties, or including
neighbors in social gatherings. Acts of righteousness such as these, per-
formed with a servant spirit, capture the attention of the unbeliever.

Would it surprise you to know that your home is part of God's
evangelism strategy—that you are to perform acts of righteousness in
and from your own home? Is it any wonder that the overseer described
in Titus is to be given over to hospitality (Titus 1:6–8)? *Hospitality* does
not mean simply having believers over for dinner. It's a compound
Greek word that means to be "a lover of strangers."

If you were to ask your neighbors to describe their greatest desire,
chances are they would say they long for intimacy, unity, and peace.
Most have given up hope of ever living in unity. Their marriages are
stressed, and their families are out of control. Many have given up
hope. As Thoreau observed, "Most men live lives of quiet desperation."

When we are hospitable, we will have opportunities to demonstrate the love of Christ in our own homes. Jesus said that when the
nonbeliever observes unity in a home and family, he gains a glimmer of
hope. He sees that there is hope in Christ. When believers are one,
Jesus said, people will know that God loves them and did indeed give
His divine Son for them.

LIGHTHOUSE THOUGHT FOR THE DAY

Acts of righteousness done for our neighbors will point them toward
Christ, the Light of the World.

JOE ALDRICH

Overcome with Jesus

They were looking intently up into the sky as he was going....
Then they returned to Jerusalem...went upstairs to the room where they
were staying...[and] joined together constantly in prayer.
ACTS 1:10, 12–14

As the disciples headed to Jerusalem, they carried in their minds the image of Jesus—risen, glorified, and ascending into heaven. What an awesome picture! I can imagine that they were so overcome by what they had just witnessed that they talked very little on their way back to the upper room. And when they arrived, all they could do was pray.

Read John's description of Jesus in Revelation 1:12–16. When he saw Him among the lampstands, eyes blazing like fire, voice like the sound of rushing waters, face shining brighter than the sun, John "fell at his feet as though dead" (Revelation 1:17). He, too, was overcome at the sight of Jesus. He immediately forgot about being hungry, tired, penniless, and alone, because in the face of *shekinah* glory, nothing else mattered.

Are you overcome with the image of Jesus, or are you preoccupied with the stuff of life? Is your focus on His majesty, or is it on your problems? What are you meditating on—financial struggles, wrongs you have suffered, a negative report? Everything pales in comparison to one real glimpse of the Son of God.

Seek after a revelation of Jesus. As you pray, ask God to teach you how to rest in His presence and discern His character. Practice waiting quietly and patiently to hear His voice. Allow yourself to become consumed by His holiness and beauty. Meditate on His righteousness and immeasurable love. Your prayers are heard through Him; your life is complete in Him; and you can know peace and joy because of Him.

LIGHTHOUSE THOUGHT FOR THE DAY

Nothing compares with just a glimpse of the glory of the Lord Jesus Christ. As lighthouses for Him, let us make it our goal above everything else to see His glory and hear His voice.

DR. TERRY TEYKL

Finishing the Race

Since we are surrounded by such a great cloud of witnesses, let us throw off
everything that hinders and the sin that so easily entangles, and let us run
with perseverance the race marked out for us. Let us fix our eyes on Jesus,
the author and perfecter of our faith.

HEBREWS 12:1–2

World-renowned golfer Gary Player once said, "Long ago I learned that there is just one thing to do after losing a tournament—and that is to forget it! In fact, that's what the game is all about: facing the adversity of defeat and then going on to the next task!"

This is good counsel for those of us involved in the lighthouse ministry. We can easily become discouraged and ineffective simply because we tend to dwell on what we believe to be past defeats. In fact, if we are not careful, we can wallow in them.

Jesus, however, teaches us to persevere regardless of how many times we think we have failed. Gary Player learned that lesson. He illustrates the principle that we must learn from our failures and then move on to whatever God is calling us to next.

In reality, we as Christians never need to feel defeated. When we commit our way to the Lord and trust fully in Him, He will use even our failures to strengthen and prepare us for more effective service.

Don't allow discouragements or defeats to impede you. Instead, invite the Lord to use them as building blocks. Our failures can help us to identify with the hurts and needs of others and to respond with deep humility and dependence on our Lord.

LIGHTHOUSE THOUGHT FOR THE DAY

Our Lord's power shows up best in our weakness. Rather than allowing discouragement to dim our lighthouse ministry, we should fix our eyes on Jesus and finish the race.

PAUL CEDAR

Abiding Prayers

*"I am the vine; you are the branches. If a man remains in me and I in him,
he will bear much fruit; apart from me you can do nothing."*

JOHN 15:5

Jesus was clear: If you want to bear fruit, if you want to be used to bring others to Jesus, you must abide in Him. As His branches, we must draw nutrients from Him, the true vine. How do we do that? Through prayer and time in the Word.

Every aspect of our lighthouse ministry, including what we share with others and how we care for them, must be bathed in prayer. If we want to bear fruit for Christ, we must abide in Him; we must rely on His strength and insight. We must listen to God and seek His direction as we reach out to those around us.

Unfortunately, it's often easy to do things in our own strength, under our own initiative. After all, we are capable people. We all have talents and abilities that would seem to lend themselves to neighborhood ministry. It is also easy to listen to the voice of guilt—that accusing voice that says, *You haven't shared with your neighbor yet. What's wrong with you?*—and jump ahead of God and His strength.

Without abiding prayer, we are prone to making hasty decisions about how to care for our neighbor. Instead, we need to seek God for just the right way to care. We need to pray: *Lord, bring me the right opportunity to share with my neighbors. Give me insights into their spiritual lives and their needs that can shape how I share with them. Show me ways to care for them that are meaningful and helpful, that clearly show Your love for them.*

LIGHTHOUSE THOUGHT FOR THE DAY

When we rely on God's strength, direction, and wisdom, we can have lighthouse ministries that bear fruit for Him. We tap into those things by abiding in prayer.

JONATHAN GRAF

Seeking and Surrendering

Then the LORD said, "The outcry against Sodom and Gomorrah is so great and their sin so grievous that I will go down and see if what they have done is as bad as the outcry that has reached me. If not, I will know."

GENESIS 18:20–21

Surrendering to God places us on the narrow road that leads to life. The broad road, which leads to destruction (Matthew 7:13–14), is populated by people who have, in essence, surrendered to their own wills and desires. This was the case with the inhabitants of Sodom.

Abraham and his family, on the other hand, had chosen to follow God even though they didn't know where He was leading them. As a result, they received His provision, protection, and blessing.

The Lord revealed to Abraham His intent to destroy the people of Sodom because of their wickedness. But Abraham's nephew Lot lived in Sodom, and Abraham was concerned for his welfare. So Abraham approached God and asked, "Will you destroy both innocent and guilty alike? Suppose you find fifty innocent people there within the city—will you still destroy it, and not spare it for their sakes?" (Genesis 18:23–24, NLT). After this "bargaining" episode, the Lord still destroyed the city, but He saved Lot and his family. Yet Lot's wife hesitated to surrender to God, so she did not share in her family's dramatic rescue .

As we see throughout Scripture, those who choose their own course and pursue their own desires inevitably encounter grave dangers. They remove themselves from His gracious protection and intervention. But when we surrender our lives to God, we enter a relationship with Him that offers safety and allows us to reach out on behalf of others.

LIGHTHOUSE THOUGHT FOR THE DAY

Shining our light for Jesus Christ means surrendering our fleshly desires to Him and seeking and obeying His guidance moment by moment.

STEPHEN ARTERBURN

Expecting Answers

If we ask anything according to his will, he hears us. And if we know that he hears us—whatever we ask—we know that we have what we asked of him.
1 JOHN 5:14–15

In Africa, just as in America, there's nothing strange about a man with a bucket and rag washing his car. But have you ever seen a man washing an invisible vehicle? Even a friendly neighbor watches and then quietly turns away, pretending not to see.

Ivy Giles smiled as her husband, John, a zonal coordinator for Every Home for Christ in Africa (EHC), was once again "faith washing" the four-by-four missions vehicle he had been claiming in prayer. John believed that a real vehicle would soon be parked outside their home. Every now and then he felt it was time to go out and "faith wash" his sure-to-come vehicle.

Then, on a recent sunny African day, twenty-eight friends from John's church came to witness the miracle. It was a brand-new, four-by-four Nissan Turbo Diesel double-cab truck with a rugged trailer specially designed for rough conditions in the bush.

Even the neighbor who had turned away earlier with a smile came by and brought some fellow church members to see the miracle. Believers in America, who had felt led to buy a vehicle for missions work in Africa, heard about the EHC need.

On their first journey with the new truck, which covered five thousand miles of rugged roads into Africa's interior, John and Ivy saw two thousand Africans come to Christ.

Productive prayer expects answers. Jesus said, "I tell you, whatever you ask for in prayer, believe that you have received it, and it will be yours" (Mark 11:24).

LIGHTHOUSE THOUGHT FOR THE DAY
Faith, it is said, is reaching into nowhere, grabbing hold of nothing, and hanging on until it becomes something. Keep holding on—answers are on the way!

DICK EASTMAN

He Welcomes "Sinners"

Now the tax collectors and "sinners" were all gathering around to hear him
[Jesus]. But the Pharisees and the teachers of the law muttered,
"This man welcomes sinners and eats with them."

LUKE 15:1–2

A pastor received and accepted a call to serve a particular church. Before his official installation, he came to the church incognito—with tattered clothes, unshaven face, unwashed hands, and smelling of sweat. Congregational members, not recognizing him, avoided him and did not welcome him back. When the pastor came the next Sunday neatly groomed, he was warmly and enthusiastically welcomed.

This congregation's response to this pastor was very telling. We tend to choose whom we welcome. We are prone to gladly receive those who are like us and live up to our standards, but we are just as prone to treat with disregard or disdain those who don't.

Jesus' behavior challenged the standards of His day—and ours. He attracted the wrong kind of people. The "tax collectors and 'sinners'" all gathered around Him. Even worse, according to the Pharisees and teachers of the law, Jesus "welcomed sinners and ate with them."

Whom do you attract? Whom do you welcome? Whom do you eat with? Are you willing to do what Jesus did: relate to those people society disdains and counts as worthless? Are you willing to take time for, listen to, and develop an interest in people who are not like you or whose standards may be different from yours?

On the day you are accused of "welcoming sinners and eating with them," rejoice and be glad, for on that day you will be like Jesus Christ.

LIGHTHOUSE THOUGHT FOR THE DAY

Ask the Lord to put a person in your path to whom He wants you to minister. Be ready to reach out to that person, whatever his or her standing in the world.

AL VANDERGRIEND

Choosing What Is Better

Jesus…came to a village where a woman named Martha opened her home
to him. She had a sister called Mary, who sat at the Lord's feet listening to
what he said…. Martha…. came to him and asked, "Lord, don't you care
that my sister has left me to do the work by myself?…" "Martha, Martha,"
the Lord answered "….Mary has chosen what is better."

LUKE 10:38–42

One of our greatest sources of anxiety is trying to do too much. Consider how the farmer in this story might feel at the end of the day.

Early one morning a farmer tells his wife he is going to plow the "south forty." He gets off to an early start so he can oil the tractor. He needs more oil, so he goes to the shop to get it. On the way to the shop he notices the pigs weren't fed, so he proceeds to the corncrib, where he finds some sacks of feed. The sacks remind him that his potatoes are sprouting, so he heads for the potato pit. On the way there he passes the woodpile and remembers that his wife wanted firewood in the house. An ailing chicken passes as he is picking up the wood, so he puts down the wood to tend to the chicken. At the end of the day, the frustrated farmer has not even gotten to the tractor, much less the field.

Ever had a day like that? Sure! Haven't we all? So what can you do to keep from having more? You can learn to set priorities.

Martha made the preparations for Jesus' visit the priority, while Mary placed more importance on a relationship with Him. Jesus' response to Mary affirmed the importance of setting priorities.

We should pray daily about how to best use our time for the benefit of the kingdom. When we do that, we will find that there are a lot of things that just aren't as important as sitting at the Master's feet.

LIGHTHOUSE THOUGHT FOR THE DAY

There is great peace in setting priorities, particularly when we ask God to show us what is most important.

STEVE DOUGLASS

The Family Business

The earth is the LORD's, and everything in it, the world, and all who live in it;
for he founded it upon the seas and established it upon the waters.

PSALM 24:1–2

This is our Father's world, and we are His heirs and residents of His world. There is a trespasser who tries to take occupancy, but he is just an intruder. Sadly, many Christians have forgotten that this earth is our heavenly Father's and that we are to be about His business.

I learned a lot about a family business by growing up on a farm.

My grandfather developed a successful family farm that was ahead of its time. It had electric lights and indoor plumbing years before rural electrification made that possible for every home and farm. Though it was located miles from the nearest town, it was a showplace.

My grandfather eventually sold the farm to my father, and I grew up there. Anyone raised on a farm knows about rising early and working long hours during the day. While the work was hard, it never seemed like work to me. I saw it as a privilege because it was part of the family business—*my* family's business.

Years after I left the farm and began work in the ministry, I prayed over the city where I ministered and was greatly moved as the Lord reminded me of life on the family farm. He impressed upon me that the city was much like the farm. Just as our farm was made up of many fields with different crops that needed attention, the city was made up of many neighborhoods with different groups of people living in them.

When we accept joint ownership of God's family farm, the Father's business becomes our business, and His business is to seek and save those who are lost. What a privilege it is to be a part of that!

LIGHTHOUSE THOUGHT FOR THE DAY

Jesus knew as a boy that He was here to "be about [His] Father's business," (Luke 2:49, NKJV), and as the Father sent Him, so has He sent us.

JIM HYLTON

Loving God for Who He Is

Rejoice in the Lord always. I will say it again: Rejoice!
PHILIPPIANS 4:4

One of the most important discoveries I have ever made is this truth: God is most glorified in me when I am most satisfied in him. This is the motor that drives my ministry as a pastor. It affects everything I do.

Whatever I do, my aim is to glorify God (1 Corinthians 10:31). This means my aim is to do it in a way that shows how the glory of God has satisfied the longings of my heart. If my preaching betrayed that God had not even met my own needs, it would be fraudulent. If Christ were not the satisfaction of my heart, would people really believe me when I herald his words, "I am the bread of life; he who comes to me shall not hunger, and he who believes in me shall never thirst" (John 6:35, RSV)?

The glory of bread is that it satisfies. The glory of living water is that it quenches thirst. We do not honor the refreshing, self-replenishing, pure water of a mountain spring by lugging buckets of water up the path to make our contributions from the ponds below. We honor the spring by feeling thirsty, getting down on our knees, and drinking with joy. Then we say, "Ahhhh!" (that's worship!), and we go on our journey in the strength of the fountain (that's service). The mountain spring is glorified most when we are most satisfied with its water.

Tragically, most of us have been taught that duty, not delight, is the way to glorify God. We have not been taught that delight in God is our duty! Being satisfied in God is not an option. It is the most basic demand of all. "Delight yourself in the LORD" (Psalm 37:4) is not a suggestion, but a command. So are: "Serve the LORD with gladness" (Psalm 100:2, RSV) and "Rejoice in the Lord always" (Philippians 4:4).

LIGHTHOUSE THOUGHT FOR THE DAY

We will bear fruit as lighthouses for Christ when we "taste and see that the LORD is good" (Psalm 34:8) and delight in who He is.

JOHN PIPER, WITH JUSTIN TAYLOR

Seeing God at a Dead End

> *Then Jesus lifted up His eyes, and seeing a great multitude coming toward Him, He said to Philip, "Where shall we buy bread, that these may eat?" But this He said to test him, for He Himself knew what He would do.*
>
> JOHN 6:5–6, NKJV

Think of Philip, sitting on the hillside with Jesus, watching thousands upon thousands of people streaming up the mountain to see the Lord and hear Him teach.

Then the question: "Where shall we buy bread?"

The question pushed poor Philip right into a dead end. He didn't have any idea what to say or what to do! Was the Lord seriously asking him for some kind of answer? Thinking that a quick crowd estimate might do the job, Philip whipped out his calculator and tried to crunch a few numbers.

> *Philip answered Him, "Two hundred denarii*
> *worth of bread is not sufficient for them, that*
> *every one of them may have a little." Then*
> *Jesus said, "Make the people sit down." (John 6:7, 10, NKJV)*

If Philip had only known it, he had just met God at a dead end. He was sitting within scant inches of the Creator of the universe. What are a few thousand loaves of bread to the One who holds all the rippling, golden wheat fields of the whole world in the palm of His hand? Philip was about to witness what God could do.

That's the way it is for us. When we come to the dead end of personal inadequacies, when we come to the dead end of depleted resources, He's right there. Not just inches away, but *inside* us! Closer than hands or feet, closer than breathing. And He will be to us all that He is.

LIGHTHOUSE THOUGHT FOR THE DAY

When we come to our own personal dead ends, God is there for us; when we "can't," God can!

RON MEHL

How Strong Is Your City?

We have a strong city; God makes salvation its walls and ramparts.
ISAIAH 26:1

I don't think many people could honestly say about their city what is said in this verse. I live in Colorado Springs, Colorado, a city that is home to more than a hundred Christian ministries and organizations. Yet Christians are still a small minority of the overall population.

Still, I believe this verse will someday be true of my city—and I believe it can be true of your city as well. But it will take prayer, prayer, and more prayer. It will take hundreds of thousands of Christians praying for the lost in their cities. It will take thousands of lighthouses for Christ praying for their neighborhoods. It will take persevering prayer—prayer over the long haul that doesn't give up when results aren't seen in a month, three months, a year, or more.

Are you ready for that kind of prayer? If there is any doubt, ask God to strengthen and sustain you through the months and years, through those times when you feel as if you are the only one praying.

Isaiah 26 goes on to say, "Open the gates that the righteous nation may enter, the nation that keeps faith. You will keep in perfect peace him whose mind is steadfast, because he trusts in you" (vv. 2–3).

As a lighthouse, you are part of that "righteous nation" entering your city. Continue to pray that salvation becomes your city's walls and ramparts, the surrounding protection of your city. Don't go by sight in your assessment of your effectiveness—remember that we walk by faith. Keep praying for your lost neighbors, and keep your faith and trust in God for the results.

LIGHTHOUSE THOUGHT FOR THE DAY
A city is only as strong as the believers who pray within it and for it. Be a persevering lighthouse of prayer for your city!

JONATHAN GRAF

Inclusiveness for Christ

"Come to me, all you who are weary and burdened, and I will give you rest."
MATTHEW 11:28

Shortly before his death, noted historical author Carl Sandburg was asked whether he believed any words to be bad. He replied by saying that he knew of only one: *exclusive*.

"To be exclusive," he said, "is to feel superior towards others and, therefore, to regard others as unworthy of one's association and friendship."

I believe Sandburg was right. *Exclusive* is a bad word, especially for Christians. Our Lord Jesus is *inclusive*. He has invited anyone and everyone to come to Him.

Unfortunately, many professing Christians are known for being exclusive—for being holier-than-thou and looking down their noses at others. Many outsiders in our culture believe that Christians are judgmental, critical, and hypocritical.

It should not be so. It *must* not be so!

Jesus was known as "a friend of sinners." He did not exclude sinners. Instead, He loved them, reached out to them—and even died for them. He did not ignore sin, nor did He condone it. He came to forgive sinners, including each one of us.

The key was His love. Authentic love always erases exclusiveness. Our Lord came into the world as love personified. And He sends us into the world to be the same.

Our lighthouses should be beacons for sinners. We have the privilege of reaching out to all around us with the love and grace of Jesus Christ as we pray and care and share.

LIGHTHOUSE THOUGHT FOR THE DAY

As sinners who have been saved by grace, we should never exclude others, but rather love them and invite them to be forgiven by Jesus.

PAUL CEDAR

What Is "In"?

> "If you knew the gift of God and who it is that asks you for a drink, you would have asked him and he would have given you living water."
>
> JOHN 4:10

Though the belief systems of Americans have changed in many ways in recent decades, the same unchanging gospel still works. Why? Because Jesus came once for all humanity—past, present, and future. He remains the central focus.

What can change, however, is the way we share our faith with others. Even Jesus and the apostle Paul varied their approaches depending on their situations. They reached people at their areas of need or understanding.

In John 3 we see the dignified but spiritually deceived Nicodemus, who came to see Jesus by night. Jesus used an analogy of physical birth to teach Nicodemus the necessity of spiritual rebirth.

The woman at the well (John 4) was deceived and depraved, but she discovered who Jesus really was. Jesus used the need for water, something she understood, to explain her spiritual need.

In Acts 17 we see Paul on Mars Hill in Athens, faced with the altar to the "unknown God." He addressed a group of people who, although they were diverse in their spiritual outlook, were all misled. For Paul, it presented the perfect opportunity to reveal who God really is.

What really is biblically "in" when you share your faith? It is always relevant to address the spiritual journey of the seeker. When we use this approach, it satisfies thirst instead of supplanting views. Once the seeker realizes the "answer," his views will change anyway. That is what true conversion is all about. It is a sovereign work of the Holy Spirit.

LIGHTHOUSE THOUGHT FOR THE DAY

We should be ready to meet the needy where they are in their spiritual lives and show them the one true way to God: Jesus Christ.

DR. DOUGLAS SHAW

The Glory of God

The heavens declare the glory of God;
the skies proclaim the work of his hands.

Psalm 19:1

One beautiful February night at our home in Minnesota, I stepped outside around ten o'clock and enjoyed a spectacular reminder of our God's glory. It was a clear, crisp, windless winter night, and I could almost *feel* the peacefulness around me.

The light from a beautiful full moon glistened off the layer of newly fallen snow, and it appeared as though someone had randomly scattered thousands and thousands of tiny diamonds all over the ground. I looked up from the snow to a brilliant night sky displaying the moon and countless bright stars, and it hit me: The Lord's glory was being manifested to me that very moment through His creation.

I was reminded that evening of the truth from God's Word, the truth that He has given us His creation as a silent reminder of His power and presence. I looked at the beautiful creation before me and felt deeply assured of His presence in my own life.

I thought that night about how creation challenges each of us to consider the reality of the person of God. Romans 1:20 says, "For since the creation of the world God's invisible qualities—his eternal power and divine nature—have been clearly seen, being understood from what has been made, so that men are without excuse."

Those are the truths each of us can take from the creation around us. It is an assurance to believers that God has a plan and purpose for our lives. For nonbelievers, it is a challenge to consider the question, "Who is God, and what does that mean to me?"

Lighthouse Thought for the Day

As you enjoy God's creation, be assured that God has a plan and purpose for your life. When nonbelievers ask the question: "How can I know Him?" be ready to give an answer for the hope that you have (1 Peter 3:15).

Bruce Schoeman

Finding Strength to Forgive

"If you do not forgive men their sins, your Father will not forgive your sins."
MATTHEW 6:15

Ralph Waldo Emerson said of Abraham Lincoln, "His heart was as great as the world, but there was no room in it to hold the memory of a wrong." There's a lot to be said for that kind of forgetfulness.

In Jesus' day, the Pharisees held that someone could be forgiven no more than three times. In Matthew 18, when Peter asked Jesus if he was supposed to forgive someone up to seven times, he was more than doubling the Pharisees' Talmudic standard. To his amazement, however, Jesus told Peter to forgive "seventy times seven," meaning that he was to place no limit on forgiveness.

Many of us have a difficult time forgiving and receiving forgiveness. But in Matthew 6:15, Jesus clearly explained the connection between forgiving those who offend us and receiving forgiveness from God.

We are to forgive unconditionally and without reservation. We are not to take the attitude that we will forgive only when the offending party asks for forgiveness or admits his or her guilt. Jesus demonstrated this at the crucifixion when He prayed for God to forgive His executioners, even though they were certainly not asking for His forgiveness or admitting any wrongdoing (Luke 23:34).

We are to forgive others because Jesus' blood was a complete payment for their sins (2 Corinthians 5:19). Refusing to forgive someone is to insist on a kind of "double jeopardy," or a second payment for sin. As lighthouses for Christ, we need to remember that Jesus has already paid the price for our sins and the sins of those who may offend or hurt us.

LIGHTHOUSE THOUGHT FOR THE DAY

Do you want to fully access God's forgiveness and effectively tell others the Good News of that forgiveness? Then forgive, forgive again, and forgive some more!

EDDIE AND ALICE SMITH

The Wisdom Factor

*How much better to get wisdom than gold, to choose
understanding rather than silver!*
Proverbs 16:16

Knowledge is power. It is the cornerstone for technology, medicine, education, and invention. Knowledge translates into financial power, too, as testified by the many reports of industrial espionage.

Knowledge is power, but it is not all-powerful. If knowledge by itself were the answer to the world's ills, we would now be living in a veritable utopia. We're deep in an information revolution, yet few would say the world is idyllic. Indeed, the Bible speaks of the increase in knowledge as a sign of the last days (Daniel 12:4).

To be effective, knowledge must be accompanied by godly wisdom. Our problem today is not a lack of knowledge, but a lack of corresponding growth in divine wisdom. The world is being negatively impacted because of knowledgeable sinners, educated fools with darkened minds, and criminals in executive positions.

Proverbs 9:1 declares that "wisdom has built her house." In other words, wisdom shows us how to build our lives, assembling the materials in a way that conforms to God's plan. In verse 10 of the same chapter, we are told that "the fear of the LORD is the beginning of wisdom." God is to be the architect and contractor of our lives.

A wise person understands that there is not enough knowledge in ten thousand universities to create and sustain one successful life. Only those who submit all they have and *all they know* to God will receive the wisdom to live life as it was designed.

Lighthouse Thought for the Day

Today I will intentionally ask for and apply godly wisdom to what I know and what I learn.

Charles T. Crabtree

Pitches of Pride

> *Humble yourselves, therefore, under God's mighty hand, that*
> *he may lift you up in due time.*
> 1 PETER 5:6

Have you ever made a commitment to fast and then found yourself unable to keep it? You're not alone. But why is it so difficult? Usually it involves our pride. Humans have a strong instinct to survive, and eating is part of that instinct. To battle that, we need to set aside our pride and humble ourselves before God.

How we approach a fast demonstrates how our pride can set us up for failure. Consider Ernest Lawrence Thayer's poem "Casey at the Bat."

> There was ease in Casey's manner as he stepped into his place.
> There was pride in Casey's bearing, and a smile on Casey's face,
> And when, responding to the cheers, he lightly doffed his hat,
> No stranger in the crowd could doubt 'twas Casey at the bat.

Can't you picture this baseball player swaggering to the plate, sure he'll hit the ball out of the park? Do you approach fasting like that? Have you fasted often and feel it's commonplace? Are you confident that you can keep your commitment in your own strength? When we're overconfident, pride throws pitches we're unable to hit. We can't get past ourselves or our bodies' need to hear God's voice. We think we can handle it on our own, but we strike out.

> And somewhere men are laughing and somewhere children shout,
> But there is no joy in Mudville—mighty Casey has struck out.

Praise God that He's able to make beauty from ashes and cause dead bones to breathe life. He isn't surprised by our weaknesses. He uses them to make us more like Christ.

LIGHTHOUSE THOUGHT FOR THE DAY

Seek God's help rather than your own strength as you fast for those on your prayer list.

TOM PHILLIPS

Ordered Steps

The steps of a good man are ordered by the LORD.
PSALM 37:23, KJV

The psalmist does not say that the steps of *everyone* or even the steps of *every believer* are ordered by the Lord. Rather, he says, "The steps of a *good man* are ordered by the LORD."

A "good man" is not only a believer, but also has yielded to the Spirit's control. He has crucified personal ambition and dreams and earnestly desires above all else to be continually at the center of God's will.

Proverbs 3 reflects this thought: "Trust in the LORD with all your heart…in all your ways acknowledge him, and he will make your paths straight" (vv. 5–6). The promise to the believer is very clear: Trust in the Lord, acknowledge Him in all ways—not only as Savior, but also as Lord—and He will "order your steps."

For years, Dr. Bill Bright of Campus Crusade for Christ has taught the concept of *divine appointment.* He believes that if we yield to the Holy Spirit's control and confess and renounce all known sin, God will order our steps in such a way that we will be put in the presence of those who need Him. If we are sensitive and yielded to the Spirit, God will open doors of opportunity every day.

Those in need may be Christians who are discouraged or are facing personal problems, or perhaps lost souls who are searching for the light. God will direct our paths to needy people, and at the moment of divine appointment, God will give us the right words to say if we are willing.

We should pray a prayer like this one from an old hymn:

> *Lead me to some soul today,*
> *Oh, teach me Lord just what to say.*
> *Friends of mine are lost in sin*
> *And cannot find their way.*

LIGHTHOUSE THOUGHT FOR THE DAY

As lighthouses for Jesus Christ, we need to ask God to direct our steps to those who need Him.

LARRY LEWIS

Shining Stars

So that you may become blameless and pure, children of God
without fault in a crooked and depraved generation, in
which you shine like stars in the universe.

PHILIPPIANS 2:15

Recently, a friend of mine commented on how difficult it is to distinguish between professing Christians and those who do not follow Jesus Christ. Christians and non-Christians seem to go to the same events, do the same things, and live, talk, and spend the same way.

Sadly, I had to agree with my friend.

The Lord wants to eliminate the blur between what is light and what is dark and what a life lived for Christ and a life not lived for Him looks like. God wants us to live lives that reflect Him in every way.

There are prerequisites to shining as lights in this world. One is a commitment to keeping ourselves from being defiled by the world and our modern culture. The children of the one living and true God are commanded to live consistently with the callings of Jesus Christ and with His character.

Imagine what our nation would look like if those who really knew Jesus communicated the message of Christ by diligently living out their faith. Would we not see healthier marriages and families, first in our churches then in our neighborhoods? Would we not see better parent-child relationships?

Being a light for Jesus means affecting the lives of those we are around on a daily basis. God wants those who know and love Jesus Christ to lead this generation out of the darkness by shining the light before them. May we each ask the Lord for grace to live lives that shine like stars before the world.

LIGHTHOUSE THOUGHT FOR THE DAY

We are called to be set apart from the world so that we can be lights to the world. Shine the light, and make your neighbors wonder why you live differently.

JARVIS WARD

Right Thinking

Whatever is true, whatever is noble, whatever is right, whatever is pure,
whatever is lovely, whatever is admirable…think about such things.

PHILIPPIANS 4:8

A few years ago the *Houston Post* reported that a lady had complained to the government that the extra sunlight created by daylight saving time was burning up her lawn. Her perspective was so distorted that she believed the government controlled the amount of daylight in a twenty-four-hour period.

Life really is determined by our perspective. With right thinking, we can face anything. Our thoughts and attitudes are our greatest assets. Walt Emerson said it this way, "What lies behind us and what lies before us are tiny matters compared to what lies within us." The Bible tells us, "As he thinks in his heart, so is he" (Proverbs 23:7, NKJV).

Unfortunately, we live in a world of crooked thinking. Therefore, we need to make sure our thinking is right. Paul knew the art of right thinking. Paul had found the way to think like Jesus, to let Him guide his thinking. He asked that we let the mind of Christ be reproduced in us.

Here are some ways to change your thinking and your attitude: Pray, letting Scripture guide you; read God's Word and other books that help shape good thinking; listen to good music and speech; and engage in good conversation.

Just as great music follows a scale, so must our thoughts follow a scale. Here is a scale by which to gauge your thoughts: "You'll do best by filling your minds and meditating on things true, noble, reputable, authentic, compelling, gracious—the best, not the worst; the beautiful, not the ugly; things to praise, not things to curse" (Philippians 4:8, MSG).

LIGHTHOUSE THOUGHT FOR THE DAY

Our thoughts our very important. They affect everything about us, including how we respond to neighbors who need Jesus Christ.

JIM HYLTON

Happy Birthday!

Something like scales fell from Saul's eyes, and he could see again.
He got up and was baptized....
He began to preach in the synagogues that Jesus is the Son of God.

ACTS 9:18, 20

What happens at the point of conversion varies greatly between people. In Acts we read of many different people confessing the Lord Jesus as Savior. It took a crisis experience to bring some of them—like Saul—to their knees. Others, like the Ethiopian eunuch, gladly trusted Jesus Christ upon hearing the gospel.

For most people, becoming a Christian is a memorable experience, and recalling when and where that decision was made enables us to counterattack Satan when he assaults us with doubts. I believe it's profitable during times of doubt to reaffirm our commitment to the Lord by telling Him, "No matter what doubts and troubles may come, I believe You're my Savior."

During our Christian pilgrimage, especially when we're younger, it's common to reinforce our decision to trust Jesus Christ. Looking back, my wife, Pat, and I both can recall saying to the Lord, "Now, Lord, you know that I accepted You years ago...." but we recommitted our lives to Him anyway. As Psalm 103:14 says, God knows our frame. He remembers what we're like. He isn't surprised when we want to make sure we're saved. It's a natural, human response to doubt.

Many Christians can remember the day they first put their trust in Jesus Christ, while others—Ruth Graham, for example—can't remember when they received Jesus, but can't remember when they didn't trust Him, either. It isn't necessary to remember a specific date when you first trusted Jesus. What is crucial is truly making that commitment and then resting in God's promises.

LIGHTHOUSE THOUGHT FOR THE DAY

As lighthouses for Jesus Christ, we need to remember that our salvation rests on God's promises, and not our personal experiences.

LUIS PALAU

Being a River of Life

On the last and greatest day of the Feast, Jesus stood and said in a loud voice,
"If anyone is thirsty, let him come to me and drink.
Whoever believes in me, as the Scripture has said,
streams of living water will flow from within him."

JOHN 7:37–38

This passage refers to the Feast of the Tabernacles, when the Jews remembered Moses bringing water from the rock for the thirsty people of Israel (Exodus 17). They thanked God for the precious, life-giving water they had received during the past year and asked Him for water for the coming year. They also remembered the prophecy of Ezekiel that life-giving water would flow out from the temple.

But in John 7:37–38, Jesus tells those in attendance that this concept was being fulfilled in their sight. He was saying to them, and to us, "If you want living water, come to me, and I will give it to you freely. And when you receive this never-ending flow of life-giving water, it will flow from you so that you will be able to pass it along to others."

Jesus said in John 7:38, "From his innermost being will flow rivers of living water'" (NASB). Jesus promises that if we put our trust in Him, He will pour out His Spirit on those we come in contact with. We will be like sponges that are so soaked with precious water that it pours out and falls on everyone around us.

Providing new life to those around us means caring for them. But before we can do that, we need to pray for the Holy Spirit to fill us and refill us. As D. L. Moody said, "We are leaky vessels." As such, we need to be refilled continuously with the living water Jesus provides.

LIGHTHOUSE THOUGHT FOR THE DAY

As lighthouses for Christ, we need to pray that God will continuously fill and refill us with His life-giving Spirit so that we can bless those around us.

ALI HANNA

Why Pray?

"You may ask me for anything in my name, and I will do it."
JOHN 14:14

For years I wrestled with this question about prayer for the salvation of the lost: Why should I pray and fast for something that God wants done anyway? As I've thought about this and looked into God's Word, I've learned these things about God's approach to soul-winning:

1. *Soul-winning is a partnership between God and His people.* God could have chosen angels to preach the gospel and win the lost, but He chose us to represent Jesus. We can't do this alone. To effectively reach others for Christ, we need to be filled with the Spirit. We cannot be filled with the Spirit apart from a close relationship with God, which we receive through prayer.

2. *Satan has great power to bind and blind lost souls.* The unsaved people around us must be released from bondage to the devil in order to receive God's Word, and God has chosen to do this through the prayers of His people.

3. *While it is true that God wants the lost to be saved, they have offended Him greatly by their sins, so they need intercessors.* When we become intercessors like Jesus was—we appeal to God on behalf of those around us for His mercy—God acts even more mercifully to win people to Himself.

God has given us the opportunity to have a part in bringing lost people to Him. Let's pray and fast, asking Him to help us be more effective in winning those around us to Jesus Christ.

LIGHTHOUSE THOUGHT FOR THE DAY

As lighthouses for Jesus Christ, we must pray for those around us, that their hearts will be ready to receive the gospel. This kind of intercessory prayer needs to become a regular part of our relationship with God.

LOWELL LUNDSTROM

Intentionality

How can they believe in him if they have never heard about him?
And how can they hear about him unless someone tells them?
Romans 10:14, TLB

C. T. Studd was a young, wealthy cricket player in England when he read these words of an atheist:

Did I firmly believe, as millions say they do, that the knowledge and practice of religion in this life influences the destiny in another...I should esteem one soul gained for heaven worth a life of suffering. Earthly consequences should never stay my hand nor seal my lips. Earth, its joy and its grief, would occupy no moment of my thoughts. I would strive to look upon eternity alone and on the immortal sounds around me, soon to be everlastingly happy or everlastingly miserable. I would go forth to the world and preach it in season and out of season, and my text would be "what shall it profit a man if he gain the whole world and lose his soul?"

After taking an honest look at these words, Studd made a full commitment to Christ. He gave up his fortune to spread the message of Jesus, and he affected two continents. When people questioned his passion, he said, "If Jesus be God and died for me, then no sacrifice can be too great for me to make for Him."

Studd was intentional in his witness. We should be, too. Not many are going to ask us directly to tell them how they can know Christ as Savior and Lord. We need to build bridges and look for opportunities. Prayer is key in turning conversation to Christ.

I want to be a good witness. I want to tell individuals "Christ died for sins once for all, the righteous for the unrighteous, to bring you to God" (1 Peter 3:18). I want to follow Christ's example, who came "to seek and to save what was lost" (Luke 19:10).

Lighthouse Thought for the Day

A Christlike life is key to our witness, but we also have to *tell* people how to enter into a saving relationship with Christ.

Bob Ricker

The Big Picture

Give thanks to the LORD, for he is good. His love endures forever. Give thanks to the God of gods. His love endures forever.

PSALM 136:1–2

One of my daughters was a whiz at putting picture puzzles together. She was good at working these puzzles because she could always keep the "big picture" (on the box top) in front of her.

For the Christian, the 136th Psalm is the big picture. *His love endures forever.* It forces us to rise above the mundane minutiae of life. It sets before us the majesty of the Creator, the sweeping vistas of creation, and the enduring love of God. When we read this Psalm, the disconnected fragments of life suddenly make sense, and the enigmas of individual personalities are better understood.

If you cannot see beyond the immediate, you can't see your function in life. Without purpose, there is no meaning. Without a vision of the big picture, life is vanity. Sadly, millions of people live meaningless lives because all they see are the pieces of life, and most of those pieces are broken.

When you are tempted to think that God is not longsuffering or merciful, read the middle verses of Psalm 136. Never lose sight of the main truth about God in the story of Israel. Those who did not see the big picture saw only the tests of faith, not the triumphs. Instead of praising God for His enduring mercy and love, they cried over adverse circumstances and temporary setbacks. Yet all the time God was at work.

May God help all of us to be big-picture people. After all, He was the One who put us in the picture.

LIGHTHOUSE THOUGHT FOR THE DAY

As lighthouses for Jesus Christ, let's be people who focus on the big picture: God is good, and His love endures forever.

CHARLES T. CRABTREE

The Whole Gospel

I am jealous for you with a godly jealousy. I promised you to one husband,
to Christ, so that I might present you as a pure virgin to him.

2 CORINTHIANS 11:2

Jesus warned His disciples that tremendous deception would be unleashed in the last days. "See to it that no one misleads you," He admonished them (Matthew 24:4, NASB). Five times He repeated this warning, saying there would be false christs, false teachers, false prophets, as well as "great signs and wonders, so as to mislead, if possible, even the elect" (v. 24, NASB).

The Lord also declared that "this gospel of the kingdom shall be preached in the whole world as a testimony" (v. 14, NASB). Underline the phrase, *this gospel.* The gospel as Jesus taught it, with its power to heal, deliver, and make people holy, will be proclaimed as a witness to all nations before His return.

Even while deception is being multiplied upon the earth, the gospel of the kingdom of God—Jesus' gospel—is also being restored.

What is this "gospel of the kingdom" Jesus talked about? It is the *whole* message of Jesus Christ. It is more demanding, more fulfilling, and more powerful than typical American Christianity. It is the gospel that costs us our all but gives us God's best.

In the midst of the worldliness, lukewarmness, and outright deceptions that have crept into the body of Christ in our times, this gospel of the kingdom is the message that we, as lighthouses for Christ, must proclaim in the last days. If we listen to anything that does not lead us to the path to God's kingdom—if we are not becoming like Jesus in holiness, love, and power—we are being misled.

LIGHTHOUSE THOUGHT FOR THE DAY

If we are to be effective lighthouses for Christ, we must keep ourselves focused on the gospel—the whole gospel—that He preached.

FRANCIS FRANGIPANE

Who Is He?

"What do you think about the Christ? Whose son is he?"
MATTHEW 22:42, NCV

After three years of ministry, hundreds of miles, thousands of miracles, and innumerable teachings, Jesus asks, "Who?" Jesus bids the people to ponder not what He has done, but who He is.

It's the ultimate question of the Christ: Whose Son is He? Is He the Son of God or the sum of our dreams? Is He a figment of our imagination?

When we ask that question about Santa, the answer is the culmination of our desires. A depiction of our fondest dreams. Not so when we ask it about Jesus. For no one could ever dream a person as incredible as He is. The idea that a virgin would be selected by God to bear Himself.... The notion that God would don a scalp and toes and two eyes.... That's too incredible. Too revolutionary. We would never create such a Savior. We aren't that daring.

When we create a redeemer, we keep him safely distant in his far-away castle. We allow him only the briefest of encounters with us. We permit him to swoop in and out with his sleigh before we can draw too near. We wouldn't ask him to take up residence in the midst of contaminated people. In our wildest imaginings we wouldn't conjure a king who becomes one of us.

But God did what we wouldn't dare dream. He did what we couldn't imagine. He became a man so we could trust Him. He became a sacrifice so we could know Him. And He defeated death so we could follow Him.

Only a God could create a plan this mad. Only a Creator beyond the fence of logic could offer such a gift of love.

LIGHTHOUSE THOUGHT FOR THE DAY

Our lighthouses should point our neighbors to the light no one could have envisioned—a free gift of love from God through the sacrifice of His Son.

MAX LUCADO

Receiving the Seed

"He who has ears to hear, let him hear."
LUKE 8:8

Jesus used the phrase "He who has ears to hear, let him hear" many times, and always as part of some important teaching. He is saying that to us today as He seeks to instruct us through His written Word and through our personal fellowship with Him.

Jesus uses this phrase in reference to receiving God's Word, which He likens to seed in the Parable of the Sower in Luke 8. In this chapter, Jesus teaches the disciples about the kingdom of God and how to live under God's rule. Jesus' point in this passage is that God speaks to His people in a way that produces great fruit in their lives, as long as they listen and obey.

Jesus taught that God's Word always remains the same, but that the soil of our hearts determines how much fruit the "seed" produces (Luke 8:8). In order for the seed to produce a great harvest, this soil has to be deep and free from any hindrance so that it may receive the seed. This is what Jesus called "good ground" or hearts that "having heard the word with a noble and good heart, keep it and bear fruit with patience" (Luke 8:15, NKJV).

It is not enough to have God give you His Word. You must receive that Word into a heart that is ready to appropriate its promises. When it is received into a hard, shallow, or divided heart, God's Word will not produce anything. But the harvest from any one of God's promises that is received into a good, fertile heart is often measureless.

LIGHTHOUSE THOUGHT FOR THE DAY

In order to be effective and productive lighthouses for Christ, we must make certain our hearts are prepared to receive His promises and commands, which are contained in His written Word.

HENRY BLACKABY

Feeling Inadequate?

That is why, for Christ's sake, I delight in weaknesses, in insults,
in hardships, in persecutions, in difficulties.
For when I am weak, then I am strong.

2 CORINTHIANS 12:10

This is what a friend of mine calls "flip-side logic." The world, our friends, our families, and our own personalities tell us that the key to success is to be strong, competent, and self-confident. But that is not God's way.

When our confidence and fearlessness come from within ourselves, we are prone to go our own direction, thinking we know what is best in a given situation. When we do that, we can easily fall prey to the deceptions of the evil one.

On the other hand, when we feel incompetent, in over our heads, and unable to do what is required, we are more apt to call on God to take over.

God does not want us at the helm. He wants to steer the boat. He wants us to turn over control to Him, just as the disciples in the storm-tossed boat, afraid for their lives, did (Luke 8:25).

When I admit my inadequacy and dependency on the Lord Jesus and His abundant love and grace, I am effective as a witness. But when I am self-confident and full of my own importance, I find I can't accomplish anything.

Successful evangelism begins with a sense of inadequacy, moves to prayer and fasting for help and guidance, then steps out in confidence, knowing that the Lord said to Paul, "My power is made perfect in weakness" (2 Corinthians 12:9).

LIGHTHOUSE THOUGHT FOR THE DAY

As lighthouses for Jesus, we need to ask God to make us dependent on Him to give us strength and guidance as we endeavor to reach others for Him.

ALI HANNA

Making Friends for Christ

> "When you give a banquet, invite the poor, the crippled, the lame,
> the blind, and you will be blessed."
>
> LUKE 14:13–14

Jesus recognized that we are prone to spend our time with those who make us feel comfortable. He never said that that is wrong, but He challenged us to move beyond our comfort zones and reach out to those who are too needy to repay us. Jesus wants us to see people not in terms of what they can do for us, but in terms of what we can do for them. He wants us to see their needs and to have the courage to reach out to meet those needs.

In *Letter to the Romans,* William Barclay points out that such love leaves a deep impression:

> There was a soldier who was wounded in battle. A padre crept out and did what he could for him. He stayed with him when the remainder of the troops retreated. In the heat of the day he gave him water from his own water bottle, while he himself remained parched with thirst. In the night, when the chill of frost came down, he covered the wounded man with his own coat, and finally wrapped him up in even more of his own clothes to save him from the cold. In the end the wounded man looked up at the padre.
>
> "Padre," he said, "you're a Christian?"
>
> "I try to be," said the padre.
>
> "Then," said the wounded man, "If Christianity makes a man do for another man what you have done for me, tell me about it, because I want it."

LIGHTHOUSE THOUGHT FOR THE DAY

May we all recognize what we need to do for others so that those around us will want what we have in Christ.

AL VANDERGRIEND

The Light of His Word

Your word is a lamp to my feet and a light for my path.
PSALM 119:105

Have you ever gotten up in the middle of the night and stubbed your toe on something hard? If you have, you're probably wincing right now.

It doesn't help to have someone tell you that the pain will go away in a minute or two. As you jump around on one foot, yelping in pain, the only benefit you can see of smacking your toe like that is that you hope you learned not to do it again—at least not on the same object.

Sin is a lot like that. When we stub our spiritual toes, it's humiliating and painful. Think back on certain painful sins in your life: Are you wincing again? How many times have you smacked a spiritual toe on that same bedpost?

What help a simple lamp is in a midnight trek across the room! In the same way, spiritual light helps you make your way through life. God's Word is a lamp to your feet and a light to your path, but "the way of the wicked is like deep darkness; they do not know what makes them stumble" (Proverbs 4:19).

I've found Scripture to be incredibly helpful when it comes to illuminating some of the paths I've taken. People who resent what God says in His Word seem to prefer groping their way in the dark to walking confidently in the light.

People with godly wisdom are grateful for the good lighting of God's Word. They've learned—through life's experiences, through the Word itself, or through a combination of both—that it is better to walk with their path illuminated by the truth of the Scriptures than to stub their way through the night.

LIGHTHOUSE THOUGHT FOR THE DAY

As followers of Christ, and as lighthouses for Him, we need to keep the light of God's written Word, the Bible, before us always. When our way is well lighted, we can lead others on the right path.

DAVID MAINS

What Is That in Your Hand?

But Moses said to God, "Who am I, that I should go to Pharaoh
and bring the Israelites out of Egypt?"

EXODUS 3:11

I don't find it difficult to identify with Moses when he told God the task was too hard for him. Like Moses, I sometimes forget that God has proclaimed, "I will be with you" (Exodus 3:12). That makes all the difference in the world! It puts the task at hand in an entirely different perspective.

Even after God reassured him, Moses was still afraid. So God asked him a question: "What is that in your hand?" (Exodus 4:2). It wasn't much. Just a common staff. But common things have uncommon uses when God gets hold of them. God can use a little to do the miraculous. A boy's lunch can feed a multitude. A sling can slay a giant. Some flour and a few drops of oil can last as long as they need to.

God took Moses' ordinary staff and used it to help orchestrate Israel's exodus from Egypt. Just as God used an ordinary staff to do miracles, He can do great things with ordinary people—like you and me.

A song talks about us being "just ordinary people." That's true. We are ordinary, but at the same time we are gifted with the Holy Spirit and with God's calling on our lives. And we are called to extraordinary living by the power of God.

God has placed something in our hands, too. It's the task of reaching the unsaved world for the Lord Jesus Christ. That starts with those closest to us—our friends, our coworkers, our family members, our neighbors.

LIGHTHOUSE THOUGHT FOR THE DAY

Whatever God has placed in your hand, you can be assured that He will be with you as you use it to accomplish it for Him.

BOB RICKER

How Bright Is Your Light?

"You are the light of the world.... Let your light shine before men,
that they may see your good deeds and praise your Father in heaven."
MATTHEW 5:14, 16

A nautical lighthouse whose light is obscured or dimmed is all but worthless to ships looking to it for direction. In fact, it can do more harm than good. The same is true of our witness for Jesus Christ.

Scripture clearly commands us to shine our light on those around us. Basically this means that we are to portray Jesus Christ—the true Light—to others. Obviously we cannot do this without the Holy Spirit's help. But that brings me to a crucial question: Do you allow the Holy Spirit to operate unhindered in you?

Psalm 66:18 says, "If I had cherished sin in my heart, the Lord would not have listened." This is a truth many believers overlook—that if we don't deal with the known sin in our lives, God doesn't hear our prayers. We can't shine the light of Christ if we are not in communion with Him. If we want to shine Christ's light effectively on our neighbors, it is crucial for us to keep the lines of communication with God open.

We should continually ask the Holy Spirit to reveal anything that comes between God and us. When He reveals a sin, we need to deal with it—confess it, ask forgiveness, and endeavor with God's help to forsake it.

When we become pure vessels that are fit for Jesus' use—lighthouses whose lights shine *brightly* on those around us—our neighbors will begin to see the light of Christ in us, and they will long to know what makes us different.

LIGHTHOUSE THOUGHT FOR THE DAY

A lighthouse for Jesus Christ whose light is obscured is useless to Him. We must be sure our light shines brightly at all times.

JONATHAN GRAF

Every Part Is Important

But in fact God has arranged the parts in the body, every one of them, just as
he wanted them to be. If they were all one part, where would the body be?
1 CORINTHIANS 12:18–19

Recently I suffered a spinal injury that caused significant pain and lack
of mobility in my neck, left shoulder, and left hand. Through a great
deal of therapy, constant prayer, and hard work, my condition
improved. But just about the time life was getting back on track, I had
a mountain bike accident. I ended up in an emergency room, and the
doctors thought that I had fractured my left shoulder. Thankfully, I
hadn't; but I had significantly damaged the ligaments and rotator cuff,
again limiting the use of my shoulder and arm.

These experiences taught me the value of every part of my body. I
found that when one segment is not working correctly or is in pain,
every other part of my body is affected. God has created our bodies so
that the parts are interdependent. When they are working in harmony,
we can accomplish wonderful things. Just watch a star athlete, a gifted
musician, a graceful dancer, or a skilled surgeon.

The apostle Paul makes it clear that such is the case in the body of
Jesus Christ—the church. The parts of the body of Christ are interdependent. An injured or sick body part affects the whole fellowship. On
the other hand, when each part of the body is healthy, the body func-
tions with incredible harmony and can accomplish amazing things for
the kingdom of God.

Each of us has unique skills, abilities, and strengths that God can
use to make the body of Christ what He wants it to be. God wants *you*
to be a healthy part of the body of Christ so that you can impact the
world for Him.

LIGHTHOUSE THOUGHT FOR THE DAY
Working together, the body of Christ can make the Lighthouse
Movement a great effort for God.

ROBERT E. RECCORD

Checking the Fuel Gauge

Be filled with the Spirit.
EPHESIANS 5:18

I'm convinced that gas tanks are designed to go from half-full to empty in a moment's time—especially when you're stuck in rush-hour traffic, which happens often in my hometown of Boston.

Years back my family and I were on our way to a church event when I realized that the red needle on the gas gauge of my car had collapsed. Already pressed for time, I thought out loud, "Oh, boy, I'd better get some gas soon. We're running on fumes!" In an instant, our then eight-year-old, Kristin, came to the rescue with a sincere recommendation.

"Dad, just cover up the empty sign!"

"What did you say?" I replied.

"You know," she repeated, "Just put a piece of paper or something over the empty sign. That's all you need to do, Dad! Just cover up the empty sign!"

As quickly as my mind registered *ludicrous* to the suggestion, my heart signaled *indicted*.

Just cover up the empty sign! How easy it is to do that when it comes to reaching others for Christ! Rather than reaching for more of God's power, we try to go it alone. The result? We fall flat on our faces!

Jesus promised that the Holy Spirit would fill us up and enable us to tell others about Him (Acts 1:8). God wants our witness for Christ do be natural and effective, and that will only happen when we are filled with the readily available power of the Holy Spirit.

LIGHTHOUSE THOUGHT FOR THE DAY

When you feel the need for more of God's power in your lighthouse ministry, don't cover up the empty sign. Instead, ask for more and more of Him.

ROBERT C. CROSBY

Faithful to His Cause

And the LORD said to Joshua, "Today I will begin to exalt you in the eyes of all Israel, so they may know that I am with you as I was with Moses."

JOSHUA 3:7

Joshua was a faithful man. When Moses sent the spies into the Promised Land, only two, Joshua and Caleb, returned ready to carry out God's plans. Because of their faithfulness, God lifted them up, and He made Joshua the leader.

Regardless of the giants in the land, Joshua did not see the obstacles in his path. Instead, he saw himself as the recipient of all the blessings God promised. He heeded the words of the Lord and acted accordingly. Joshua demonstrated his faithfulness by believing that God was who He said He was and that He would accomplish all that He had promised.

From the example of Joshua, we see that faithfulness is a two-way street. As we are faithful to God, He is faithful to us. Therefore, our faithfulness in serving God in our ministry of praying, caring, and sharing can bring others into a deeper relationship with Christ.

How often are we fearful that we cannot meet the giant needs of others? That kind of fear can paralyze us. But if we believe that God is who He says He is and that He rewards those who seek Him, we can pray with confidence and share God's love with people knowing that the Word of God doesn't go out in vain. The joy of faithfulness is in knowing that God is the one who will complete the work.

LIGHTHOUSE THOUGHT FOR THE DAY

We need to focus on being faithful in praying, caring, and sharing the gospel of Jesus Christ. Fallow ground is softened through faithful prayer and faithful, consistent, and unconditional caring for others.

TOM PHILLIPS

An Amazing Design

From him the whole body, joined and held together by every supporting
ligament, grows and builds itself up in love, as each part does its work.
EPHESIANS 4:16

While speaking to a large Latvian church one night, I explained to the congregation what we really mean when we use the word *church:* "Your forefathers built beautiful edifices for God. Riga was home to church buildings many centuries old until World War II bombers destroyed nearly all of them. Did God allow that in order for you to learn that *you* are the temple of God?"

The apostle Paul spelled this out when he wrote, "The body is a unit, though it is made up of many parts; and though all its parts are many, they form one body. So it is with Christ. For we were all baptized by one Spirit into one body—whether Jews or Greeks, slave or free—and we were all given the one Spirit to drink. Now the body is not made up of one part but of many" (1 Corinthians 12:12–14).

The church is not the building made with human hands. It's something far more amazing. It's a body, assembled by God, made up of individual believers who work together for the glory of God and for the good of one another.

As members of the body of Christ, it is important that we spend time together so that we can strengthen each other. The writer of Hebrews knew this very well. He wrote, "Let us not give up meeting together, as some are in the habit of doing, but let us encourage one another—and all the more as you see the Day approaching" (Hebrews 10:25).

LIGHTHOUSE THOUGHT FOR THE DAY

As lighthouses for Christ, we must never underestimate the importance of fellowship in the church. It is in that setting that we strengthen and energize ourselves and those around us.

EDDIE SMITH

The Witness of Your New Life

If any man be in Christ, he is a new creature: old things are passed away;
behold, all things are become new.
2 CORINTHIANS 5:17, KJV

There are several powerful witnesses to you and those around you that your decision for Christ was real. One is the change that has taken place in your life.

Certain life goals that had once seemed terribly important no longer interest you. Activities that once amused you have lost their appeal and perhaps even annoy you. Old habits now bring you shame. Now there is a feeling of discomfort when you do things you know are wrong. In short, you have begun to learn the truth of 1 John 5:18, which tells us, "We know that anyone born of God does not continue to sin."

When you came to faith in Jesus Christ, your relationships began to change too. While you are still fond of your old friends, you now wince when they use the name of Jesus as a curse word, and you now say no to things you happily did with them before. Now you desire more and more to be with those people who love your Savior. To your surprise, those "religious" people you once avoided—or laughed at—are now your very dear friends. This is another witness to the reality of your new life. As the apostle John said, "We know that we have passed from death unto life, because we love the brethren" (1 John 3:14, KJV).

When you look at the changes God has brought about in you, you can say with confidence that you are truly a child of the living God!

LIGHTHOUSE THOUGHT FOR THE DAY

The changes in your heart, mind, and behavior are evidences of your true relationship with Jesus Christ—to you and to those around you.

PAT ROBERTSON

Trimming the Wick

Fan into flame the gift of God, which is in you.
2 TIMOTHY 1:6

A major responsibility of lighthouse keepers of yesteryear was to trim the wick in the burner at the top of the lighthouse tower. This had to be done often because once a wick became overburned, its flame became too dull to project a strong, bright light. In that case, the lighthouse became useless. Trimming the wick to remove the ashen remains of the previous fire exposed new material to the flame so that it again burned strong and bright.

As lighthouses for Jesus Christ, we need to do something very similar. So often we as Christians are more prone to *reflect* on yesterday's flame than to *tend* to today's:

> *I remember what it was like when I first was saved.*
> *God was really moving back then.*
> *Church is just not what it used to be.*

The works of God in the past are precious memories, but we must remember that these things are now a part of history. They will not bring the light our world so desperately needs to see *this* day.

Are you banking on yesterday's experiences with God, or are you praying for fresh ones today? Paul trimmed the wick of yesterday's remains and refreshed the flame in his own soul: "I do not count myself to have apprehended; but one thing I do, forgetting those things which are behind and reaching forward to those things which are ahead, I press toward the goal for the prize of the upward call of God in Christ Jesus" (Philippians 3:13–14, NKJV). We need to do the same.

LIGHTHOUSE THOUGHT FOR THE DAY

Although we can draw encouragement from past works of God in our lives, we need fresh fire in our hearts to light our world for Jesus today.

ROBERT C. CROSBY

Strength in Helplessness

*That is why, for Christ's sake, I delight in weaknesses, in insults, in hardships,
in persecutions, in difficulties. For when I am weak, then I am strong.*

2 CORINTHIANS 12:10

The methods and values of the kingdom of God are totally contrary to
the world's. To the natural mind, God's wisdom seems backward.
Perhaps nowhere is this contrast more fully manifested than in Christ's
entrance into this world. I find it astonishing that God became a baby,
that He who is all-powerful became totally helpless. Talk about a
shocking display of vulnerability! A young virgin, an infant babe, a
homeless couple, a fetid stable—God used all of these things to bring
into the world its only hope for salvation.

But this is the way of God's kingdom: He who is most dependent is
most empowered. The world places a premium on self-reliance and
independence. Not so in the kingdom of God. When we reach a point
of acknowledging our helplessness, then the authority of heaven is at
hand for us. For, as 2 Corinthians 12:10 tells us, it is at the point of
greatest helplessness that we are at our point of greatest receptivity to
divine empowerment.

This is wise, you see, because a dependent person is one who can
be trusted. By *dependent* I don't mean the kind of parasitism where
people suck other people dry. Rather, I mean a sincere vulnerability, an
absence of self-reliance, a spirit of cooperation, an honest sense of
need.

Let's not despise the times God leads us into places of helplessness,
for it is in those places that He cultivates true spiritual authority in us.

LIGHTHOUSE THOUGHT FOR THE DAY

If you want to access God's power, you have to come to a place of
acknowledging that on your own you are helpless—that without Jesus
you can do nothing.

STEVE FRY

Adding Power to Prayer

She never left the temple but worshiped night and day, fasting and praying.
LUKE 2:37

Andrew Murray, a missionary and author of the late nineteenth and early twentieth centuries, once wrote: "Prayer grasps the power of heaven; fasting loosens the hold on earthly pleasure."

Believers have always recognized the value of fasting as part of their prayer lives. Fasting adds power to prayer. Jesus Himself fasted (Matthew 4), and He promised that God would reward the believer who fasts with the right motivation (Matthew 6:16–18). Jesus teaches us that both prayer and fasting are important to a life of faith. Abstaining from food or exercising discipline in what we consume helps to focus our attention on communication with God.

Fasting should be a part of every lighthouse for the Lord Jesus Christ. It is one thing to pray consistently, but when we add fasting, we demonstrate to God—and ourselves—that we are serious about tapping into His power, which is essential for us to be effective witnesses for Him.

There are a number of ways you can fast. You can start by fasting one day a week, or if you struggle with fasting that long—and many people do—try fasting one meal one day a week, then increase the number as your body becomes accustomed to missing meals.

As you fast, remember most of all that you are to seek God's face, not His hand. Fasting is a means to draw closer to God and to see what He can do through you as you dwell in His presence.

LIGHTHOUSE THOUGHT FOR THE DAY

As you establish your lighthouse ministry, consider making fasting a part of your prayer life. You will be amazed at the difference it makes!

VONETTE Z. BRIGHT

In Need of Shelter

When Jesus spoke again to the people, he said,
"I am the light of the world. Whoever follows me will never walk in darkness,
but will have the light of life."
JOHN 8:12

The snow fell more heavily with every passing mile of our drive through Michigan. We passed several restaurants glowing warmly in the darkness, and one marquee tempted us with the message, "Come in and escape the winter." We longed to pull off the road, if just for a cup of tea, but in our desire to make our destination before morning, we kept moving.

Soon, the snow turned to sleet, and our car's defroster could no longer keep up with the rapidly forming sheet of ice on the windshield. The highway quickly became packed with snow and ice, making driving treacherous.

As we pressed on, a thought struck me. I had driven this road many times, had passed the small towns and roadside restaurants, but I had never taken much notice of them. But now, out in this darkness, even the smallest light from a place of shelter or rest stood out.

I thought about Jesus' teaching about the importance of light in places of darkness and how He metaphorically referred to the life He offers as "light." I thought about all the people in the world who are just like I was that night—in the dark and in need of shelter.

As lighthouses for the Lord Jesus Christ, we need to pray for those around us who are lost in darkness and need the shelter of God's love. We need to pray that the Holy Spirit will draw these precious souls to the light of Jesus, and we need to let that light shine into the world from our own lives.

LIGHTHOUSE THOUGHT FOR THE DAY

God is not willing that anyone stay in darkness (2 Peter 3:9). Let's pray for, care for, and share the light of Jesus with our neighbors so that they will be drawn to the light of Christ.

MARY L. MARR

Preparing for the Wedding

*"The wedding of the Lamb has come,
and his bride has made herself ready."*
REVELATION 19:7

The days leading up to a wedding are a time of great joy. As the big day approaches, the anticipation heightens as the bride readies herself to begin a new life with her groom.

Likewise, there is great joy in heaven now as marriage supper plans are being made and the table is being set. Jesus, the Son of God and King of Glory, is about to celebrate His marriage in the presence of God the Father, the Spirit, and the holy angels. And we are the bride! God says that we are to be getting ready for the royal wedding (Revelation 19:7; 21:2). But how should we be dressed?

First, we should be clothed in faithfulness. We are to be a faithful bride, giving ourselves to no other lord, so enthralled by our Groom that we lose sight of worldly things. He is to be the sole object of our affection.

Next, we are to be adorned with intimacy. Christ wants a bride whose heart beats in rhythm with His own and whose thoughts are like His thoughts. To begin that intimacy here in our relationship with Him, we must commune with Him constantly (1 Thessalonians 5:17).

Finally, we are to be dressed in holiness. Why? Because He is holy (1 Peter 1:16). We are to be a bride who reflects the character of the Bridegroom.

It is time for us to seriously consider our betrothal to the Son of God. Let's live today as one who is destined for His throne!

LIGHTHOUSE THOUGHT FOR THE DAY

The process of preparing ourselves to be the bride of Jesus Christ will make our light shine more brightly to our neighbors.

EDDIE AND ALICE SMITH

Fighting the Isolation

If we love one another, God lives in us and his love is made complete in us.

1 JOHN 4:12

It's been said that one of the greatest indicators of where our sense of community has gone in the past several decades is the demise of the front porch. This tells me that in our culture we now place less value on meeting as neighbors than we once did. I believe that this has contributed to an increased sense of alienation and isolation in our communities. Not only do we not befriend our neighbors, most of us don't even *know* them! What a change from just a few decades ago!

This sense of isolation is a problem in the church as well. Our cultural mind-set causes individuals to migrate to larger and larger congregations, where a one-man pastoral staff cannot possibly provide the depth of friendship each person in the congregation needs. To make matters worse, many laypersons do not recognize the need to become the "hands" of the local church.

In our culture it is difficult to slow down and make time for our friends and loved ones, let alone our neighbors. Nevertheless, one thing has not changed: People need to have a sense of belonging. Without it, they will never respond positively when we tell them the Good News of the gospel.

We make Jesus real to others when we respond to their felt needs, but we will never know what those needs are unless we take the time to reach out to our neighbors and make them feel that we care for them. It can be done. But first, we need to find a way to build new "front porches," where we can become friends with those who live around us.

LIGHTHOUSE THOUGHT FOR THE DAY

To reach others for Christ we must first break down the walls of isolation that have been erected by a changing culture.

MARY L. MARR

Up All Night

He will not let your foot be moved, he who keeps you will not slumber.
PSALM 121:3, RSV

The worship team and prayer teams gathered around me and prayed for me before I preached. Our worship leader remarked that God was up all night working on this service and the people who would be there—including me. He thanked the Lord and praised Him for His unwearying work on our behalf.

Oh, what a truth! For every Christian! The Psalmist said it plainly: "My help comes from the LORD, who made heaven and earth. He will not let your foot be moved, he who keeps you will not slumber" (Psalm 121:2–3, RSV). The one who helps you never sleeps. He stays up all night, every night.

Do you need help? I do. Where do you look for help? When the psalmist lifted up his eyes to the hills and asked, "From where does my help come?" he answered, "My help comes from the LORD"—not from the hills, but from the God who made the hills. So he reminded himself of two great truths: One is that God is sovereign over all the problems of life; the other is that God never sleeps.

God is a tireless worker. We are prone to think of ourselves as workers in God's life. But the Bible wants us first to be amazed that God is a worker in our lives: "From of old no one has heard or perceived by the ear, no eye has seen a God besides thee, who works for those who wait for him" (Isaiah 64:4, RSV).

God is so eager to work for us that he goes around looking for more work to do for people who trust Him: "The eyes of the LORD run to and fro throughout the whole earth, to show his might in behalf of those whose heart is blameless toward him" (2 Chronicles 16:9, RSV).

LIGHTHOUSE THOUGHT FOR THE DAY

As lighthouses for Christ, we need to remember that our God is a God "who works for those who wait for him" (Isaiah 64:4, RSV).

JOHN PIPER, WITH JUSTIN TAYLOR

The Power of Holiness

Just as he who called you is holy, so be holy in all you do.
1 PETER 1:15

Have you ever met a truly holy person? There is a power in such people's godliness that is plainly visible to all. Every aspect of their lives seems to reflect their relationship with the holy God. True holiness is *that* powerful.

It can be easy to fake holiness—at least in the short run. But unless we reach for true holiness, our perceptions of God will be skewed, possibly to the point that we think that the Almighty no longer requires holiness or godliness. When that happens, we compromise the standards of His kingdom and slip into disobedience. When we stop obeying God, we begin faking holiness.

We must understand that true holiness starts with the true knowledge of the Lord. This is not some ten-week course to be passed, but an unfolding experience of realizing that Jesus Christ dwells within us. It is a process that starts with rebirth through faith in Jesus and continues on as we learn to walk in and partake of Christ's holiness, power, and perfection.

When this happens, the cross stands upright before us, confronting us with our own Gethsemanes, our own Golgothas. But it also supplies us with our own resurrections, through which we ascend spiritually into the true presence of the Lord. It enables us to say with Paul, "I have been crucified with Christ; and it is no longer I who live, but Christ lives in me" (Galatians 2:20, NASB). That's what true holiness is all about! When Christ lives in you, and you in Him, you will have a holy and powerful life.

LIGHTHOUSE THOUGHT FOR THE DAY

There is great power in walking in holiness before God. As lighthouses for Jesus Christ, we must make true holiness the top priority in our lives.

FRANCIS FRANGIPANE

Thy Will Be Done

"Lord, teach us to pray."
LUKE 11:1

The prayer life of Jesus was so beautiful that the disciples realized that they simply did not understand true prayer. They came to Him for help. Their request was not, "Lord, teach us to be successful" or "Lord, teach us to impress people," but "Lord, teach us to pray."

True prayer begins with the certainty that God is there, listening. God as a philosophical theory or a religious concept has no power. But believers have been born of God and therefore have an intimate relationship with Him. We bear His name—a name that is synonymous with holiness and honesty. That changes everything!

True prayer acknowledges the sovereignty of God over His kingdom and manifests a desire for His will to prevail. It is at this point that we decide if our prayers will be self-centered or God-centered. How can they be the latter? Only as we submit our plans, ambitions, desires, and everything else to God and say, "Lord, You take over. I want Your will more than my own because I know You know best."

A shift from "my rule" to "Thy will" must take place if our prayer life is to be powerful. His will must become our prayer, and that can only take place as the rule of self comes to an end. When that happens, Satan's will is thwarted.

In that sense, our prayers will be the kind Jesus wants to answer through us—the kind He would teach us to pray.

LIGHTHOUSE THOUGHT FOR THE DAY

I will be an effective lighthouse for Christ when I live with an attitude of prayer that says, "Not my will, but Thine, be done."

CHARLES T. CRABTREE

A Lesson from the Farm

"I sent you to reap where you didn't sow;
others did the work, and you received the harvest."

JOHN 4:38, TLB

Using truths from the farm, Jesus reminded His disciples that reaping is not the hard labor. Farmers would certainly agree. The time of reaping is usually preceded by months of cultivating, weeding, irrigating, and feeding.

Evangelism involves cultivating, sowing, and reaping. The apostle Paul said it this way: "I planted, Apollos watered, but God gave the increase" (1 Corinthians 3:6, NKJV). Virtually all converts had a multiplicity of influences that preceded their decision to follow Christ—a mother who prayed for thirty years, a pastor who faithfully taught God's Word, a neighbor who cared.

Cultivating is an appeal to the heart through righteous acts done with a truly serving heart. Can you bake a cherry pie, fix a water heater, mow a lawn? Do those things to build a strong relationship with your neighbor.

Sowing, the communication of biblical truth, is an appeal to the mind. Sowers keep a stream of biblical communication flowing into the lives of seekers. A tract, a well-written book, or a word of testimony sows seeds of truth that can grow in their lives. The sower is a resource center for searching people.

Reaping appeals to the will in anticipation of a response. Many believe that evangelism means only reaping, and so many believers feel pressured to actually lead someone to Christ. However, not all are called to do that. Some of us may be the cultivators or sowers who do the hard labor.

LIGHTHOUSE THOUGHT FOR THE DAY

Our effectiveness as lighthouses for Christ will soar if we affirm one another's giftedness, then reach out in our own way to love and nuture those around us.

JOE ALDRICH

The Key of Compassion

[Jesus] was moved with compassion for them.
MATTHEW 9:36, NKJV

Jesus was filled with compassion for the people around Him. He felt people's pain—emotionally, physically, socially, and spiritually—and the conditions of their lives touched His heart. He also knew their eternal condition. Seeing them "like sheep having no shepherd" (Matthew 9:36, NKJV)—with no one teaching them the truth or caring about their awful condition—He was moved to the point of suffering *with* them.

Jesus wept, prayed, and labored—preaching, teaching, and healing—before the watching eyes and hearing ears of the disciples. The salvation of the people rested on each disciple having a heart of compassion like His.

There is no other explanation for the total yielding of the disciples' lives to take the Good News of God's great salvation to "Jerusalem, and in all Judea and Samaria, and to the ends of the earth" (Acts 1:8) than the compassion they learned from Jesus. As Paul exclaimed, "The love of Christ compels us" (2 Corinthians 5:14, NKJV).

Jesus' disciples today have an even deeper compassion because Jesus, our living Lord, dwells within us through the Holy Spirit and expresses His heart to us and through us to our lost and dying world. It is therefore impossible to live "in Christ" without compassionately caring for our lost families, neighbors, and world. It is impossible to live "in Christ" and not yield our lives to Him so that He can reach out in His saving love to others through us.

LIGHTHOUSE THOUGHT FOR THE DAY

As lighthouses for Jesus Christ, we are compelled to reach out in compassion to those around us who need His saving love.

HENRY BLACKABY

Choose Your Weapons

For though we live in the world, we do not wage war as the world does.
2 CORINTHIANS 10:3

The Word says, "For the weapons of our warfare are not carnal but mighty in God for pulling down strongholds" (2 Corinthians 10:4, NKJV). Tearing down spiritual strongholds sounds like violent stuff: people with faces contorted, straining under physical pressure and expending enormous human energy as they rage against demonic enemies.

But the ultimate battle over spiritual forces looked nothing like that. It was a battle fought by a gentle Savior who in simple obedience surrendered to the will of the Father, suffered in silence, and laid down His life for us. By the world's standards, Jesus was not an impressive warrior. But He won the greatest battle of history, and in so doing, He demonstrated the weapons of our warfare: compassion, sacrifice, simple obedience, and extraordinary love.

Unfortunately, we often square off against an unbelieving world as if the very people we're trying to reach were the enemy. We're too easily drawn into a battle of wills, a struggle for control, or debate of ideas, when Jesus simply wants us to reach out in gentleness, selflessness, and love.

This battle rages inside every human heart. But when we conquer our self-will and self-centeredness by humbling ourselves and taking the role of a servant, the power of heaven rushes in to work wonders—and serious damage is done to the kingdom of darkness.

LIGHTHOUSE THOUGHT FOR THE DAY

Use the weapons of your warfare today. Your simple acts of kindnes, sacrifice, and love will tear down the walls between you and others and, perhaps, for the first time in their lives, the people around you will see the light of Jesus.

TOM PELTON

Deeper Intimacy with God

> "I have come that they may have life,
> and that they may have it more abundantly."
>
> JOHN 10:10, NKJV

In the wee hours of the morning on June 6, 1981, Doug Whitt and his new bride, Sylvia, were escorted to their hotel bridal suite. In the lovely room the honeymooners saw a sofa, chairs, and a table—but no bed. Then they discovered that the sofa was a hide-a-bed. They opened it and climbed in. The mattress was lumpy, the springs sagging. It wasn't the night of romantic bliss they had long dreamed of. They spent their first night of married life tossing and turning, and in the morning both awoke with sore backs. The new husband felt that they deserved a lot better, and his bride agreed, so he went to speak to the desk clerk.

Mildly upset, Doug complained about the room. With a puzzled look on his face, the clerk asked, "Did you open the door in the room?"

"The door? Uh, no," Doug responded, "I thought it was a closet."

Returning to the room with the groom, the clerk opened the door, and there, complete with a fruit basket and chocolates, was a beautiful bedroom with a lovely, big bed. Right behind the door was a veritable honeymoon paradise. The couple had not ventured far enough. They had settled for too little.

Something similar often happens to Christians. They settle for salvation and don't venture further to experience the joy of true intimacy with God. They think getting saved is all there is, so they never open the door to the spiritual paradise God has ready and waiting for them.

LIGHTHOUSE THOUGHT FOR THE DAY

Lighthouses for Jesus Christ are Christians who will take one more step, open one more door, in their endeavor to know and love God more deeply.

WOOD KROLL

Spiritual Discipline

But I discipline my body and bring it into subjection, lest, when I have preached to others, I myself should become disqualified.

1 CORINTHIANS 9:27, NKJV

"I lost forty pounds in thirty days! Call 555-5415 for details."

We've all seen the ad. My first response was "Sign me up!" For years I've wrestled with culinary indiscretion, and I dream of being able to erase in a month all the evidence of my losing struggle. Help is but a phone call away. Even so, gravity eventually wins. *Sigh.*

There really is no quick and easy way to get and keep our bodies in shape. Doing so requires that we master certain areas of our lives. In many ways, the same is true in the spiritual realm.

Paul mastered his body so that he would not be disqualified in the race for the prize. In essence, he said, "Body, listen up! You get tired; you get sick; you can be lazy; you get bogged down with your besetting sin. I remind you, mortal flesh, that through the Spirit's power I no longer have to succumb to your call. I do not have to respond to temptation." Like Paul, we need to discipline ourselves to say no to our fleshly longings and to say yes to acts of righteousness that bring glory to God.

Fasting is one of those righteous acts. It is a way of praying and waiting on the Lord with a spirit of expectancy. Fasting demonstrates an intensity of desire, a seriousness of intent. It puts aside normal fleshly pleasures in the pursuit of God. In fasting with prayer, we say no to the flesh to concentrate on God, His character, and what He wants to do through us in our world.

LIGHTHOUSE THOUGHT FOR THE DAY

Fasting shows that we are seriously seeking God for something—perhaps the salvation of a friend, relative, or neighbor.

JOE ALDRICH

Workplace Prayer

"For God so loved the world that he gave his one and only Son, that whoever believes in him shall not perish but have eternal life."

JOHN 3:16

Of the 132 instances recorded in the Gospels, 122 of Jesus' interactions with people took place in homes or places of business, not in places of worship. He prayed and healed and ministered in the midst of daily life —in the streets of the marketplaces and in the family kitchens. He may have said, "Come to me," but in truth, He went to people and touched them where they lived and worked.

As you pray for those whose lives you touch, determine how you might pray for workplaces in your area as well. Ask God to make you sensitive to the needs and hurts of people you encounter at the dry cleaner, the pharmacy, or your favorite restaurant. Know that He wants the lazy checker at the grocery store to experience the depths of His love. Practice saying, "Can I pray for you?" when you encounter people in various workplaces and businesses.

You'll be surprised at how open people are to receiving prayer in the workplace. Today the workplace is experiencing a wave of spiritual receptivity as more and more people carry their spiritual hunger to work and as companies discover the value of investing in the spiritual health of their employees. Large corporations are hiring chaplains to minister to their workers, and Bible studies and prayer groups are cropping up in offices and break rooms all over the country. If enough lighthouses extended their prayer reach beyond the neighborhoods to the businesses in their communities, we might just see a revival sweep through the marketplace of America!

LIGHTHOUSE THOUGHT FOR THE DAY

Your daily contact with people in the workplace gives you the opportunity to pray for them and care for them.

DR. TERRY TEYKL

What's Your Story?

So then every one of us shall give account of himself to God.
ROMANS 14:12, KJV

The Bible tells us that we will one day give account of ourselves—a history of our transactions—to almighty God. When you get to heaven and stand before the Lord, what account of your relationship with God will you give?

Because your story is unique, it is an irrefutable account of your relationship with God. Sharing your faith means telling others the history of that relationship. This story is so important that you should record it permanently for your friends, family, and others. Can you tell your story?

It started when you first became aware that God is real. Somewhere along the line, all believers came to their first realization of the reality of God. My strict, godly parents didn't let me fall into gross sin, but my attitude toward God was awful, and when I was nine years old I came under deep conviction about it.

Your story has a point of decision. That decision might have taken place in a day, or it may have occurred over a long period as guilt and fear moved you toward conviction, confession, and a step of saving faith. When you took that step, you committed yourself in faith to Jesus Christ.

Your story also includes a history of changes that came because of your faith in Christ—changes for the better in how you lived and thought. Enumerate those changes and be ready to tell those around you about them. The things that God has done in your life are the things that will draw others to Jesus Christ.

So, what's your story?

LIGHTHOUSE THOUGHT FOR THE DAY

Your unique "light" is the account of your relationship with God. Developing your story and presenting it to those with whom you share Jesus Christ will help make you a living witness for Him!

DR. CORNELL HAAN

Losing the Timidity

For God did not give us a spirit of timidity, but a spirit of power, of love and of self-discipline. So do not be ashamed to testify about our Lord.

2 TIMOTHY 1:7–8

At times I have wished that the New Testament were more forthcoming about the warts and foibles of the church's heroes. The New Testament portrays people of God who consistently lived out their faith on a much higher plane than I do.

Musing on this apparent lack of clay feet among New Testament leaders, I recently rediscovered Timothy. There is a lot in Paul's second letter to Timothy to suggest that the young minister had slowly slid into a morass of discouragement that threatened to paralyze his ministry.

Paul urges Timothy not to be ashamed to preach the gospel. Why would Timothy be ashamed to preach? Perhaps he was losing his confidence. Maybe he was facing a gnawing sense of his own inadequacies and feeling like a hypocrite.

It's not too great a stretch for most of us to identify with Timothy. But how was he to put aside timidity? How are we to do the same? Paul gives us the key: "For God has not given us a spirit of fear, but of power and of love and of a sound mind" (NKJV).

This spirit of power that God has so generously imparted is His ability to work on our behalf. Because God is all-powerful, He is always working for us somewhere, assaulting the walls of impossibility and timidity that confine us. The spirit of power He gives us is the ability to discern where He is working, to recognize the breaches in the walls before us, and to boldly break them down as we recognize this power at work in our own lives.

LIGHTHOUSE THOUGHT FOR THE DAY

It is the power of God that breaks through the walls of our timidity so that we can boldly preach the Word of God.

STEVE FRY

The Power Source

Peter replied, "Repent and be baptized ...in the name of Jesus Christ.... And you will receive the gift of the Holy Spirit.
The promise is for you and your children and for all who are far off—for all whom the Lord our God will call.

ACTS 2:38–39

Approximately two thousand years ago, Peter and the other apostles proclaimed the truth that is at the very heart of the lighthouse ministries. The gift and ministry of the Holy Spirit is the most important truth any believer can receive.

The great evangelist Dwight L. Moody knew this well. "One day in New York—what a day!" he once declared. "I can't describe it. I seldom refer to it. It was almost too sacred to name. I can only say God revealed Himself to me. I had such an experience of love that I had to ask Him to stay His hand.

"I went to preaching again. The sermons were no different. I did not present any new truth. Yet hundreds were converted. I would not go back where I was before that blessed experience if you would give me Glasgow."

The Holy Spirit is the key to revival and awakening because He is the key to supernatural living. Apart from living in the fullness of the Spirit, the believer has no power to introduce others to Christ. The Holy Spirit is convicting many Christians of their lethargy, their coldness of heart, their unbelief, the loss of their first love. A spiritual explosion is spreading the Good News of Christ far and wide throughout the world. There is a resurgence in evangelism unparalleled in church history, as we endeavor—in the power of the Holy Spirit—to help fulfill the Great Commission.

LIGHTHOUSE THOUGHT FOR THE DAY

Through the power of the Holy Spirit, lighthouses for Christ are beaming the greatest of all news not only to their neighbors, but also to "all who are far off."

BILL BRIGHT

Choosing the Extraordinary

"'Who is he who will devote himself to be close to me?' declares the LORD."
JEREMIAH 30:21

William James said, "The best use of life is to spend it for something that outlasts life."

If we are not careful, the demands of what *seems* important can crowd out what is important. In a classic biblical example, Jesus pointed out that Martha was "worried and upset about many things, but only one thing is needed" (Luke 10:41–42). Martha missed it. But not Mary. She chose "what is better, and it will not be taken away from her" (v. 42). Mary was living close to the Lord.

We can miss it too. We are called to overcome what is ordinary for what is extraordinary. We can overcome. The psalmist said, "I have set the LORD always before me" (Psalm 16:8, NKJV). I like the intentionality of "Let us fix our eyes on Jesus" (Hebrews 12:2). Perhaps David said it best when he wrote, "Whom have I in heaven but you? And earth has nothing I desire besides you.... God is...my portion forever" (Psalm 73:25–26).

A popular columnist said that she had never heard of a person who said on his deathbed that he wished he had spent more time at the office. That says a lot about the choices we should make. We are always choosing. I want to choose well. I don't want to just begin the race—I want to finish it and finish it well. I want to choose that which cannot be taken away. I want to be one of those who "devotes himself to be close" to the Lord.

From now into eternity, if we choose what is best, it will never be taken away.

LIGHTHOUSE THOUGHT FOR THE DAY

As lighthouses for Jesus Christ, let's choose daily to devote ourselves to being close to our Lord.

BOB RICKER

What Does Jesus Expect?

While we were still sinners, Christ died for us.

ROMANS 5:8

Expectations create conditional love. "I love you, but I'll love you more if...."

Now I know what you're thinking. Shouldn't we expect the best out of one another? Shouldn't we encourage each other to strive for excellence and never settle for anything else? Absolutely.

But it was Christ who taught us how to use expectations. Does He demand a lot? You better believe it. Does He expect much? Only our best. Does He have expectations? Just that we leave everything, deny all, and follow Him. The difference? Jesus' expectations were accompanied by forgiveness and acceptance.

Study attentively these words written by Paul: "While we were still sinners, Christ died for us." When did He die for us? When we reached perfection? No. When we overcame all temptation? Hardly. When we mastered the Christian walk? Far from it. Christ died when we were still sinners. His sacrifice, then, was not dependent on our performance.

When we love with expectations, we say, "I love you. But I'll love you even more if...." Christ's love had none of this. No strings, no expectations, no hidden agendas, no secrets. His love for us was, and is, up front and clear. "I love you," He says, "even if you let Me down. I love you in spite of your failures."

One step behind the expectations of Christ come His forgiveness and tenderness. Tumble off the tightrope of what our Master expects and you land safely in His net of tolerance.

LIGHTHOUSE THOUGHT FOR THE DAY

Alone, expectations can be bullets that kill; but buffered by acceptance and forgiveness, they can bring out the best in us and those around us.

MAX LUCADO

Prayer Makes a Difference

*"Call upon Me in the day of trouble; I will deliver you,
and you shall glorify Me."*

PSALM 50:15, NKJV

The Battle of Dunkirk was one of the turning points of World War II. Hitler had blitzed through France, isolating British, French, and Belgian soldiers in a northern segment of France along the English Channel. They were utterly trapped, and all evidence indicated that the Germans would slaughter them in a matter of days. If the Allied soldiers tried to escape across the Channel in ships, Hitler's submarines or his Luftwaffe would sink them at sea.

In desperation, England's King George VI decreed a day of fasting and prayer throughout the British Empire. Millions of Christians united to pray on behalf of the trapped soldiers. God answered immediately!

On the German side of the Channel, a violent storm grounded every plane, and tanks bogged down in the mud. The storms held the Germans captive. On the British side, the sea was as smooth as glass, and the sky was crystal clear. The English people, having focused on God's will through fasting and prayer, sensed God's awesome miracle and quickly began to send thousands of boats of all sizes to retrieve the trapped soldiers. Within hours, they had plucked 330,000 Allied soldiers from Hitler's hands.

When they arrived on English soil, many soldiers formed circles of prayer to thank God for His deliverance and for being so faithful to His promises.

LIGHTHOUSE THOUGHT FOR THE DAY

If prayer and fasting can change the course of history, they can certainly change the course of the lives of your family, neighbors, relatives, and work associates.

ROBERT E. RECCORD

Creative Communication

"This is why I speak to them in parables: 'Though seeing, they do not see; though hearing, they do not hear or understand.'"

MATTHEW 13:13

In our postmodern age, when people value experience over explanation, we need to find fresh approaches to communicating God's truth. This is a particularly vital issue since sin tends to build up its own defenses, which can cause a certain imperviousness to truth. Jesus often used parables to scale the defenses of sin, and like Him, we can use stories to slip past its sentries.

First, we need to listen carefully to the *seeker's* story; otherwise, we won't be able to help that person see faith's relevance to his or her life.

Next, we should try to connect one of *God's* stories to the person's life. I once met a woman who described in painful detail how her mother envied her. I said, "You know, there's someone in the Bible who was just like your mother."

"Aw come on! Someone in the Bible like *my mother?*" she asked incredulously. "This I've got to hear."

We spent an hour talking about Saul's horrible envy of David and how David found not only solace in his relationship to God, but the power to forgive.

Lastly, when it's appropriate, share something of *your* story as well. People hunger to know if God is there. They want to know if we have personally experienced the truths we are sharing. We can do this when we share our own Christian experience.

LIGHTHOUSE THOUGHT FOR THE DAY

Ask Jesus to help you learn to ask good questions, to listen, and to tell God's stories, just as Jesus did when He was on earth.

REBECCA MANLEY PIPPERT

Love Conquers Fear

*Who shall separate us from the love of Christ? Shall trouble or
hardship or persecution or famine or nakedness or danger or sword?*

ROMANS 8:35

I don't know about you, but I am always more afraid of the unknown
than of the known. The uncertainty associated with new activities,
even fairly simple ones, can make me feel insecure and inadequate. So
it is with evangelism. The idea of knocking on a neighbor's door—perhaps a neighbor I don't know well or have never actually talked to—
can fill me with dread. *What will I say? What if I say the wrong thing?
What if this is a bad time for them?*

If you are like me, you dread the thought of being laughed at—and
that can certainly happen when you talk to people about Jesus Christ.
This fear can be deep-seated and not easy to overcome.

We need to pray for our neighbors, but we also need to pray for
strength for ourselves. We need to ask for God's protection as we
attempt to pray for, care for, and share Christ with our neighbors—not
because doing so is inherently dangerous, but because we are incredibly weak. When we read this verse and contemplate the difficult things
that Paul had to contend with, we see that God is able to do a lot more
than give us a little courage: He also gives us strength to overcome
adversity.

Nothing can separate us from the love of Christ. It is through that
love that we are empowered and emboldened to reach out for Him to
our friends and neighbors.

LIGHTHOUSE THOUGHT FOR THE DAY

As lighthouses for Christ, we need to remember to ask God to give us a
sense of His love for us and His presence with us as we reach out to
others in the name of the Lord Jesus Christ.

ALI HANNA

The Heart of the Matter

*"Why do Your disciples transgress the tradition of the elders?
For they do not wash their hands when they eat bread."*

MATTHEW 15:2, NKJV

A teacher is judged by his students' conduct, and leaders of their day saw Christ's disciples as products of their mentor. Their behavior reflected on Jesus, who had authority over their lives and the way they were conducted.

The Pharisees complained that Jesus' disciples did not wash their hands before they ate, as the Pharisees themselves did in accordance with ceremonial tradition. The complaint was not that the disciples were unsanitary, just *unceremonial*.

The lustration, or ceremonial washing of hands, was not for the purpose of cleansing hands prior to eating. Although people came to the table with clean hands, laving in a ceremonial manner while uttering the proper prayer took place many times during a meal. It was a practical tradition because silverware had not been invented, and people ate with their hands. But, as happens so often, a practical matter became a ceremonial one. Then the ceremony overshadowed the practical purpose it connoted.

Jesus could have answered the Pharisees' complaints that His disciples did not follow the washing ceremony by pointing out that they were not Pharisees. But rather than defend His disciples, Jesus got to the heart of the matter: Obedience to God's commandments was far more important than following human tradition (Matthew 15:3–11).

LIGHTHOUSE THOUGHT FOR THE DAY

As lighthouses for Jesus Christ, we need to make certain that our actions demonstrate obedience and commitment to our Lord, not to human tradition.

MOISHE ROSEN

Humble by Choice

Humble yourselves before the Lord, and he will lift you up.

JAMES 4:10

True discipleship begins not with adherence to rules, but with forsaking pride. Purity begins with our determined refusal to hide the condition of our hearts. Honest self-discovery brings forth humility, from which true holiness grows.

As lighthouses for Jesus Christ, we are called to this kind of humility.

If we cannot see the depravity of our old nature, we become "Christian Pharisees"—self-righteous hypocrites who, like those the Master described, "trusted in themselves that they were righteous, and viewed others with contempt" (Luke 18:9, NASB).

Every time we judge or criticize another, we demonstrate a self-righteous attitude. Contempt is the motive behind our words each time we criticize another church. Ironically—and sadly—too many churches today look upon each other with identical attitudes of superiority. The modern church has too many people who think they are holy but are the exact opposite because they lack humility.

The humility we are to walk in is drawn from a well deeper than just an awareness of our needs. Even in times of spiritual fullness, we must delight in weakness, knowing that all strength is the product of God's grace. Our humility must go beyond the pattern of proud living that is interrupted only momentarily by intervals of self-abasement. Meekness must become our way of life. Like Jesus, we must delight in becoming "lowly in heart." As Christ's disciples, we must delight in humility. We must be humble by choice.

LIGHTHOUSE THOUGHT FOR THE DAY

Effective lighthouses must not only accept humility, but they must follow the lead of our Lord, who delighted His Father in heaven by choosing humility.

FRANCIS FRANGIPANE

Making Progress

*I want to know Christ and the power of his resurrection and
the fellowship of sharing in his sufferings, becoming like him in his death,
and so, somehow, to attain to the resurrection from the dead.*

PHILIPPIANS 3:10–11

A commercial airline pilot turned on the intercom to make an announcement. "Ladies and gentleman, I have some good news and some bad news. The good news is that we have a 150-mile-per-hour tailwind, and we are breaking all the speed records. The bad news is that our communications system is out, and we are lost."

If you lose direction, *progress* isn't necessarily a good thing. The farther you go—particularly in your Christian journey—the more lost you become. Many Christians have a tendency to seek experience rather than real spiritual progress. This problem grows out of a desire to be touched emotionally or receive a blessing, not out of a scriptural desire for true growth. However, the Christian life is not speed, activity, or seeking after experience. It is a direction. It is the way.

Jesus said, "'Man shall not live by bread alone, but by every word that proceedeth out of the mouth of God'" (Matthew 4:4, KJV). The Word of God is where we find true life. Test everything by the Word. You can trust it. It is our compass. Do not waste your life by living outside the boundaries and direction provided in the Scriptures. Life goes by so quickly that it would be a tragedy to make record time but wind up somewhere you never meant to go.

LIGHTHOUSE THOUGHT FOR THE DAY

My lighthouse will shine ever more brightly as I seek God in His Word and ask Him to bring me one step closer to my all-consuming goal—to be like Jesus in thought, word, and deed.

CHARLES T. CRABTREE

When You Fast

"But you, when you fast, anoint your head and wash your face."
MATTHEW 6:17, NKJV

Notice, Jesus did not say, *"If* you fast," but rather, *"When* you fast." He assumed that His listeners would fast as an important spiritual discipline—not in the self-righteous, self-promoting manner of the Pharisees, but with a humble spirit, even as He Himself had done when He fasted forty days in the wilderness.

Sadly, many Christian disciplines are neglected in today's church. Few of us pray as much as we ought, read the Bible as regularly as we should, witness as faithfully as we could, or give as generously as we might. Some of us even falter in the discipline of regular and faithful church attendance.

Until recently the spiritual discipline of fasting has not only been neglected, it has been almost forgotten. This seems very strange since the Bible is replete with references to it. In the Old Testament, we see that Moses, Elijah, David, Ezra, Daniel, Nehemiah, and Jehosaphat all observed periods of fasting. On several occasions, the entire nation of Israel observed extended periods of fasting and prayer. In the New Testament, we find that not only Jesus fasted, but so did Anna, Cornelius, Paul, and the rest of the apostles.

So what is so important about fasting? What is it's value? The most important value of fasting is the spiritual power it holds. When the disciples were unable to cast out the evil spirit from the demon-possessed boy, Jesus rebuked them for their lack of faith and power and said, "This kind does not go out except by prayer and fasting" (Matthew 17:21, NASB). Jesus indicated that fasting is essential to maximum spiritual power and victory.

LIGHTHOUSE THOUGHT FOR THE DAY
To have a powerful lighthouse prayer ministry, make fasting a regular part of your spiritual discipline.

LARRY LEWIS

Searching for the Sheep

*"'For this is what the Sovereign LORD says: 'I myself will search for my sheep
and look after them. As a shepherd looks after his scattered flock
when he is with them, so will I look after my sheep. I will rescue them
from all the places where they were scattered.'"*

EZEKIEL 34:11–12

Sheep need a shepherd. Defenseless as they are, sheep are sure to be scattered, confused, and vulnerable to predators if there is no one to guide them and watch over them. People who do not know Jesus are like sheep without a shepherd.

Lost sheep are of great concern to Jesus Christ, the Good Shepherd. He is moved with compassion at their condition because they are "harassed and helpless" (Matthew 9:36). God places great priority on finding lost sheep, and there is great rejoicing in heaven when just one is found (Luke 15:3–7).

Christ is also in the business of healing and restoring sheep once they have been found: "I will bind up the injured and strengthen the weak" (Ezekiel 34:16). He is always ready to make them lie down in green pastures, to lead them beside still waters, and to restore their souls (Psalm 23).

Our Lord has also appointed us, His sheep, as undershepherds to help Him find and enfold the lost sheep and care for their needs. Look for them in your family, neighborhood, or workplace. How does the Shepherd feel about them? He asks us to be His feet in the search for His lost sheep. He asks us to be His hands in binding up the injured and strengthening the weak. He asks us to be His voice in calling them to follow the Shepherd. He asks us to care as He cares.

LIGHTHOUSE THOUGHT FOR THE DAY

The lost sheep who matter so much to the Good Shepherd should also matter to us, His undershepherds. What does He want you to do in order to rescue them?

AL VANDERGRIEND

God's Sovereign Plans

The LORD will reign forever and ever.
EXODUS 15:18

Judy was a senior at the University of Texas when she got engaged to a young man named Bob. As the wedding got closer, Judy felt increasingly uneasy about going through with it. It was not because she didn't love Bob—she did—but because she felt that God had called her to join the staff of Campus Crusade for Christ, and Bob wasn't open to that.

Judy had a lot of anxiety, including some sleepless nights, until she yielded to what she knew God wanted her to do. When she announced her change in plans, Bob was heartbroken and her family disappointed.

Why did God prompt Judy to break off the engagement? Because He had different plans for both her and Bob. Judy joined the staff of Campus Crusade for Christ and eventually became the director of the ministry's publications department and the editor of its publication, *The Worldwide Challenge*. Bob later told Judy that the broken engagement was one of the best things that ever happened to him because the heartbreak caused him to grow much closer to the Lord.

By the way, I am very grateful that God led Judy to break that engagement and join the staff of Campus Crusade. You see, some years later, Judy became my wife!

God is not only in charge of the universe, He also has a special purpose for each of us who know Him. Knowing that, we can have God's peace in tough circumstances as we walk in His protection and His wonderful plan.

LIGHTHOUSE THOUGHT FOR THE DAY

We will shine forth for Christ if we will trust that He knows what's best for us and submit to His leading.

STEVE DOUGLASS

Enriching Growth

And we pray this in order that you may live a life worthy of the Lord...
bearing fruit...growing in the knowledge of God.

COLOSSIANS 1:10

"I am better or worse as I pray more or less," wrote missionary E. Stanley Jones. "It works for me with mathematical precision."

Prayer is, as author Samuel Zwemer suggests, the gymnasium of the soul. No athlete would think of entering competition without some level of preparation. Regular exercise is vital to achieving athletic excellence. So it is with prayer in the believer's life: Faithfulness in prayer begets spiritual growth.

Prayer, of course, doesn't save us. Only Christ's shed blood does that. Thus, to pray an hour every day for the next year will not make someone "more" saved. However, it will certainly help that person grow in Christ.

Charles Spurgeon observed, "All the Christian virtues are locked up in the word *prayer.*" It shouldn't surprise us, then, as we develop a lighthouse of prayer focusing on our neighbors, that we, too, will grow in the process.

Jude urged his readers, "Build yourselves up in your most holy faith and pray in the Holy Spirit" (Jude 1:20). This suggests that prayer, when empowered by God's Spirit, enriches growth. Believers can no more hope to grow in Christ without prayer than a plant can hope to grow without nutrients. Indeed, we grow as we pray and we pray as we grow. As E. Stanley Jones said, it works with mathematical precision.

LIGHTHOUSE THOUGHT FOR THE DAY

When as we pray for others, we grow in Christ in such a way that our own personal lights shine even more brightly. Before long the light from our growth in Christ may well set our whole neighborhood aglow. What a blessing! Through prayer we grow and we glow!

DICK EASTMAN

Triple Security

*"I give them eternal life, and they shall never perish;
no one can snatch them out of my hand".*

JOHN 10:28–29

In *What Is a Real Christian,* an evangelistic booklet published by Multnomah Press, I told of a meeting I had with some Scottish ministers several years ago. During a break, a man who had been in the ministry for seventeen years came to me and said, "Luis, I don't know if I have eternal life."

As we talked, he told me that two of my team members had visited him and his wife the evening before. Both mentioned their assurance of eternal life. After they left, the minister asked his wife, "Dear, do you have eternal life?"

She said, "Phil, I don't know. Do you?"

"You know I don't," he replied. "What are we going to do?" She suggested that he talk with me the next day. Phil received eternal life as we talked. Soon afterward his wife did too. Like Phil and his wife, you can know with "triple security" that you have eternal life.

Concerning those who receive Him in faith, Jesus said, "I give them eternal life, and they shall never perish; no one can snatch them out of my hand" (John 10:28).

Notice the three parts of your eternal security. First, He says, "I give them eternal life." Second, "They shall never perish." And third, "No one can snatch them out of my hand."

What more could you want? What blessed assurance there is in knowing the Lord Jesus Christ!

LIGHTHOUSE THOUGHT FOR THE DAY

Because of the assurance Jesus gives us in His Word, we can know with triple certainty that we have eternal life.

LUIS PALAU

Relinquishing Our Losses

So Rachel died and was buried on the way to Ephrath (that is, Bethlehem).
Over her tomb Jacob set up a pillar,
and to this day that pillar marks Rachel's tomb.
GENESIS 35:19–20

Whether it involves a loved one, a relationship, a dream, or something of material value, we tend to carry our losses with us. Part of spiritual renewal involves releasing to God our losses and the circumstances surrounding them.

Abraham and his grandson Jacob both lost loved ones as they traveled to the Promised Land. When Sarah died, Abraham wept for her and then buried her there in Canaan (Genesis 23:1–4, 19). A generation later, Jacob was given a new name, Israel, and the promise of a great heritage in the Promised Land. On his way there he, too, lost his beloved wife when she died giving birth to their son Benjamin. The Bible tells us that Jacob grieved over his loss, then moved on (Genesis 35:20–21).

Personal losses are inevitable as we journey through life. When we suffer loss, we need to do as Abraham and Israel did: acknowledge them, grieve openly over them, forgive if necessary, give them a proper burial, and then move on. We may even build our own kind of memorial to remind us of what we loved and lost, but at some point we must give it over to God.

After we relinquish our losses, we can press on to accomplish what He has called us to do: glorify Him in our own lives and ministries as we reach out to others in His name.

LIGHTHOUSE THOUGHT FOR THE DAY

Loss is an inevitable part of life. As Christians and lighthouses for Christ, we can model God's power by learning to properly grieve over our losses and then move on in joy and victory.

STEPHEN ARTERBURN

Before Talking about God...

And into whatsoever house ye enter, first say, Peace be to this house.
LUKE 10:5, KJV

"Before you talk to your neighbor about God, talk to God about your neighbor," says Ed Silvoso, founder of Harvest Evangelism.

This is what we call prayer evangelism—and it works! God promises us that when we pray according to the will of the Father, He hears and answers us. And what could be more in His will than to see those around us come to Him?

When we intercede on behalf of those who don't know God, we become advocates before Him for those who may not even know they need Jesus Christ. We invite the Holy Spirit to touch the hearts of those who don't know their hearts need touching. We ask God to bless sinners by bringing them to Him.

When you pray blessings on your neighbors and friends, expect surprises! My wife and I were praying for a certain set of our neighbors. Shortly after that, they got into a fight, and the situation became so volatile that the police were called. About a month later, one of them came over and asked if we would help them mend the relationship. It provided an opening to talk about Jesus.

Prayer is politically correct. By that I mean that few people will be offended if you offer to pray for them. I've been doing this for years, and the most negative response I've had is: "Well, I guess it can't hurt!"

You can start your prayer evangelism efforts today by thinking of people to pray for. Pray for their homes and workplaces. Pray for open hearts to hear the message of Jesus Christ. Pray blessings on them!

LIGHTHOUSE THOUGHT FOR THE DAY

Prayer is the vital groundwork of any kind of evangelism, including the push for witnessing that we call the Lighthouse Movement.

DR. CORNELL HAAN

Restoring the Prodigals

"But while he was still a long way off, his father saw him and was filled with compassion for him; he ran to his son, threw his arms around him and kissed him. [But] the older brother became angry and refused to go in."

LUKE 15:20, 28

The parable of the prodigal son is not an easy one for us to process because in many ways it does not seem "fair." When we encounter people who have deliberately turned away from God and made poor lifestyle choices, it is tempting to identify with the older brother who became angry at the whole scene. He was indignant that his father gave the younger son a party instead of the thrashing he deserved. He wanted justice to be administered, not grace.

In downtown Los Angeles there is a place known as the "Dream Center," a renovated fifteen-story hospital where the powerful drama of the Prodigal Son is replayed again and again. Each of the fifteen floors is dedicated to one particular group of prodigals—prostitutes, drug addicts, homeless, runaways. They come seeking shelter and a hot meal; what they find is the unconditional love and compassion of Jesus.

Not only does Jesus want to welcome prodigals home, He is expectantly looking for them. He sees them coming when they are still a long way off and runs to meet them with outstretched arms. They are His lost children who have found their way home, and He does not spare any expense in the celebration.

When we see a prodigal return to God, we should do the same.

LIGHTHOUSE THOUGHT FOR THE DAY

As a lighthouse for Jesus Christ, which will you offer to the one who has strayed—justice or grace? Which is more likely to bring the person back into the family of God? Pray prodigals home, and do not spare the fattened calf when they make it.

DR. TERRY TEYKL

Going to Training

We proclaim to you what we have seen and heard,
so that you also may have fellowship with us.
And our fellowship is with the Father and with his Son, Jesus Christ.
1 JOHN 1:3

Baseball is a great spectator sport for two reasons: the spectators and the ballplayers. The players are the ones the spectators go to the ballpark or sit down in front of the TV to watch. Without them, there would be no spectators.

In order for a baseball player to make himself worthy of his major league status (not to mention the pay he receives and the adoration of his fans), he needs preparation. He prepares during the off-season by keeping himself in shape and making adjustments in his game. He then fine-tunes his game during spring training.

Just as a professional ballplayer needs training to prepare for competition, Christians need training so they can live the life Christ commands them to live. I see the church as "training camp," the pastor as the manager, and the teachers, facilitators, and others serving in the body as his coaching staff. It is on this "training field" that believers learn how to relate to one another and to the unsaved world around them.

As believers, we need fellowship and teaching in order to prepare us for ministry outside the walls of the church. Christianity, unlike baseball, is not a spectator sport. It is only as we learn to be a part of the body of Christ that we can show the rest of the world the life in Christ.

LIGHTHOUSE THOUGHT FOR THE DAY

As I draw strength from the fellowship and teaching that I enjoy in church, I am more prepared to be a lighthouse for Jesus Christ outside the walls of the church.

CHARLES T. CRABTREE

Loving Even When It Hurts

"Today you will be with Me in Paradise."
LUKE 23:43, NKJV

In unspeakable agony, Jesus hung dying on the cross. Yet He made the effort to speak the Good News from His Father to a repentant sinner who was dying on a cross next to Him. Jesus took His eyes off His own condition and reached out with words of compassion and assurance to someone in need.

Now here is an incredible picture of compassion and love! What a Savior we serve!

Jesus alone had the Good News that every person needed to hear, so He expressed it to sinners and saints alike, the religious and the irreligious. He knew firsthand that the Father was "not willing that any should perish but that all should come to repentance" (2 Peter 3:9, NKJV), so He spoke with a thief and a murderer, even while He was dying on a cross!

Given the love of the Father within Him, it was inevitable that Jesus would share with a lost, dying person. The Father had sent Him to love each person in His presence. There was never any hesitation, no "time out!" At all times, under all conditions—even the worst—Jesus was prepared to reach out with the love of God.

Jesus fills our hearts with exactly this kind of love when He comes to take up residence within us. It is recorded in the Scriptures how earnestly He desires to live out His life from within us so we can reach the hurting and lost world around us.

LIGHTHOUSE THOUGHT FOR THE DAY

As lighthouses for Jesus Christ, let us have His heart of compassion for the unlovely and the undeserving.

HENRY BLACKABY

Long-Range Plans

Behold, the Lord GOD shall come with a strong hand, and His arm shall rule for Him; behold, His reward is with Him, and His work before Him.

ISAIAH 40:10–11, NKJV

Isaiah knew that God had long-range plans for His people and that they were good plans. And all the while, whether Isaiah could see progress or not, God was working. In the meantime, Isaiah needed to stay put. He needed to stay faithful. He needed to work with the flock. He needed to keep people his priority. The reason the Lord had put him there was to be light among them.

No matter what your calling in life—whether you're a pastor, a missionary, or someone who checks water meters all day—it's people that count. God has you where you are to touch the lives of those who cross your path. God has you where you are to hold your light high, like a city on a hill.

Many of the people I've counseled through the years have lost their focus and become discouraged because they have focused on other things—on organization, financial portfolios, profit and loss, professional fulfillment, or other outward signs of success.

Sometimes, such things are completely necessary. But you and I can't forget that ultimately—*wherever* we work, *whatever* we do—God has placed us where we are to have vital contact with the people around us. And results don't always happen overnight, in a week, in a year, or even in our lifetime.

That might mean talking to folks who don't seem responsive, picking up a future deacon out of the gutter, or delivering the Good News to a neighbor in a small house with a very large Rottweiler.

LIGHTHOUSE THOUGHT FOR THE DAY

Keep holding out your light. When the King comes in the clouds to call for you, nothing else will matter.

RON MEHL

Courting Rejection

*And he went and lived in a town called Nazareth. So was fulfilled
what was said through the prophets: "He will be called a Nazarene."*
MATTHEW 2:23

Jesus' hometown of Nazareth was in Galilee, which the rest of the
Jewish community held in derision because of its racial mixture. To live
in Nazareth was to court rejection.

Rejection is one of God's favorite tools for equipping His servants.
All the great biblical saints endured the crucible of rejection: Moses,
David, Paul—even Jesus. But a common thread runs through the lives
of all of them: The breadth of their influence was proportionate to the
depth of their rejection.

We should feel blessed when we are misunderstood, ostracized, or
rejected. I'm not talking about rejection due to our own character
weaknesses, but about that which comes when we have given our all
and reached out the most. I'm talking about the kind of rejection Jesus
spoke of: "Blessed are you when men hate you, when they exclude you
and insult you and reject your name as evil, because of the Son of
Man" (Luke 6:22). Rejection is a blessing because it is the evidence that
we are giving something. If we never give, we never risk rejection—
and Jesus has called each of us to give ourselves to others to further His
kingdom.

We won't always be rejected when we give, but some rejection is
sure to come if we make giving a lifestyle. That's okay. We just need to
keep giving more. We need to give freely, concerning ourselves only
with bringing people into God's kingdom. Doesn't that sound a lot like
a certain Savior we know?

LIGHTHOUSE THOUGHT FOR THE DAY
When we are rejected on account of Christ, we can rest assured that
we're doing something right.

STEVE FRY

Finding Courage in Battle

"'You will not have to fight this battle. Take up your positions;
stand firm and see the deliverance the LORD will give you....
Do not be afraid; do not be discouraged.'"

2 CHRONICLES 20:17

How do you usually react when faced with a seemingly impossible situation? Do you tend to hide your head? Or do you grit your teeth and press ahead, no matter how insurmountable the obstacle may seem?

We can find encouragement by viewing our battles from God's perspective. Doing so reminds us of three things. First, regardless of outward circumstances, we do not battle against flesh and blood. Second, the battle is God's, not our own. Third, and most importantly, despite the bruising we may receive in the midst of a battle, God has already won.

How much easier it is to move forward courageously when we see the battle from God's point of view. When we do, fear leaves us, and we can pray more diligently and confidently, certain that God hears and that He will answer.

In the eyes of the world, time on our knees is time wasted. But the prayers of believers supernaturally unleash God's power against our enemy. In some miraculous way, our prayers become agents of power. Angels unsheathe their swords and the battle rages. We can't see it, but we know the principalities are at war, and there is no fear. God is in control, the ultimate victor. We can enter combat focused on God and believing that He will accomplish all that He intends.

LIGHTHOUSE THOUGHT FOR THE DAY

We acquire courage only through time spent with God in prayer. Through it, He enables us to see the battle and to stand in the gap for others.

TOM PHILLIPS

The Shepherd's Prayer

*"I pray also for those who will believe in me through [the disciples'] message,
that all of them may be one, Father, just as you are in me and I am in you."*
JOHN 17:20–21

Jesus has "other sheep" not yet in the fold, and He prayed for them. The apostle Paul did too: "My heart's desire and prayer to God for the Israelites is that they may be saved" (Romans 10:1). Later, Paul urged that "requests, prayers, intercession and thanksgiving be made for everyone" so that people might "be saved and…come to a knowledge of the truth" (1 Timothy 2:1, 4). The prayers of today's undershepherds—believers in Jesus Christ—change hearts.

A pastor from California and his wife, together with another couple, formed a lighthouse of prayer and prayed for unsaved neighbors. As they prayed, a husband and wife who lived across the street, then three children who lived down the street came to Christ. As they prayed for an elderly woman on their street, she, too, came to faith, though she had been in the service of Satan.

Two lighthouses of prayer in Michigan saw six new commitments to Christ in their neighborhood in one year's time. In addition, people were released from addictions and healed from diseases; dysfunctional families were helped; demons were cast out; and a Bible study was started.

God has chosen to work in people's lives in response to the prayers of His people. The Father, in response to Jesus' prayer, is still bringing people to faith. And He will continue to do so until the end of time. Jesus invites us, His undershepherds, to join Him in praying for those who are yet to believe.

LIGHTHOUSE THOUGHT FOR THE DAY
Ask God to give you His burden for those who live and work around you. He will show you how to pray for what He wants to accomplish in their lives.

AL VANDERGRIEND

The Communicator

"Therefore go and make disciples of all nations."
MATTHEW 28:19

John Bass, the former President of Christian Booksellers Association (CBA) said, "The constant flow of communication exposes others to the challenge and motivates them to accomplish." The challenge our Lord has laid out for us, our most important job here on earth, is to communicate the gospel to others.

This communication hinges on how well we know the Lord ourselves. The apostle Paul's greatest desire in life was to know Jesus Christ. "I want to know Christ and the power of his resurrection and the fellowship of sharing in his sufferings, becoming like him in his death" (Philippians 3:10). After that, Paul's mission was to make Jesus known to the world.

Communicating the gospel also requires that we make time in our lives to pray for other people and for our attitude toward them. How do you view the people God brings into your path? Do you see them as a burden, or as a blessing from God?

Jesus didn't treat people as burdensome interruptions. For example, when He heard that John the Baptist had been beheaded, He withdrew to be alone, but the crowds followed Him anyway. What would you have done? Jesus' response was to hear the Father's voice and feed the people who were hungry—both physically and spiritually. The people were not an interruption; they were His ministry.

We are God's communicators—His transmitters and receivers. As we live in faith and obedience before others, we will point them to Jesus Christ.

LIGHTHOUSE THOUGHT FOR THE DAY
Look for ways to make time in your day for others.

TOM PHILLIPS

Is Christianity Intolerant?

*Jesus answered, "I am the way and the truth and the life.
No one comes to the Father except through me."*

JOHN 14:6

There is much talk today about our pluralistic society. From a worldly perspective, tolerance is seen as the greatest good. But today's society has twisted the meaning of tolerance, making it practically synonymous with relativism. True tolerance is treating people decently regardless of how they may differ from you. The false tolerance demanded by today's society requires that we accept all beliefs as equally true. To suggest that someone else's religious belief might not be true is wrongly labeled as intolerance.

By the world's standards, therefore, the Christian belief that Jesus is the only way of salvation is perceived as intolerance, even bigotry. Whenever we proclaim that Jesus is the Way, the Truth, and the Life, the inference is that all other ways are false, and therefore those who trust anyone or anything other than Jesus for salvation are mistaken. You don't have to tell people they are wrong; the message itself pronounces them wrong. Those who don't believe will always view this as intolerance. And those who are considered intolerant can expect some rejection.

God wants us to be loving and humble when we tell others about Him. Yet even the most inoffensive manner cannot guarantee that people will not take offense at what we have to say. Ultimately, people decide the basis upon which they will or will not be offended.

LIGHTHOUSE THOUGHT FOR THE DAY

If you are rejected for being a lighthouse for Jesus, remember that you are standing for the Savior and that it is not you being rejected, but Him.

DAVID BRICKNER

From the Inside Out

Surely you desire truth in the inner parts;
you teach me wisdom in the inmost place.

PSALM 51:6

A man in Long Beach, California, went into a fast-food chicken fran-chise to buy lunch for himself and the woman with him. He took their orders, and they drove to a nearby park for a picnic. When he opened the box, he was surprised to see money instead of chicken. Apparently the manager kept the earnings in a chicken box to prevent robbery until the armored truck arrived. He had inadvertently handed the wrong box to the unsuspecting customer.

The man quickly returned his picnic basket of cash to the store manager. Elated, the manager said to him, "Stick around! I want to have the newspaper take your picture. You are the most honest guy in town!" The man refused. When the manager asked him why he wanted to avoid publicity, the man said, "Well, I am a married man, and the woman I am with is not my wife."

Integrity is much more than superficial honesty. It's a commitment of inward character that directs every area of our lives. It's at the core of what God's church is all about because it's where Christians hold one another accountable. The Bible says, "As iron sharpens iron, so one man sharpens another" (Proverbs 27:17). Simply put, Christians need one another to ensure the growth and continued strength of inner character.

Often believers fail spiritually because they try to handle weak areas of their lives alone. An accountability partner will help you grow from the inside out.

LIGHTHOUSE THOUGHT FOR THE DAY

Integrity is a vital character quality for the believer, and we can build it through accountability with fellow believers.

ROBERT E. RECCORD

My Example

Do your best to present yourself to God as one approved,
a workman who does not need to be ashamed
and who correctly handles the word of truth.

2 TIMOTHY 2:15

My grandfather died when my father was only eleven. As the eldest in the family, my dad had to drop out of school to run the family farm and an excavating business. He learned how to do both very successfully. However, one thing Dad never learned to do well was read.

But that never prevented him from studying God's Word. I can remember walking into the kitchen for breakfast and seeing my father sitting at the table eating his breakfast with his Bible open on the table next to him. Since he could barely read, it often took him ten to fifteen minutes to read just one verse. Often he would call me to his side and ask, "What is that word?"

I've taken speed-reading courses and have my doctorate. Like most people, I can read several verses in less than a minute. It took my father fifteen minutes to do what I can now do in just seconds. But my nearly illiterate dad shames readers like you and me every day when we do not take even a few minutes to read the Bible—God's message to mankind!

My dad read his Bible every day. That prepared him to share his faith, which he did whenever he got the chance. Whenever we would stop for a coffee break or lunch, he would find a place to sit where he could talk to someone. He would listen to that person, and within five minutes be sharing his faith.

What an example he was for me!

LIGHTHOUSE THOUGHT FOR THE DAY

We prepare to share the light of Jesus by reading the Word of God daily.

DR. CORNELL HAAN

A "Fasted" Life

Religion that God our Father accepts as pure and faultless is this: to look after orphans and widows in their distress and to keep oneself from being polluted by the world.

JAMES 1:27

Fasting is a vitally important aspect of the ministry of the Lighthouse Movement. Whether for one meal or over a period of days, it shows that we're serious about influencing our neighborhoods, our homes, and our workplaces for God.

For some of us, though, giving up food for a few days is the easiest form of fasting. The real challenge is living a daily life that's entirely yielded to God. For this reason we should think about other forms of fasting that will challenge us and change how we approach the people around us.

If we aren't careful, something we think of as "spiritual"—even fasting—can become deceptively self-centered and replace genuine devotion to God. We never know what our motives truly are until we challenge ourselves to do something for someone else, particularly someone who cannot reciprocate.

In the Old Testament, God's people were continually caught up in fasting, and yet God had to challenge them repeatedly to remember the lifestyle implications of devotion to Him: "Is not this the kind of fasting I have chosen: to loose the chains of injustice and untie the cords of the yoke, to set the oppressed free and break every yoke? Is it not to share your food with the hungry and to provide the poor wanderer with shelter—when you see the naked, to clothe him, and not to turn away from your own flesh and blood?" (Isaiah 58:6–7). Fasting is merely a rehearsal for living a life that's entirely yielded to God. That is a "fasted" life.

LIGHTHOUSE THOUGHT FOR THE DAY

The spiritual disciplines of fasting and prayer are to prepare us to work on the behalf of others.

TOM PELTON

Be Anxious for Nothing

Don't worry about anything; instead, pray about everything; tell
God your needs and don't forget to thank him for his answers. If you do this
you will experience God's peace, which is far more wonderful
than the human mind can understand.

PHILIPPIANS 4:6–7, TLB

Recently, I've seen the value of living by Paul's instructions to the Philippian church to not worry about anything. In less than a week's time, I heard of four major crises in families of dear friends. It was during that time that I clung to how the Living Bible presents Paul's words: "Don't worry;…instead, pray."

The truth here is that we can trust God to handle all our needs, all our problems, all our concerns. Jesus said He would never leave us nor forsake us, and we find peace in that promise, knowing that He's there to take care of us.

God wants His people whole, and in order for us to be whole, we need to learn to release to Him all our cares and concerns, knowing that He has what is best for us and for His kingdom in mind. When we do that, we can be a bright, shining light for Christ before our family, friends, and neighbors.

Sadly, many Christians never seem to lay hold of this truth. Rather than being filled with God's indescribable peace and assurance, they are gripped with fear, unbelief, discouragement, and worry. They don't know how to rest in God's promises, and they can't grasp the fact that, no matter how circumstances look, our God will never fail us.

In the midst of all that, I just hear Christ calling to them above the tumult, "Trust in Me! I will never turn My back on you!" Christ desires to saturate each of us in His love and to give us that peace that surpasses understanding.

LIGHTHOUSE THOUGHT FOR THE DAY

When followers of Christ live and walk in His peace, we shine brightly for Him in a lost and desperate world.

BOBBYE BYERLY

From Start to Finish

*Being confident of this, that he who began a good work in you
will carry it on to completion until the day of Christ Jesus.*

PHILIPPIANS 1:6

One of the greatest men of prayer I have ever known was Manley Beasley. For most of his adult life he suffered with complications from lupus. Many times when he was near death, God raised him up. He used Manley to do mighty works, but He never healed him. It seemed that Manley was like the apostle Paul, in that the more he suffered, the more God's power was evident in his life.

Our church once invited Manley to speak at a conference on prayer and faith. His theme was, "What God Initiates, God Completes." Through him, God did a mighty work in our church, which was facing the challenge of relocating.

While he was there, Manley invited me to go to Switzerland to help him with a revival conference for pastors from Eastern Europe. "God has told me that He is going to give revival in Eastern Europe in my time," he said. "I am trying to help pastors prepare for what God is going to do." At the time, Eastern Europe seemed far from revival. I didn't say it to Manley, but I thought, *Are you sure God told you this? I don't see God doing anything in Eastern Europe.*

Our relocation project kept me from going. But do you know what happened about two months before Manley died? The Berlin Wall came crashing down, the Romanian dictator was executed, and revival spread across Romania. Before long, Billy Graham was preaching crusades in Eastern Europe.

Manley had sought God in prayer, and God had revealed to him what He would do. And as Manley told our church, what God initiates, God finishes.

LIGHTHOUSE THOUGHT FOR THE DAY

Through prayer we get to know the heart of God, and He allows us to get in on what He is doing.

DARRELL ROBINSON

A Meditation on Thirst

"Whoever drinks of the water that I will give him shall never thirst; but the water that I will give him will become in him a well of water springing up to eternal life."

JOHN 4:14, NASB

As I knelt that morning in my study, I said, "O Lord, have mercy on me, a sinner. Help me. Please come and restore my soul." Than I asked quietly, "Lord Jesus, what did You mean that those who drink the water that You give will never thirst again? I thirst this morning. Almost every believer who comes into my office thirsts. Have we not drunk?"

The Lord answered the only way I know Him to answer: He opened my eyes to see the meaning of what He said in the Bible. I had rememorized the verse early Sunday morning for my own soul and for possible use in the pastoral prayer. So as I prayed, the materials of divine communication were in place. He showed me the rest of the verse and shed on it a light I had never seen before.

As I cried out, the second half of the verse spoke. "But the water that I will give him will become in him a well of water springing up to eternal life." With it came an answer. Not an audible voice, but the voice of Jesus in the Word illumined and applied by the Holy Spirit.

It went like this: When you drink My water, your thirst is not quenched forever. If it were, would you feel any need of My water afterward? That is not My goal. I do not want self-sufficient saints. When you drink My water, it makes a spring in you that satisfies thirst not by removing your need for water, but by being there to give you water whenever you get thirsty. So drink, John, drink.

LIGHTHOUSE THOUGHT FOR THE DAY

In order to become a spring of water whose waters do not fail (Isaiah 58:11), let us continually drink deeply from the river of His delights (Psalm 36:8).

JOHN PIPER, WITH JUSTIN TAYLOR

Rest for the Weary

"Come to me, all you who are weary and burdened, and I will give you rest.
Take my yoke upon you and learn from me, for I am gentle
and humble in heart, and you will find rest for your souls.
For my yoke is easy and my burden is light."

MATTHEW 11:28–30

This world offers plenty of roads to spiritual renewal and transformation, but only one road leads in the right direction. Unfortunately, many of us have exhausted ourselves traversing one false road after another in search of spiritual refreshment. We desperately need rest for our souls, but instead of finding the rest we seek, we end up feeling even more weighed down by life.

Proverbs tells us, "There is a path before each person that seems right, but it ends in death" (Proverbs 14:12, NLT). In other words, the fact that a way *seems* right doesn't mean it will lead toward true spiritual renewal. It could lead to a dead end. In fact, any spiritual path that does not lead us to Jesus Christ will *not* lead to true spiritual renewal—no matter how right it seems.

Those of us who have taken many paths but still find ourselves weary need to come to Jesus, who assures us that we *will* find rest in Him—that He will take our burdens on Himself and provide balance in our lives.

Jesus Christ Himself is our way (John 14:6). The burden He calls us to bear is light, and the yoke of His expectations fits us perfectly. When we put our lives back under His control, Jesus promises us rest for our souls—true spiritual renewal.

LIGHTHOUSE THOUGHT FOR THE DAY

Jesus Christ is the only way to true spiritual refreshment. He stands with arms opened wide, inviting us to place our burdens on Him.

STEPHEN ARTERBURN

Extraordinarily Ordinary

Then Jesus said to Simon, "Don't be afraid; from now on you will catch men."
So they pulled their boats up on shore, left everything and followed him.

LUKE 5:10–11

Jesus always found a way to enable ordinary people to do extraordinary things.

He called the most unlikely men to become His friends and brothers. They were simple fishermen who left their boats to follow Him. Seminary for them was the University of Serving Others. It was not a "prep school" that trained them for the future, but a "purpose school" for doing the Father's will right then and there.

John Wesley was a lot like the disciples in this respect. The door of the organized church closed to him, but he and George Whitefield found that the fields of England were ripe for reaching people. Wesley said, "Our societies were formed from those who wandered upon dark mountains, that belonged to no Christian church but were awakened…by Methodists, who pursued them through the wilderness of this world to the highways and the hedges—markets and fairs—to the hills and the dales—who set up the standard of the cross in the streets and the lanes of the cities, in the villages.…"

Like Wesley, we can become like Jesus' first disciples by giving up our "boats," just as they did. Our boats come in all shapes and sizes, but when we give them up to Jesus, He uses us to reach people.

The original disciples were extraordinarily ordinary. The bolt of cloth from which they were cut was as ordinary as the one from which we are cut. It is the grace of the Lord that enables us, as it did them, to be used by Him in extraordinary ways.

LIGHTHOUSE THOUGHT FOR THE DAY

Ordinary people like us can do extraordinary things for Jesus if we will give Him all that we have.

JIM HYLTON

Fasting Over Neighbors

*There, by the Ahava Canal, I proclaimed a fast, so that we might
humble ourselves before our God and ask him for a safe journey for us
and our children, with all our possessions. So we fasted and petitioned
our God about this, and he answered our prayer.*

EZRA 8:21, 23

In this story, a group of exiled Israelites were about to return to
Jerusalem. It would be a dangerous trip. They were carrying a lot of
cash and would have to pass through bandit-infested terrain. The most
obvious human solution to the problem was to ask the king for help.
Instead, Ezra and the people fasted and prayed for God's protection.

Their fasting was a sign of humility. It said to God, "We mean business.
We know that we will not make it without Your protection and
help every step of the way." This wasn't just a passing "Lord, help us on
this trip" prayer. It was a fervent time of prayer and fasting, asking God
to meet a life-and-death need.

My question is: How serious are you about the salvation of your
neighbors? Oh, I'm sure you pray, but are you concerned enough
about their souls to take a more radical step? A more humbling step?
Are you serious enough to fast?

You may ask, "What will fasting do?" I believe that besides showing
God our seriousness, it opens more widely the lines of communication
with Him. When we humble ourselves in this manner, our ears seem
to hear God more clearly. He is more likely to give us insights into our
neighbors' condition and direction on how to care for them and share
the gospel of Christ with them.

LIGHTHOUSE THOUGHT FOR THE DAY

Why not fast just one meal a week and use the time to pray for your
neighbors? Try it, and see what God will do in both your own life and
in the lives of your neighbors.

JONATHAN GRAF

"Other" Sheep

"I have other sheep that are not of this sheep pen.
I must bring them also.
They too will listen to my voice, and there shall be
one flock and one shepherd."

JOHN 10:16

It's easy for us to think of our own church group as specially favored—as "God's flock." Jesus, however, refuses to be limited by our narrow perspectives. He thinks of others who are not yet in the fold.

Jesus thinks of the "other sheep" as already belonging to Him. He told the disciples, "I *have* other sheep." These sheep haven't yet come to saving faith. They may not even know that they are His sheep, but He knows they are, and He has set His love upon them. He laid down His life for them. Jesus also knows they are going to respond to Him: "They...*will* listen to my voice," He said.

We are prone to write off some people as impossible. But no one is beyond the Good Shepherd's reach. No heart is too hard. No one is so deep in sin that he cannot be rescued. We can invite people to trust Christ with the absolute confidence that His sheep will hear His voice.

Those who respond to the Shepherd's voice will become part of the one church. Some of them are our neighbors, friends, relatives, coworkers, or fellow students. Jesus wants His other sheep found and enfolded. We may think in terms of various denominations, but Jesus thinks of "one flock" and "one Shepherd," with one faith and one hope.

All who hear His voice are His sheep and have a place in the fold—the same fold you are in.

LIGHTHOUSE THOUGHT FOR THE DAY

Pray that some of Jesus' other sheep hear the Shepherd's voice soon and become part of the one flock under one Shepherd.

AL VANDERGRIEND

Bringing the Water

Whosoever drinketh of the water that I shall give him shall never thirst.
JOHN 4:14, KJV

Millions of people right here in America thirst for the living water that Jesus gives. Many have nearly everything they have ever dreamed of—nice houses, big cars, good jobs—yet they remain unfulfilled. They have found these worldly things to be as "broken cisterns that can hold no water" (Jeremiah 2:13, NKJV).

What do we know of the Samaritan woman in John 4? She was of a different race and culture than Jesus, so the race barrier was strong. She was also a wayward and wicked woman. But her race, social status, and sinful condition didn't matter to Jesus. What was important to Him was that she was unhappy, empty, and searching. That day Jesus demonstrated that no matter how terrible a sinner a person is, He is always there, only a prayer away.

Jesus began a conversation with her by asking her to give him a drink of water. "How is it that you, being a Jew, ask a drink from me, a Samaritan woman?" she asked. Ignoring her sarcastic question, Jesus said simply, "If you knew the gift of God, and who it is that says to you, 'Give me a drink,' you would have asked of Him, and He would have given you living water."

That she drank of the living water is obvious because this disreputable woman suddenly became an evangelist. She ran to the nearby city of Sychar and invited anyone who would listen to come and see Jesus. The entire population rushed to the well to see and hear Him, and the Scripture says, "Many of the Samaritans of that city believed on him for the saying of the woman...."

Isn't it amazing that one person, having drunk the living water, can bring a city to Jesus?

LIGHTHOUSE THOUGHT FOR THE DAY

Every Christian who has drunk the living water can lead many others to it.

LARRY LEWIS

Doing Good—Habitually

Let us not become weary in doing good, for at the proper time
we will reap a harvest if we do not give up.

GALATIANS 6:9

Which do you think is harder to break: a good habit or a bad habit? Although most people would respond, "a bad one," the surprising truth about habits (which are any behaviors repeated again and again) is that a good one is just as hard to break as a bad one.

For example, if you have the habit of brushing your teeth every morning, it won't be easy to leave the house without doing so. Go to church Sunday after Sunday for a few months, and it becomes a habit. Even when you're away on vacation you may look for a place to worship. Experts say that actions repeated daily for five or six weeks start to become habits. So if you want to develop a good one, you're probably not as far from doing so as you might think.

For too many years too many Christians have shown too little interest in their neighbors' spiritual condition. As a lighthouse for Jesus Christ, you need to make it a habit to pray for, care for, and share the gospel with those around you. You may get discouraged at times, especially if you aren't seeing the results you want, but if you diligently continue your efforts, this will become a habit, and you will see results.

So keep at it. Let it become a part of who you are. Let it become a good habit with eternal consequences.

LIGHTHOUSE THOUGHT FOR THE DAY

If praying for, caring for, and sharing the gospel with those around you seems uncomfortable, even unnatural, stay at it. In time it will become part of who you are. And then you'll find it hard not to do it.

DAVID MAINS

The Hinge of Time

"Of Him all the prophets bear witness that through His name
everyone who believes in Him receives forgiveness of sins."

ACTS 10:43, NASB

Just as a hinge is the pivot upon which a door opens, so the momentous occasion when God came to earth in the flesh was the hinge of history upon which the kingdom of God opened to all who would enter. Who split time from B.C. to A.D.? Jesus!

Unlike us, Jesus did not recognize His birth as the event that split time. Before He ascended back to heaven, He said that the things about Him in the Old Testament were fulfilled when He died and rose again, making the resurrection the hinge of time between the past and the future (Luke 24:44–47). So what changed when B.C. became A.D.?

When Jesus died, the temple's veil was rent in two. This meant that instead of only allowing the high priest to enter once a year, all could enter freely. Everyone had immediate access directly to God's throne room because the blood of Christ had paid for individual forgiveness of sin. With the death of Christ, not His birth, the Father delivered us from the domain of darkness and transferred us to the kingdom of His beloved Son, Jesus (Colossians 1:13–14).

Someday, human reckoning of time will be over and "there should be time no longer" (Revelation 10:6, KJV). Eternity will stretch out, with Jesus, the hinge of time, reigning forever and ever as King of kings and Lord of lords. Where we spend that "forever" beyond time will hinge on whether we accept Him while there is still time.

LIGHTHOUSE THOUGHT FOR THE DAY

Jesus has supernaturally opened the door to A.D. time and to heaven for you—and for your neighbors.

EVELYN CHRISTENSON

No Matter What

"My sheep listen to my voice; I know them, and they follow me.
I give them eternal life, and they shall never perish;
no one can snatch them out of my hand."
JOHN 10:27–28

God never gives up on us, even when we fail Him—and all of us will have moments of failure at some point in our walk with Jesus.

Jesus said, "My sheep listen to my voice; I know them, and they follow me" (John 10:27). This means that a Christian is first of all someone who trusts Jesus Christ, believes Him, and relies on Him. Second, a Christian is someone who obeys the Lord. To open your heart to Jesus Christ is not just to believe in Him, but to obediently follow Him.

But what about those times of failure? People have told me, "If I give my life to Christ, I'm afraid I won't follow Him and that I'll fail Him. I don't want to be a hypocrite. I already see too many people like that."

It doesn't catch God off guard when we fail. He has provided a way for restoration: "If we confess our sins, he [God] is faithful and just and will forgive us our sins and purify us from all unrighteousness" (1 John 1:9).

Until we see the Lord face-to-face, we won't be totally without sin. But we can be confident "that he who began a good work in you will carry it on to completion until the day of Christ Jesus" (Philippians 1:6). Part of God's good work in us is to accomplish good works through us (Ephesians 2:10). As Christians, we can be sure that we are God's workmanship, a new creation in Christ Jesus.

LIGHTHOUSE THOUGHT FOR THE DAY

God doesn't give up on us, even when we are at our worst. When we fail, we can confess it and receive His forgiveness, and then move on to be mightily used of Him.

LUIS PALAU

Wanted: Intercessors

But Moses sought the favor of the LORD his God.
"O LORD," he said, "why should your anger burn against your people....
Turn from your fierce anger; relent and do not bring disaster
on your people." Then the LORD relented.

EXODUS 32:11–14

God has always looked for intercessors: passionate advocates to stand before Him and plead for the people. Both Testaments contain outstanding examples of those who interceded passionately on behalf of the people.

Moses was a daring and selfless intercessor for the rebellious Israelites. He even said that he was willing to give up his own salvation for them (Exodus 32:32). We see that same intercessory passion in the apostle Paul, who was so desperate for the good of his people that he declared, "For I could wish that I myself were cursed and cut off from Christ for the sake of my brothers, those of my own race, the people of Israel!" (Romans 9:3–4).

Today more than ever before, God is looking for true prayer warriors, people who will stand in the gap and offer fervent intercessory prayer. Indeed, we are in a spiritual war, and the outcome hinges on prayer.

Maybe God is looking to you to be a mighty intercessor today. What a great privilege to colabor with our Lord! Through the nationwide prayer-care-and-share effort that we call the Lighthouse Movement, you can network in prayer with like-minded Christians so that by God's grace we can influence our neighborhoods, communities, and nation for Jesus Christ.

LIGHTHOUSE THOUGHT FOR THE DAY

It is a tremendous privilege and a solemn responsibility to make your home a lighthouse of intercessory prayer for your neighbors, friends, family members, and coworkers.

THOMAS WANG

Gifted to Evangelize

There are different kinds of gifts, but the same Spirit.

1 CORINTHIANS 12:4

After many years of teaching personal evangelism in churches across our nation, I have come to the conclusion that most Christians have developed negative—and incorrect—stereotypes of evangelism and evangelists.

When we hear that we are all to evangelize, we think of the most nightmarish examples of televangelists, or we think we have to be another Billy Graham. Let me assure you, this is not what I mean when I say that you are called to evangelize.

What do most evangelists look like? Well, to start with, they look like the same people who helped bring you and me to faith in Jesus. They are the people who prayed for us, cared for us when we needed it, and helped us come to an understanding of the call of Christ upon our life. In short, they are people just like you and me!

Everyone who knows Jesus Christ personally is called to evangelize, and each of us is gifted in some area that makes us suitable for different kinds of evangelism. Just as there are many different personalities and gifts in the body of Christ, there are also many different facets to evangelism. The key for us is our willingness to be used of God.

The first step we must take in this process is making ourselves—our gifts, our talents, even our shortcomings—available to be used in whatever way God sees fit. How about you? Are you ready to make your gifts available?

LIGHTHOUSE THOUGHT FOR THE DAY

Evangelism is the responsibility of everyone who knows Jesus Christ as Lord and Savior. Ask yourself what gifts God has given you to help you meet that responsibility.

DALLAS ANDERSON

A Sense of Acceptance

No one has ever seen God; but if we love one another,
God lives in us and his love is made complete in us.

1 JOHN 4:12

Rejection hurts. From the earliest days of our childhood we do what we can to avoid it, and we spend much of our lives seeking the approval of others. The world system in which we are raised gives us the impression that if we appear good, perform well, and have a certain social status, we will be accepted. But try as we might to fit in, we always seem to come short. Even self-acceptance withers under criticism.

Unconditional love and acceptance is one of the most basic needs of every human being, yet no matter how hard we work, we cannot win it. We find it only in God. The Bible tells us that God is love (1 John 4:16). Therefore He loves us because it is His nature to do so. As we become partakers of His divine nature, however, we become like Him. When we walk with Him, we should find ourselves beginning to reach out to those around us in unconditional love.

People without Christ feel rejected because, by definition, they lack meaning and acceptance. When Jesus was on the earth as a man, He said that His mission was to seek and save that which was lost (Luke 19:10). Paul told us that God is reconciling the world to Himself through Jesus and that it is our task to make that opportunity known (2 Corinthians 5:19–20).

Your neighbors need to know that the unconditional acceptance they're longing for is in fact available. Better still, it's free of charge, and you can take them to it.

LIGHTHOUSE THOUGHT FOR THE DAY

Only in Christ can we reach out to our neighbors and give them a true sense of unconditional love and acceptance.

NEIL T. ANDERSON

Fear Not!

Say to those with fearful hearts, "Be strong, do not fear;
your God will come, he will come with vengeance;
with divine retribution he will come to save you."
ISAIAH 35:4

Several years ago, God called me to launch PrayUSA!—a national forty-day prayer initiative leading up to Easter. Frankly, the weight of the responsibility terrified me. The way I saw it, there were too many "giants in my path."

When I told a friend about my fears, she said, "I will pray that God will give you the measure of faith that this job requires." This friend understood an important truth: Faith in God casts out fear of the unknown.

The day my wife, Alice, and I arrived in Chicago to present the PrayUSA! initiative to thirty-five national prayer leaders, my knees were knocking. But as Alice and two pastors prayed for me that morning, their faith was literally transferred into my heart. PrayUSA! resulted in unprecedented participation that first year and each year since.

We are to be people of faith, yet sometimes we fret over life's cares. God says, "Fear not" (Isaiah 35:4, RSV), yet we allow fear to paralyze us. God says to us, as He said to Moses and Joshua, "I will never leave you nor forsake you" (Joshua 1:5), yet we sometimes feel abandoned. We know that God has promised to meet our needs (Philippians 4:19), yet we still worry.

Fear is not the opposite of faith; it is our having more faith in the obstacles before us than in the God we serve. Be encouraged today. If God is saying something today that is contrary to your fears, make a decision to believe His truth and not the lies of the enemy.

LIGHTHOUSE THOUGHT FOR THE DAY

Let's declare our lighthouses for Jesus "Fear-Free Zones." We can find help in overcoming our fear through the Word, through prayer, and, as I did, through fellowship in the family of God.

EDDIE SMITH

Discipline

Train yourself to be godly.
1 TIMOTHY 4:7

As in athletics, our walk with God requires training and discipline. Listen to a few examples from the Word:

- If anyone competes as an athlete, he does not receive the victor's crown unless he competes according to the rules. (2 Timothy 2:5)
- Do you not know that in a race all the runners run, but only one gets the prize? Run in such a way as to get the prize. (1 Corinthians 9:24)
- Let us throw off everything that hinders and the sin that so easily entangles, and let us run with perseverance the race marked out for us. (Hebrews 12:1)

We must not duck the discipline of holiness of living: "But just as he who called you is holy, so be holy in all you do; for it is written: 'Be holy, because I am holy'" (1 Peter 1:15–16). Holiness is part of winning the race.

Once when I spoke with a friend about sexual fidelity, he said with finality, "I made that decision years go." That's a good attitude. Allowing ourselves to become entangled in sin leads to casualties. You don't need to give into temptation; you don't have to be a casualty. It's a choice.

Many times, the words of 2 Timothy 2:20–21 have challenged me: "In a large house there are articles not only of gold and silver, but also of wood and clay; some are for noble purposes and some for ignoble. If a man cleanses himself from the latter, he will be an instrument for noble purposes, made holy, useful to the Master and prepared to do any good work." I want to be disciplined in holiness—prepared for any good work. Don't you?

LIGHTHOUSE THOUGHT FOR THE DAY

How we choose to live determines the success of our ministries here on earth. Let's choose to be holy.

BOB RICKER

Instruments of Mercy

Dear friends, since God so loved us, we also ought to love one another.
1 JOHN 4:11

A mother once asked Napoleon to pardon her son, who was scheduled for execution. The general answered that since it was the young man's second offense, the law required that he be put to death. "But sir," the mother urged, "I'm not asking for justice, I'm begging for mercy." Napoleon replied, "Your son doesn't deserve mercy," to which the mother cried, "Sir, it would not be mercy if he deserved it!" Napoleon relented and spared her son.

We all need mercy, and God has showered it on us endlessly. Because of the sacrifice of His Son on the cross, God can spare us the death sentence the law says we deserve because of our rebelliousness. That's what His grace is like: giving to us freely what we in no way deserve.

Jesus loved us to the point of laying down His life for us (John 3:16). The book of 1 John tells us that we love God because He first loved us (4:19) and that our love for Him is demonstrated in our willingness to lay down our lives for one another as we give of ourselves to meet one another's needs (3:16–18).

In light of what God has done for us—in light of the mercy we have received—how can we selfishly bottle up the love and mercy He has shown us? On the contrary, we must become channels of the blessing of God's love to our neighbors. Like the woman who pleaded for her son's life, we must be instruments of mercy.

LIGHTHOUSE THOUGHT FOR THE DAY

Your neighborhood is full of people like the condemned young man whose life Napoleon spared—people who will justly and righteously perish if they do not receive mercy. As a lighthouse for Jesus Christ, it is up to you to make sure they know that they can be spared.

EDDIE AND ALICE SMITH

Destroying Strongholds

Then Esther told them to reply to Mordecai, "Go, assemble
all the Jews who are found in Susa, and fast for me; do not eat or drink for
three days, night or day. I and my maidens also will fast in the same way."
ESTHER 4:15–16, NASB

In this passage, Queen Esther called her people to fast. This act released God's power into the otherwise hopeless situation and miraculously spared the Jewish people from individual death and racial oblivion.

We should be equally willing to fast and intercede for those in our communities so that they may be saved from spiritual death. One of the most powerful and effective things you can do for the people around you is to fast and pray for them. The combination of fasting and prayer is the spiritual weapon our Lord has given us to help destroy the strongholds of evil in our world.

I had fasted from solid food many times, but never for as long as forty days—until God led me to do so in 1994. I knew He would not so lead me without a specific purpose, so I entered my fast with expectancy. God had burdened me with the sins of America and the church. During the fast, the Lord continually encouraged me, and I sensed His presence and was overwhelmed with His joy as never before. Most importantly, the Lord gave me assurance of a coming great spiritual awakening. Each year since 1994, I have engaged in a forty-day fast with similar results.

Ask the Lord how He wants you to fast and for how long. As you fast and pray, you will break down spiritual strongholds of evil in your personal life and in your community.

LIGHTHOUSE THOUGHT FOR THE DAY

As a lighthouse for Jesus Christ, I will fast and pray for my community, knowing that the eternal lives of people are at stake.

BILL BRIGHT

Open Your Eyes!

"Do you not say, 'Four months more and then the harvest'? I tell you,
open your eyes and look at the fields! They are ripe for harvest."

JOHN 4:35

A minister was talking to a Christian who said he was bored with life and found no meaning in it. The minister decided to challenge him.

"Tell me," the minister asked, "how many children does the door-man in your apartment have?"

"I don't know if he has any children," the man replied. "He just opens and shuts the door."

"How about the elevator operator?" the minister continued, "What does her husband do?"

"I don't know if she has a husband," the man replied.

The questions went on. It was soon apparent that this man was blind to the people and the needs around him. Challenged to "open his eyes," he began to learn about the needs of the people he met and to look for ways he could be of help to them. Within a few weeks, his life changed dramatically. By taking an interest in the people around him and trying to show them the love of Christ, he found new joy and real meaning in life.

When Jesus looked around, He saw real people, real needs, and real opportunities. His eyes were open. He saw the potential of a harvest that would bring glory to God. Jesus invites us to "open our eyes and look at the fields"—our neighborhoods, workplaces, and our relational networks.

Are your eyes open?

LIGHTHOUSE THOUGHT FOR THE DAY

Give people around you opportunity to tell you about their lives; then look for opportunities to meet their needs.

AL VANDERGRIEND

Thank You!

Give thanks in all circumstances, for this is
God's will for you in Christ Jesus.
1 THESSALONIANS 5:18

Giving thanks is one way we worship. A godly man recognizes this and strives to maintain "an attitude of gratitude" in his heart and home, regardless of circumstances. As praising the Lord in the midst of difficulty often releases the power of heaven, so thanksgiving in times of trouble expresses faith that pleases God and that He is eager to reward.

Note that 1 Thessalonians 5:18 does not tell us to give thanks *for* all circumstances, but *in* all circumstances. The believer recognizes that "in all things God works for the good of those who love him" (Romans 8:28). Therefore, when tough times come, he is able to thank the Almighty for His continual goodness, while entreating His help. Of course, we should be quick to thank God for His many answers to prayer and blessings to us. The Lord notices when we neglect thanking Him for all His benefits (Luke 17:11–19).

Every day is a gift from God, and we should begin—and end— each one by lavishing our thanks upon Him. We are to thank Him for the "small" things, including our daily meals, as well as for "big" things like salvation.

Whenever we pray, we are to first express appreciation: "Enter his gates with thanksgiving and his courts with praise; give thanks to him and praise his name" (Psalm 100:4).

LIGHTHOUSE THOUGHT FOR THE DAY

If you and your family aren't already in the habit, begin consciously thanking God for everything He does for you. Thank Him for His goodness when you first open your eyes in the morning and before you close them at night.

BILL MCCARTNEY

He's Jesus!

For we do not have a high priest who is unable
to sympathize with our weaknesses.

HEBREWS 4:15

He was the kind of fellow you'd invite to watch the Rams-Giants game at your house. He'd wrestle on the floor with your kids, doze on your couch, and cook steaks on your grill. He'd laugh at your jokes and tell a few of His own. And when you spoke, He'd listen to you as if He had all the time in eternity.

And one thing's for sure, you'd invite Him back.

It is worth noting that those who knew Him best remembered Him not as Jesus Christ or Lord Jesus, but as Jesus. Think about the implications. When God chose to reveal Himself to mankind, what medium did He use? A book? No, that was secondary. A church? No. That was consequential. A moral code? No. To limit God's revelation to a cold list of dos and don'ts is as tragic as looking at a Colorado road map and saying that you've seen the Rockies.

When God chose to reveal Himself, He did so (surprise of surprises) through a human body. The tongue that called forth the dead was a human one. The hand that touched the leper had dirt under its nails. The feet upon which the woman wept were calloused and dusty. And his tears…oh, don't miss the tears…came from a heart as broken as yours or mine ever has been.

So people came to Him. My, how they came to Him! Why? Because He refused to be a statue in a cathedral or a priest in an elevated pulpit. He chose instead to be Jesus.

LIGHTHOUSE THOUGHT FOR THE DAY

The Jesus we serve in our lighthouses is not some religious icon or set of rules. He's Jesus, and if we show our neighbors who He really is, some will come to Him.

MAX LUCADO

Made to Endure

"Therefore everyone who hears these words of mine and puts them into practice is like a wise man who built his house on the rock."

MATTHEW 7:24

Nautical lighthouses are towers of strength, engineered to withstand the most terrible of storms. The lighthouses on the coast of New England must endure the infamous nor'easters, some of the most violent storms any ocean serves up.

Lighthouses are strong for three reasons: They are built on rock; their structure has integrity; and they have a deep and broad foundation. We are strong in Christ for the very same reasons.

A lighthouse stands up to the most violent of storms partly because it is built upon solid rock. It's the same with us. To be strong, we must anchor ourselves to the Solid Rock, Jesus Christ. Being a Christian isn't about simply being a better person or working harder at it. It's being a person whose life is anchored on a relationship with Jesus.

The shape of most lighthouses is similar—tall and cylindrical. There are no corners, no seams, and no breaks in the structure. In other words, it has structural *integrity*. It is built to hold together no matter what. Likewise, our witness for Christ is the brightest when we live lives that reflect His character.

Finally, lighthouses are built upon a deep and broad foundation. The part of a lighthouse that gets most of the attention, of course, is its bright beacon. However, the foundation—the part you cannot see—is what holds it firmly in place. Likewise, we lighthouses for Christ need to pay attention to the foundations of our lives, the places only God sees.

LIGHTHOUSE THOUGHT FOR THE DAY

If you want to be an enduring light for Christ, you need to anchor yourself in Him and live a life that reflects His character.

ROBERT C. CROSBY

We Have Authority!

"All authority in heaven and on earth has been given to me."
MATTHEW 28:18

The Bible tells us that Satan has blinded the minds of the unbelieving (2 Corinthians 4:4). But the Word also tells us that we are to be lights—light*houses*, if you will—that cut through that darkness (Matthew 5:14). That's a high calling indeed. So what steps should we take to meet that calling?

The good news for those of us who already believe is that we are not only forgiven, but we are alive in Christ and seated with Him in the heavenly places (Ephesians 2:4–6). Because of our position in Christ, we have the authority to do God's will: "In Him you have been made complete, and He is the head over all rule and authority" (Colossians 2:10, NASB).

Satan has no authority over God's children who are committed to doing His will. On the other hand, because of our position in Christ, we have authority over the kingdom of darkness.

We have the power to do God's will. The problem is that we either don't understand this truth or we don't believe it. The apostle John wrote, "The Son of God appeared for this purpose, to destroy the works of the devil" (1 John 3:8, NASB). This means we don't have to defeat the devil, because Jesus has already done that. Therefore, we are not called to completely dispel the darkness; we are called to turn on the light.

To stand against Satan's blinding, we must simply take our place in Christ, proclaim the truth in love, and pray authoritatively against it.

LIGHTHOUSE THOUGHT FOR THE DAY

Satan has blinded those of our neighbors who don't know Jesus. As children of God, we have both the authority to pray against that blinding and the light that can pierce their darkness.

NEIL T. ANDERSON

Standing Up for Others

> "Whenever Aaron enters the Holy Place, he will bear the names
> of the sons of Israel over his heart on the breastpiece of decision as
> a continuing memorial before the LORD."
>
> Exodus 28:29

During and after the Vietnam War, many Americans wore pieces of jewelry called "MIA (Missing In Action) bracelets." Each person who wore a bracelet was an advocate for those in enemy hands who could not be advocates for themselves.

The MIA bracelet illustrates the second step of intercessory prayer. After we align ourselves with God's will for our neighbors, the Spirit may call us to serve as their advocates before the throne of grace. God intends that by our prayers, and out of our love for others, we reason with Him about their destiny.

Exodus 28 gives us a biblical illustration of advocacy prayer. Every time the high priest came into the tabernacle, on his vestment he bore across his heart the names of the tribes of Israel, inscribed on twelve stones. Like the MIA bracelet, these stones were a constant remembrance before the Lord (and to the priest) that the Israelites had no hope unless God acted on their behalf.

When we gather to pray, we, too, need to come wearing on our hearts, as it were, names of those around us for whom God has given us personal responsibility in prayer. We love them through prayer as we plead for them the way we would for any loved one who was trapped in a prison. As advocates for others in prayer, we cry out to God for them: "They need what You have to give them, so, I'm praying for those who cannot yet pray for themselves."

Lighthouse Thought for the Day

As you pray for those around you, ask the Father to write their names upon your heart. Then, remember to advocate for them every single time you walk into His presence to pray.

David Bryant

Confronting Sin

He is the atoning sacrifice for our sins, and not only for ours
but also for the sins of the whole world.

1 JOHN 2:2

One of the biggest challenges in communicating the gospel is how to talk about sin without alienating seekers. This is particularly challenging in our happiness-oriented, self-absorbed modern culture. We live in a therapeutic age that believes that our problems are rooted either in addiction or emotional woundedness.

The problem is not that this analysis is wrong, but that it doesn't go deep enough. So how do we talk about sin to people who may believe our biggest problem is low self-esteem? How do we keep people listening when we say they've done something that is actually morally wrong? How do we not shrink from naming sin and still be bearers of grace?

People can only recognize sin when they are confronted with the depth of God's love for us as revealed in Christ. "But that's impossible!" we say. "How can we talk about sin and communicate God's love at the same time?" We do it by our style of communication and by the substance of our message.

First, we need a style that reflects the love of Jesus and identifies with the problems and hopes of others. Unbelievers need to sense that we understand and are sensitive to the complexities of human frailty. Second, we communicate God's love by our message. We talk about the Cross because it was what set us free, and we know it has the power to set others free, too.

LIGHTHOUSE THOUGHT FOR THE DAY

As lighthouses for Christ, we have compassion for the weaknesses of others because we know that we "have not a high priest who is unable to sympathize with our weaknesses, but one who in every respect has been tempted as we are, yet without sin" (Hebrews 4:15, RSV).

REBECCA MANLEY PIPPERT

Mission Impossible

> *"'I am the LORD your God; consecrate yourselves*
> *and be holy, because I am holy.'"*
> LEVITICUS 11:44

What? Me holy? If you're like us, that sounds like "mission impossible"! A 1960s television series by that name was about a team of specialists who took on jobs that seemed impossible to accomplish, but somehow they always found a way to carry out their mission.

Holiness is not an impossible mission for the believer because Jesus Christ has already made us holy. That's right! We are holy because God the Father made Jesus, His righteous Son, to be sin for us. He has made us—who were unrighteous and incapable of being so—holy! (Colossians 3:4). In fact, the writer of Hebrews says that God has perfected us forever (Hebrews 10:14). This is what theologians call the "principle of position." There is nothing unholy "in Christ," and that includes us.

Unfortunately, there is often a difference between our spiritual position in Christ and our earthly condition. Our position in Christ is often at odds with our behavior. The solution? Living so surrendered to Christ that His life becomes our life. The Spirit-filled life in us is nothing more (and nothing less) than Christ's life being exhibited in our own. The evidence that we are Christ-filled is that we are more like Him than like ourselves.

Today, let's pay close attention to what we say and do in front of our neighbors. Let's ask ourselves: Is it Christ's life seen in us, or our own?

LIGHTHOUSE THOUGHT FOR THE DAY

God has declared us holy through the sacrifice of His Son. It is up to us to take the steps to walk in holiness before God, our families, our friends, and our neighbors.

EDDIE AND ALICE SMITH

Accepting the Truth

O LORD, you have searched me and you know me.
PSALM 139:1

Most of us wish we were in some way different from the way we are—perhaps in personality, appearance, or physical abilities. Often we wish we were more like someone we know or someone we see in the media. While it is good to admire positive qualities in others, the desire to be like someone else can actually be a form of covetousness, which God condemns.

To be effective lighthouses to our residential or vocational neighbors, it's important that we learn to accept ourselves as God made us and utilize the gifts He has given us. And before we can truly accept ourselves, we must first recognize both the gifts and the limitations God has given us. Otherwise we will constantly struggle to be someone we are not.

One good place to start is to read Psalm 139. In it the writer rejoices, "Thank you for making me so wonderfully complex! Your workmanship is marvelous—and how well I know it" (v. 14, NLT). As God's "workmanship," we are beautiful masterpieces—works that ought to be highly valued.

Though no one is perfect, each of us is unique and special—created, embraced, and accepted by God Himself. Spiritual renewal cannot begin until we choose to accept ourselves as God made us and live in a spirit of thanksgiving for our God-designed attributes. Once we accept the truth about ourselves, we can bring great glory to God through our examples of gratitude and inner peace.

LIGHTHOUSE THOUGHT FOR THE DAY

When you acknowledge that God has made you with unique abilities—all for the purpose of serving Him—you will discover a new level of joy and effectiveness as you share Christ's love with those around you.

STEPHEN ARTERBURN

Control vs. Security

Yet you are enthroned as the Holy One; you are the praise of Israel.

PSALM 22:3

We are all tempted to control our own lives in one way or another. Some of us try to control our relationships, and others of us try to control our ministries. Almost all of us have some "territory" we want to control. Over time, the emotions and attitudes that spring from the desire to control can erode our faith and confidence, rendering us ineffective for the Lord.

I believe that wholehearted worship of God is the antidote to this contagion. Psalm 22:3 suggests that worship opens us up to the lordship of Christ and keeps us sensitive to the control of Jesus. To the degree that we yield control of our lives to Him, we will not feel the need to control our lives ourselves.

We try to control things because we are insecure, and I think that insecurity comes from not quite knowing where we stand with the Lord—from feeling we are somehow unacceptable to God. When we don't know for sure that God accepts and loves us, we feel insecure, and when we feel insecure, we feel the need to control our lives for ourselves.

There is no reason to feel insecure about anything when we consistently abide in a place of worship. For it is there that we cultivate sensitivity to the Master's voice. It is there we can know precisely what we are to do. It all comes to this elementary truth: Worship + Obedience = Security

Worship tunes us in to the lordship of Christ, and His control literally squeezes out of us the need to control for ourselves. Worshipers walk in freedom to listen as the Lord speaks to their hearts and freedom to obey when He speaks.

LIGHTHOUSE THOUGHT FOR THE DAY

Our ability to minister for Christ comes from our security in Him, and that security springs from a life of worship and obedience.

STEVE FRY

A "Quiet" Fast

Be still before the LORD and wait patiently for him.

PSALM 37:7

When was the last time you heard the sound of falling leaves? How long has it been since you sat still long enough to enjoy a cup of coffee before it got cold? Can you recall a moment in your life when the sound of silence felt comforting?

It's easy in today's society to overdose on noise and activity. We are "noise-aholics," and we are in constant motion. But we desperately need regular interludes of peaceful solitude so that our spirits can be refreshed. We need sacred times to talk to God and listen for His voice.

Your heavenly Father yearns to spend time with you, but He will not force His way into your schedule. Take a hard look at your daily planner. Are you allowing yourself any time at all to get still with the Lord? Consider five ways you can take control:

1. Decide to embark on a special kind of fast—giving up unnecessary noise and activity. Say to yourself, "I will embrace solitude."
2. Have the courage to turn something off! Do whatever it takes to eliminate all distractions.
3. As you begin to sense the silence, do not panic. Resist the urge to grab the car keys or the remote control.
4. Schedule time to be still every day, even if it is only for a few minutes. Five minutes a day adds up to two and a half hours per month.
5. Try to still your mind, not just your body. If this is difficult, try humming a favorite praise song or simply whispering the name of Jesus.

LIGHTHOUSE THOUGHT FOR THE DAY

Fasting from noise and activity may not come easily in our society, but God will use it to refresh and empower us.

DR. TERRY TEYKL

God's Prescribed Fast

"Is not this the kind of fasting I have chosen:
to loose the chains of injustice and untie the cords of the yoke,
to set the oppressed free and break every yoke?"

ISAIAH 58:6

Fasting is depriving yourself of something, usually food, for a set time while focusing on God for a particular purpose. It commonly involves an intense time of concentrated prayer. The fast that God prescribes has much to do with living sacrificially in order to oppose injustice and to minister to the poor, oppressed, and needy.

If you really want to light up your world for the Lord, you will be concerned not only about your own things or even your own family, but also with the good of others in your neighborhood, your community, and your nation. On a local level, you will seek to find a need and meet it. In particular, when you become aware of an injustice, you won't seek to avoid or ignore it, but you'll be eager to get involved in doing something about it. The Good Samaritan Jesus talked about in Luke 10 is the perfect example of this. He went out of his way to help someone (of another race) who had been victimized and left to rot.

As Isaiah 58 indicates, part of the purpose for fasting is to prepare our hearts to minister to the poor, oppressed, and needy. Part of it is also to prepare ourselves to promote justice and righteousness in our society and to reach beyond our comfort zones and personal convenience to help the less fortunate among us.

LIGHTHOUSE THOUGHT FOR THE DAY

Regular times of fasting and dedicated prayer should include praying for known needs among neighbors, the community, and the nation.

BILL MCCARTNEY

Look—Love—Level

"'For I was hungry and you gave me something to eat, I was thirsty and you gave me something to drink, I was a stranger and you invited me in.'"
MATTHEW 25:35

There is an obvious key to being a caring witness for Christ: You have to be in contact with those who need care. This means forming relationships with unbelievers.

This sounds simple, but I meet many believers who tell me that they don't have any significant relationships with non-Christians. Sadly, many of us get so involved with the body of Christ that we do nothing to cultivate relationships with those who need to know Christ. I am sure that thrills the evil one. We need to get out of this "holy huddle" mentality and start forming relationships—even friendships—with those who have yet to come to Jesus Christ.

Here are three basic principles that will help you foster relationships with someone who needs to be loved into the kingdom of God. I call them *the three Ls:*

1. *Look* for relationships. Many of us know people from work, from school, from recreational activities, or from our neighborhood with whom we have something in common. Find those connections, and take some time to reach out.
2. *Love* them beyond the expected. It takes a consistent and sometimes sacrificial love to convince many people that you really care about them. They need to see how Christ cares for them through you.
3. *Level* their misconceptions about Christians. It has been said that between the Cross and where an unbeliever stands, there are about fifteen caricatures of Jesus. Spend time with them to help them come to know the real Christ.

LIGHTHOUSE THOUGHT FOR THE DAY

We can't reach someone for Christ until we are ready to embrace that person as a friend and truly care for him or her.

DALLAS ANDERSON

Focused on the Word

But his delight is in the law of the LORD,
and on his law he meditates day and night.

PSALM 1:2

Though I am usually health-conscious, every once in a while I just like a big, sumptuous, old-fashioned meal—like the Sunday family dinner with roast beef, potatoes, gravy, a few vegetables, and bread. It's warm, filling, and satisfying.

I can't imagine, however, eating a meal only one day a week, no matter how big it might be. I feel starved just thinking about it. No matter how full I might get, I would still have to eat again.

We often treat God's Word, our daily bread, as though we can eat a big meal on Sunday morning, then make it through the week without starving. Just as the Israelites gathered manna daily, we need God's Word as our daily spiritual portion. Feeding on it daily will fill us with His character and bear the spiritual fruits of love, joy, peace, patience, kindness, goodness, gentleness, and self-control. It is that fruit in our lives that will draw others into God's presence.

God's Word also shines the light of conviction into our hearts. As lighthouses for Jesus Christ, we need a clean heart to hear God's direction and be a vessel fit for His use. King David cried out to God to "create in me a pure heart" (Psalm 51:10). After his plea, David acknowledged his position as a lighthouse for God when he said, "Then I will teach transgressors your ways, and sinners will turn back to you" (v. 13).

Our call is the same: to focus on the Word of God and allow it to guide us and convict us. Then we will see the tremendous results of touched lives.

LIGHTHOUSE THOUGHT FOR THE DAY

A worn Bible is a sign to others that our lives are focused on God.

TOM PHILLIPS

Embracing Weakness

*But he said to me, "My grace is sufficient for you, for my power is
made perfect in weakness." Therefore I will boast all the more gladly
about my weaknesses, so that Christ's power may rest on me....
For when I am weak, then I am strong.*

2 CORINTHIANS 12:9–10

"When I am weak, then I am strong"? How unlike our natural thinking! We tend to think of strength as the opposite of weakness. We reason that just as someone is either tall or short, big or small, or rich or poor, they are either strong or weak. They can't be both!

But God's Word tells us that when we are weak, we are actually strong. How could that be? For one thing, it's only when we recognize our own weakness that we realize we need Christ to be our strength. In light of this, we should never reject, regret, or shun our weakness; rather we should *embrace* it. We should let it be the wonderful reminder that we need Christ every day. Our weakness is our assurance that Jesus is there for us. He wants to replace our weakness with His strength. *His strength for my weakness?* you ask. That's right! What a deal!

Christ has promised that His grace is sufficient, that He is all we need to do the things that bring Him glory. Let your weakness be your assurance that Christ loves you, has a plan for your life, and is working out in your life that which is well pleasing in His sight.

Also, let your weakness be God's alarm alerting you to the fact that you need more of His strength. Invite Him today to replace your weakness with His strength. You can be assured that He will do it.

LIGHTHOUSE THOUGHT FOR THE DAY

Let's start embracing our weakness as God's reminder that we need more of Him!

BRUCE SCHOEMAN

The Depth of Repentance

*"I am the voice of one calling in the desert,
'Make straight the way for the Lord.'"*

JOHN 1:23

The Bible tells us that prior to the beginning of Jesus' ministry, "There came a man sent from God, whose name was John" (John 1:6, NASB). God sent John the Baptist to prepare the way for Christ.

John's baptism of repentance was not the last event of the Old Covenant; it was the first event—the groundbreaker—of the New Covenant. His purpose was to immerse Israel in an attitude of repentance (Acts 19:4). He was called to go before Christ to "prepare" and "make ready the way of the LORD" (Mark 1:2–3, NASB).

Repentance always precedes the living Christ. It's purpose is not merely to cleanse us from sin or make us sorry, but to prepare us for an outpouring of God's love in our lives and make us ready to bear fruit for the kingdom. True repentance is likened in Scripture to turning soil over to prepare it for a new planting (Hosea 10:12). It is the depth of repentance that determines the fullness of Christ.

John's command was to "produce fruit in keeping with repentance" (Matthew 3:8). In effect, John was saying, "Cease not your turning away from pride until you delight in lowliness. Continue repenting of selfishness until love is natural to you. Do not stop mourning your impurities until you are pure." He called people to repent and to continue repenting until fruit was manifested.

LIGHTHOUSE THOUGHT FOR THE DAY

Today, as we position ourselves as lighthouses for Jesus Christ, let us continue our attitude of repentance so that our hearts can be prepared to bring Jesus to our friends and neighbors.

FRANCIS FRANGIPANE

Oh, Grow Up!

As newborn babes, desire the pure milk of the word,
that you may grow thereby,
if indeed you have tasted that the Lord is gracious.

1 PETER 2:2–3, NKJV

Babies are cute; they can do no wrong even when they do wrong. We love them. We overlook their bowel behavior. We laugh when they scrunch up their faces. We're alarmed at the first sign of fever. We put up with all the messes they make.

Newborns may be fun, but they wear on us. There are only so many diapers you can change and still enjoy it. There are only so many times you can strap the baby into a car seat before the novelty wears off. As much as we love these little ones, we don't want them to be babies forever.

It's the same way with spiritual newborns. We all rejoice when someone is born into the kingdom of God. We overlook their weaknesses so they can grow (1 Peter 2:2). But how long should they drink milk without taking in solid food? How long should the born-again person remain a spiritual babe?

Too many Christians today are stuck in spiritual infancy. They are alive in Christ, but they have never grown. When offered the meat of the Word, they are more than content with pabulum. As someone once said, "You are young only once, but you can stay immature indefinitely."

If you want to be spiritually mature, you need to establish good growth habits so you can grow out of spiritual infancy. These habits include the proper diet of God's Word and the exercises of prayer, church attendance, and witnessing to others.

LIGHTHOUSE THOUGHT FOR THE DAY

Lighthouse ministry requires that we move toward spiritual maturity, and that means we have to pay attention to our diet and exercise.

WOOD KROLL

Lighthouse Intercessors

*I urge, then, first of all, that requests, prayers, intercession
and thanksgiving be made for everyone.*

1 TIMOTHY 2:1

The apostle Paul pointed out to young Timothy something all of us need to lay hold of: We as children of the living God have the privilege and responsibility to pray prayers of intercession for those around us.

That is an awesome challenge for those of us who are taking part in the Lighthouse Movement. We don't need to travel far beyond our own neighborhoods to see people who need a touch from God and who need us to intercede with Him on their behalf.

We need to pray for those persecuted for their commitment to Christ (Psalm 91:14–16). We should pray for prisoners of drugs, alcohol, immorality, obscenity, pornography, crime, prejudice, unbelief, depression, and despair (Matthew 5:44–45; John 8:31–32, 36; Romans 6:19–23; 1 Corinthians 10:13; 2 Corinthians 3:17), and we should lift up prisoners of poverty and hunger (1 Samuel 2:8; Job 5:15–16; Psalm 34:10; 50:14–15; 69:33; 72:12–13; 107:41; 140:12; 146:7; Philippians 4:19). We should also pray for the sick and discouraged (Psalm 118:5–6; 121:2; Matthew 4:23–24; Acts 3:16, 19; 2 Corinthians 12:8–10; Ephesians 3:20; Philippians 2:27; James 5:14–15; 1 Peter 5:7).

We should go into God's presence with a spirit of expectancy that He will reveal His glory and character to us in a deeper way, knowing that He desires to meet the needs of those for whom we intercede.

LIGHTHOUSE THOUGHT FOR THE DAY

If we are to be lighthouses for the Lord Jesus Christ, we need to enrich our personal spiritual lives by making intercession a regular part or our prayers.

VONETTE Z. BRIGHT

What Do You See?

Men of Issachar, who understood the times and knew what Israel should do.
1 CHRONICLES 12:32

In the Old Testament, God pointed to specific individuals—the men of Issachar—as individuals who had a special ability to understand the times they were in. Their understanding led them to know exactly what to do in certain situations.

As a light for Jesus Christ, you need to ask God to make you a "man or woman of Issachar." Ask Him for insight into your neighbors' lives. Ask Him to show you what you can do to care for them. Then start honing your abilities to "see things." Without trying to be a snoop or a nosey neighbor, learn to pay attention to things that might signal that your neighbors need prayer.

Some of the signs are obvious. Several days' worth of newspapers piling up indicates a trip or an illness. A police car with lights flashing in front of a neighbor's house could be a sign of a burglary, a domestic dispute, or other trouble. A car missing for a long time might mean a marital separation. Children who used to be very friendly and are now more withdrawn could be sending the message that there are real problems in the home. A lawn that isn't as well cared for as it used to be could signal that the dad is overworked.

These could all be signals of things to pray about. We should go to special prayer, seeking God for direction on how to minister.

Keep watching and keep asking God to help you understand what you should do when you notice different things. If you bathe the situation in prayer and listen for God's direction, He will show you how to reach out.

LIGHTHOUSE THOUGHT FOR THE DAY

We need to be alert for times when our neighbors may need prayer or a caring word or deed.

JONATHAN GRAF

The Life of Joy

*Even though you do not see him now, you believe in him
and are filled with an inexpressible and glorious joy.*

1 PETER 1:8

Ludwig van Beethoven, the great composer, is quoted as once having said, "Oh God, may I live to have just one day of unsullied joy!"

Joy. It's one of our deepest desires. Yet so few seem to be living a life filled with joy. God desires His children to live every day with an unsullied, perfect joy. The kind of joy our Lord offers us is inexpressible and glorious (1 Peter 1:8). My grandfather emigrated from Sweden. He used to talk about the "yoy" of the Lord. And he not only talked about it, he experienced it day by day. He overflowed with the joy of the Lord.

This inexpressible, glorious joy is available to all of us. It is one manifestation of the fruit of the Spirit. It comes as we allow Jesus Christ to live in us and through us in the person of the Holy Spirit.

If you live the life of authentic joy, other people are going to ask you about it. That will give you the wonderful opportunity to tell them about the source of your joy—Jesus Christ! That is one of the most natural and believable ways to share the Good News of the gospel through your lighthouse.

LIGHTHOUSE THOUGHT FOR THE DAY

The joy of the Lord will not only be your strength, but it will be used of God to woo and draw others to Himself.

PAUL CEDAR

Convinced and Confident

My heart is steadfast, O God, my heart is steadfast.

PSALM 57:7

My wife, Dee, and I were watching a Christian video, noting the joy and wholesomeness of the people in it. Dee asked, "Why would anyone want any other life?"

People who revel in their relationship with Christ will ask that "why" question. Actually, they know the answer. But there is a veil keeping the unregenerate from the truth of Christ. I am glad the sovereign work of Christ has graciously removed that veil from my eyes (2 Corinthians 3:14–18).

I see people trying to find what Christ alone offers without looking to Him. I see them trying to create outside the church what can be found in it. I see character traits that I know would be improved if the person were in Christ and among those who "'in him...live and move and have [their] being'" (Acts 17:28).

The exchanged life, in which "I no longer live, but Christ lives in me" (Galatians 2:20), can bring rest, identity, and purpose to lost, confused souls.

God calls to Himself imperfect people like us: "Not many of you were wise by human standards; not many were influential; not many were of noble birth. But God chose the foolish things of the world to shame the wise; God chose the weak things of the world to shame the strong" (1 Corinthians 1:26–27).

Without Christ I have nothing; with Him I have everything. Without Christ I am hopeless and helpless; in Christ I have "become the righteousness of God" (2 Corinthians 5:21). Without Christ I would live a barren and powerless life; with Christ I can live abundantly and powerfully through prayer.

LIGHTHOUSE THOUGHT FOR THE DAY

As lighthouses for Jesus Christ, we have the privilege of presenting to those around us a new life that is second to none.

BOB RICKER

Defeating Your Doubts

Then the eleven disciples went to Galilee, to the mountain where Jesus had told them to go. When they saw him, they worshiped him; but some doubted.
MATTHEW 28:16–17

It is amazing how some of the disciples doubted Jesus. How could this be? Hadn't they walked side by side with our Savior for three and a half years, beholding His great miracles? Didn't they remember His promise that He would "raise this temple within three days"?

The tomb where they buried our Lord was empty, and several, including Peter and Mary Magdalene, had reported seeing Jesus alive. And now the Master was with them and sharing His final instructions before ascending back to heaven. Still, some of them doubted.

The phrase "but some doubted" tells us a lot about Jesus. First, it tells us that He doesn't reject us when we're having a difficult time believing. It also tells us that He is willing to work with us until our faith is restored or strengthened. Jesus did just that with His doubting disciples, and they went on to shake up the world for Him. The Bible says, "After the Lord Jesus had spoken to them, he was taken up into heaven and he sat at the right hand of God. Then the disciples went out and preached everywhere, and the Lord worked with them and confirmed his word by the signs that accompanied it" (Mark 16:19–20).

When you struggle with doubt, begin sharing the faith you have— no matter how weak it may seem to you—with others. As you do this, Jesus will work within you and confirm His presence in your life.

LIGHTHOUSE THOUGHT FOR THE DAY

The disciples, who personally witnessed Jesus' earthly ministry, weren't above doubting, and neither are we. Let's follow their example and move out and exercise the faith we have.

LOWELL LUNDSTROM

Christ Is Our Strength

Finally, be strong in the Lord and in his mighty power.
EPHESIANS 6:10

Sometimes life de-powers us. It saps our energies, depletes our courage, and drains our patience. It is at these times that we need an infusion of God's power. We need strength to think more clearly, love more creatively, endure more consistently—strength that fills us to overflowing.

Christ is our strength. Our heavenly Father has delegated Him to care for us, abide in us, and give us exactly what we need each day in order to do what He has assigned us to do. Our Lord has the authority to forgive us and restore us when we fail, and He knows precisely what we need to accomplish the tasks He puts before us. And because He knows what is ahead, He prepares us by giving us precisely the strength we need for each day's demands.

But how do we access this power? By having quiet time alone with our God. The prophet Zephaniah gives the secret of lasting strength: "Be silent in the presence of the Lord" (Zephaniah 1:7, NKJV).

There is nothing that will energize and strengthen us like being quiet in the presence of God. When we pray and spend time in His written Word, He renews our spirit and prepares us for what lies ahead.

God's strength is unlimited, and because He has made it readily available to us, we need never run out of strength to do the things that please and glorify Him.

LIGHTHOUSE THOUGHT FOR THE DAY

We need strength to be effective lighthouses for Jesus Christ. Through His Son, Jesus Christ, God has made available to us His own unlimited strength.

BOBBYE BYERLY

Pursuit Prayer

Never be silent day or night.
You who call on the LORD, give yourselves no rest, and give him no rest
till he establishes Jerusalem and makes her the praise of the earth.

ISAIAH 62:6–7

In the early '80s, theologian David Wells stunned some of us with an article in *Christianity Today* titled: "Prayer: Rebellion Against the Status Quo."

Did you ever think of prayer that way? Jesus observed: "The kingdom of heaven has been forcefully advancing, and forceful men lay hold of it" (Matthew 11:12). At times in our prayers, there arises an intense engagement with God that looks and feels like "rebellion"—not against God, but against the status quo condition of our neighbors, our churches, our generation. In essence our prayers say to Him: "Father, the time has come for You to act. There must be delay no longer. We honor You by pursuing You for the answers and not letting up until they come."

Some call this having a "burden of prayer." Others, "the gift of faith." This kind of prayer is diligent, fervent, constant, persevering, determined, convinced, unstoppable. It is the kind of longing that John Knox revealed when he prayed, "Give me Scotland or I die!"

We need to be ready for the Spirit to ignite such a burden in us for specific people or situations. It may be one of the primary ways God calls you to suffer for one of your neighbors, as you learn how to hurt and cry for that person about the things that break God's heart.

LIGHTHOUSE THOUGHT FOR THE DAY

Don't be afraid of the Holy Spirit giving you a "burden of prayer" for someone—this may be a sign that a breakthrough for the gospel is about to happen in the one for whom you "take no rest and give God no rest."

DAVID BRYANT

Look Deeper

"Man looks at the outward appearance, but the LORD looks at the heart."
1 SAMUEL 16:7

On a recent flight, I was in an aisle seat with no one next to me. As the plane was loading, I quietly asked the Lord to keep the center seat open. I had so much work to do. I had no sooner uttered those words than there appeared a twenty-something woman who informed me that the seat next to me was hers.

As I got up to let her in the row, I noticed that she had several ear-rings in each ear, one in her eyebrow, one in her nose, and another in her tongue. When the flight attendant came by with drinks, I smiled and passed one to her. Looking at her, I couldn't help but wonder how she got through the metal detectors.

I could tell she noticed that I was looking at her pierced ears, eyebrow, and nose. So I said with a loving smile, "I've been thinking about doing that."

She belly-laughed and said, "I wouldn't do that if I were you!"

"Why is that?" I asked. "Did it hurt?"

"No, not very much," she said. "But if you did that your friends would not talk to you."

This was a young woman who understood about different cultural values. I told her of Christ, and before we landed she prayed and made Jesus her Savior.

She was a lovely young lady. Yet so many people would never see beyond the decorations she had put on her face. What church would welcome her without condition or reservation? Some might hold her up like a trophy, saying, "We've got one of these!" But if she said, "I have about fifty friends; could I invite them to church also?" many churches would not be so eager.

LIGHTHOUSE THOUGHT FOR THE DAY

In a nation with so many different cultural values, we must be careful not to judge others and miss out on the opportunity to invite them to church or share the gospel with them.

DR. CORNELL HAAN

Meditate on Scripture

If your law had not been my delight, I would have perished in my affliction.
PSALM 119:92

It was Good Friday, 1978. I went up to my dad's room to wake him up so we could go together for the cancer treatment he was to have that morning. When I entered his room, he wasn't moving. I'd just seen him up a half hour before, and I rushed to his bedside and sought to revive him. But it was to no avail. My father had died.

I loved my dad. He lived with my wife and me at the time of his death. I knew he had cancer, and I knew it would probably take his life. Still, the moment of his death was an emotional, stark, harsh reality.

As you might imagine, I endured periods of great anxiety during the weeks that followed Dad's death. At the same time, though, the Word of God gave me incredible peace. I read the Scriptures and listened to them being sung in Christian songs. Every time I felt distressed at missing Dad, I read from the Word or played a tape so I could listen to what God had to say. The Word of God literally became my delight and lifted me out of my affliction.

Sadly, we are all greatly tempted to set aside only a certain time of day to study the Bible, or to go to the Word only during times of trouble. But when we do this, we can miss the powerful comfort the Word can give us throughout our lives. That is why we are to "delight ourselves" in the Word of God.

Rather than immersing ourselves in our grief or anxiety—or as the Scripture says, "perishing in our afflictions"—we should meditate on and delight in His Word at all times.

LIGHTHOUSE THOUGHT FOR THE DAY

A lighthouse for Jesus Christ knows the value of God's Word—during times of stress as well as times of peace.

STEVE DOUGLASS

What's in a Name?

However, if you suffer as a Christian, do not be ashamed,
but praise God that you bear that name.

1 PETER 4:16

My son-in-law is a fine Christian man with a great deal of responsibility. Since it is necessary for him to begin his day by 5 A.M., sleep is a precious commodity.

One evening he was awakened by the neighbor's dog. The barking went on and on until he could stand it no longer. He threw open the window and screamed, "Shut up, you stupid dog!" Unbeknownst to him, my seven-year-old grandson, awakened by the ruckus, was standing behind him. As my son-in-law closed the window, my grandson, with hands on hips and in his best preaching voice, said, "And you call yourself a Christian!" Out of the mouth of babes!

What does it *really* mean when you call yourself a Christian? Here are some things to remember.

You are under new management. In a very real sense, when a person becomes a Christian, he or she decides to transfer the title of life from self to Jesus Christ.

Your life reflects on the name of Christ and all other believers. Christians are bearers of a wonderful name and representatives of a glorious church. What they are in the world defines Christianity to those who are not yet believers.

You are on twenty-four-hour duty. Too many Christians separate their faith from "real life." They delegate their Christianity to the hour or two a week they spend in church. Believers need to understand that the church is not just a building, but the people of God. When the lights go out on Sunday, the church goes home to be the light of the world and the salt of the earth.

LIGHTHOUSE THOUGHT FOR THE DAY

The word *Christian* identifies who I am, not just my religion. As a Christian and a lighthouse, I will be salt and light to those around me.

CHARLES T. CRABTREE

Where Is the Light Now?

"I have come as Light into the world, that everyone
who believes in Me will not remain in darkness."

JOHN 12:46, NASB

A striking prophecy about light coming to the world is found in Isaiah 9:2: "The people who walk in darkness will see a great light; those who live in a dark land, the light will shine on them" (NASB). That prophecy was fulfilled when God sent His Son to minister in that dark land beyond the Jordan (Matthew 4:13–17).

John's gospel reveals Jesus as that Light who shines in darkness and enlightens every man (John 1:4–5, 9). Jesus ministered as the Light of the World for just over three years before His enemies snuffed out that Light on the cross. Then they buried and sealed it in a pitch-black tomb. Where was the Light then?

Suddenly—on that first Easter—they had the Light back! Jesus, the Light of the World, was alive! Risen from the dead! The Light had once and for all shattered the darkness!

For forty days, Jesus' followers again took in their beloved Master's teaching and instruction. But then He was taken back to heaven right before their eyes (Acts 1:9). Jesus, the Light of the World, was gone again. But did that mean the Light was gone for good?

At one time, Jesus had warned the disciples that He would be with them only a little while longer. He also had given them the solution: "You are the light of the world" (Matthew 5:14). The light of Jesus—the world's only hope for salvation—was passed on by them so the whole world could have His light in them too.

LIGHTHOUSE THOUGHT FOR THE DAY

Remember, our purpose as lighthouses for Christ is to shine Jesus Himself, the Light of the World.

EVELYN CHRISTENSON

An Antidote for Loneliness

Then he said to Jesus, "Lord, remember me when
You come into Your kingdom." And Jesus said to him,
"Assuredly, I say to you, today you will be with Me in Paradise."
LUKE 23:42–43, NKJV

It hardly seems possible that Jesus, in all His torment on the cross, could think of anything but His own suffering. But at the foot of the cross, Christian fellowship was born. In His dying moments, He saw to it that His mother would have a home with John the Beloved. He saw to it that the repentant thief at His side would have a home with Him in heaven.

When Jesus saw His mother, for one brief moment He forgot His own cross and remembered hers. When the thief cried, "Lord, remember me when you come into Your kingdom," He knew there was someone far worse off than He. For unless He responded to that cry, the thief must surely die without hope.

Loneliness can be like a silent alarm, reminding you to write that note of encouragement, pick up that phone to call a lonely friend, or walk down the street to visit at a retirement home. I recently heard of a widow in her seventies who spends several days a week in the therapy pool at a children's hospital, helping little ones stretch and exercise their injured bodies. Her apartment is still dark and lonely when she comes home at night, but the fresh memories of smiles and laughter and little reaching hands tend to warm the long evenings.

There isn't the slightest current of loneliness that blows through our hearts that our loving Father doesn't see and understand. Before you turn to frantic activity, empty noise, or blank despair, lift your eyes and see if there is something He might want to say to you in those lonely moments.

LIGHTHOUSE THOUGHT FOR THE DAY

When you are lonely, try asking God what He wants to say to you and what He might want you to do or say for your neighbors.

RON MEHL

Extra Effort

Blow the trumpet in Zion, declare a holy fast, call a sacred assembly.
JOEL 2:15

In his bestselling book *Leading Change,* Harvard professor John Kotter writes, "By far the biggest mistake people make when trying to change organizations is to plunge ahead without establishing a high enough sense of urgency."

Here's another way to put that: It will take a Herculean effort to pull off a program like the Lighthouse Movement, with its goal of having people making major life changes. It will require a huge change of focus and strategy within the church. It may even require that we add fasting to our prayer efforts for our neighbors.

As ingenious as the lighthouse prayer-care-and-share approach is, it still requires extra effort on the part of those who put it into practice. Reaching our neighbors for Christ isn't always easy. For example, our prayers for our neighbors don't always quickly reveal how we can care for them in a way that leads to an opportunity to share Christ. So what should we do when we don't see results when we pray for our neighbors?

In Scripture, when people felt an urgent need to see God break down walls of resistance, they relied on fasting. Queen Esther asked her people to join her in fasting when it seemed the enemy was on the verge of a decisive victory.

Fasting intensifies a prayer effort, taking it to the next level. I believe fasting will be necessary if we hope to eventually see the church make the Lighthouse Movement all that it can be.

LIGHTHOUSE THOUGHT FOR THE DAY

Fasting works hand in hand with the Lighthouse Movement. We need to make use of the spiritual power available to us as through fasting as we follow our calling to share the love of God with those around us.

DAVID MAINS

Sharing the Gospel

"But you will receive power when the Holy Spirit comes on you;
and you will be my witnesses in Jerusalem,
and in all Judea and Samaria, and to the ends of the earth."

ACTS 1:8

After His resurrection, in what is known as the great commission, Jesus said to His disciples, "Go into all the world and preach the good news to all creation" (Mark 16:15). Helping to fulfill this calling is a life mission for every Christian.

Jesus didn't expect His disciples—men He had personally trained for three years—to witness in their own strength. They had to wait until the power of the Holy Spirit came upon them. They did, and it turned the world upside down! That same power is available to us today and can enable us to be witnesses of the Good News of salvation.

Just as the disciples were told to begin in their own "backyard" of Jerusalem, so we should start at home and with those nearest to us—our neighbors. That's really what the Lighthouse Movement is all about: sharing the gospel of Christ with every person in America, house by house, one neighbor at a time.

Jesus also commanded the disciples to preach to those "in Samaria." Samaritans were a racially mixed group despised by the Jews for cultural and religious reasons. But Jesus commanded His followers to reach beyond their comfort zones to break down walls of racism and sectarianism to proclaim the gospel to "all creation." We also need to be willing to share Christ with those who are of another race, religion, or culture. It may take a little courage, but we have the power of the Holy Spirit and the assurance that Christ is with us.

LIGHTHOUSE THOUGHT FOR THE DAY

Make a list of five people in your "Jerusalem" for whom you will pray regularly, then stand prepared to share the gospel with them if given the opportunity.

BILL MCCARTNEY

Courage to Step Out

When the disciples saw [Jesus] walking on the lake, they were terrified.
"It's a ghost," they said, and cried out in fear.
But Jesus immediately said to them: "Take courage! It is I. Don't be afraid."
MATTHEW 14:26–27

Do you tend to take safe, comfortable, or familiar spiritual paths only to find that these don't take you where you long to go?

Transforming our lives requires that we step out in faith, believing that God is able to turn even the watery depths of the ocean into a pathway to Himself and His plan for us. With our eyes fixed on Jesus, we can face our fear of the unknown and move beyond where we are.

Courage isn't the absence of fear. It is a frame of heart and mind in which we take advantage of what strength we do find within us, find little ways to encourage ourselves, and stubbornly follow God's direction. Courage means we find enough strength to take a step in the right direction despite our fears.

The disciples were terrified when they saw Jesus walk on the water. But Peter called to Jesus, "Lord, if it's really you, tell me to come to you by walking on water" (Matthew 14:28, NLT). Jesus told him to come, so Peter stepped out of the boat and walked on the water toward Jesus. When he took his eyes off Jesus and looked at the wind and waves, he became terrified and began to sink, but Jesus reached out and lifted him up.

People who criticize Peter for taking his eyes off the Lord forget that he was the only disciple who dared take a step in the Lord's direction. We need to do the same. If we get in over our heads, Jesus will give us the help we need.

LIGHTHOUSE THOUGHT FOR THE DAY

Courage to do great things for God does not mean an absence of fear. It means we look to God for strength to step out despite our fear.

STEPHEN ARTERBURN

God of the Small Things

*Always be prepared to give an answer to everyone who asks you
to give the reason for the hope that you have.*

1 PETER 3:15

Not too long ago, I went to a hair salon I'd not been to before. I was introduced to a beautiful hairstylist named Meg. As we chatted, Meg laughingly mentioned that her older brother was a devout Christian who had read every Christian book there was. I told her that I was a Christian and had written Christian books. She said she would ask him the next time they spoke if he had read any of my books.

On my next visit, Meg said, "Wow, my brother was over the moon that I'm doing your hair. He read *Out of the Salt Shaker* ten years ago and said it changed his life. Isn't it an amazing coincidence that he read something that you wrote?"

Later, as I was about to leave, Meg said, "I'm not sure I should tell you this, since it might make you feel uncomfortable."

"What is it, Meg?"

"Well, after I told my brother I'd met you, he told me something…amazing. He said that when he read your book ten years ago, he prayed that someone just like you would come into my life. Last week he said, 'Meg, I prayed for someone like Becky. I had no idea He'd send Becky herself!'"

As I got in my car, with tears in my eyes, I asked, "Lord, how do You do this?" From the outside it all looks so haphazard. All I did was call to get a haircut, yet I just happened to get the person who just happened to have been the object of her brother's prayer ten years ago. What a brother! What a prayer! *What a God!*

LIGHTHOUSE THOUGHT FOR THE DAY

Open my eyes, Lord, and guide me to the seekers that faithful believers have already prayed for.

REBECCA MANLEY PIPPERT

Loving Your Neighbors

*If I speak in the tongues of men and of angels, but have not love, I am only
a resounding gong or a clanging cymbal. If I have the gift of prophecy
and can fathom all mysteries and all knowledge, and I have a faith
that can move mountains, but have not love, I am nothing.*

1 CORINTHIANS 13:1–2

One of our goals as lighthouses for Jesus Christ is to love people. One of the most important truths I've learned as a believer is that I must love—love God with all my heart, soul, and mind; my neighbors as myself; and even my enemies.

There was a time when reading 1 Corinthians 13, the Bible's "love chapter," frustrated me. I wondered how I could possibly reach such a high standard of spiritual maturity. I had learned that love is important, but no one ever explained to me *how* to love.

One day, God opened my mind to understand that we love just as we receive the gift of salvation or do anything else in the Christian life—by faith.

Two very important words have helped me. Since God has commanded us to love, we know for certain that it is His will (John 15:12). With that *command* comes a wonderful *promise,* that if we ask anything according to His will, we know that He both hears us and will grant what we ask for (1 John 5:14–15).

I suggest that you reach out in love, faith, and obedience to every neighbor and acquaintance. Demonstrate to them the *agape* kind of love described in 1 Corinthians 13. By faith claim God's love for all, including those from whom you may be alienated. By faith claim God's supernatural provision to lovingly meet the needs of your neighbors and others around you.

LIGHTHOUSE THOUGHT FOR THE DAY

The most important thing I can do to shine my light for Christ before my neighbors is to love. I want my lighthouse to be a beacon of God's love. May all lighthouses for Christ do the same.

BILL BRIGHT

Leave the Light On!

*"Therefore go and make disciples of all nations, baptizing them
in the name of the Father and of the Son and of the Holy Spirit."*
MATTHEW 28:19

As I walked out the church door late one night, I reminded the people who were still in the building to be sure that all the lights were turned off before they left. The moment the words left my mouth, I realized how much my Christian life was like that—turning out the light as I left church.

It's easy for us to let our lights shine where there is already a lot of light. In church we sing, pray, praise, and enjoy wonderful fellowship. In church we pray for those who don't know Christ. When we finish doing all that, we pick up our Bibles, say "so long" to our brothers and sisters in Christ, and head back into the real world, looking forward to meeting again next Sunday.

We turn off the lights before we go.

That night, I realized that I had almost unconsciously made sure my light was turned off (or at least dimmed) before I left church so that the world would not see me as a fanatic. I am afraid, however, that the world didn't see much of Christ in me either.

We are called to go and take the gospel into the world, not to expect the world to come to us. If the world is ever to see Jesus, we need to make sure we leave the light switch in the "on" position when we walk out the front door of the church.

LIGHTHOUSE THOUGHT FOR THE DAY

Jesus never said, "Wait at church and make disciples of those who show up every Sunday morning." He told us to go out into the world and take His light to those who are in darkness. As we go, let's make sure we take the light of Christ with us.

DALLAS ANDERSON

Pray for Your Neighbor

"For my eyes have seen your salvation,
which you have prepared in the sight of all people."
LUKE 2:30–31

What Adam and Eve lost because of sin was life—eternal and spiritual life. But Jesus came to restore what was lost. He said, "I am the resurrection and the life; he who believes in Me will live even if he dies" (John 11:25, NASB). In other words, those who believe in Jesus will continue to live with Him spiritually even when they die physically.

Eternal life is not just something we get when we physically die; it is something God gives us the moment we receive Christ. The apostle John wrote, "He who has the Son has the life; he who does not have the Son of God does not have the life" (1 John 5:12, NASB). Those who are not born again before they physically die have nothing to look forward to but eternal separation from God in hell.

We have been placed here, near these unbelieving neighbors, to be a light for them. If we desire for them to find the abundant, eternal life we have found in Christ, we must pray for them. First John 5:14–15 says, "If we ask anything according to His will, He hears us. And if we know that He hears us in whatever we ask, we know that we have the requests which we have asked from Him" (NASB). Whatever we pray according to God's will, He will grant. If God desires your neighbor to be saved and you pray for that, it will happen.

LIGHTHOUSE THOUGHT FOR THE DAY

Pray that God will give the free gift of eternal life to your unbelieving neighbor.

NEIL T. ANDERSON

Giving Away Your Faith

I pray that you may be active in sharing your faith, so that you will
have a full understanding of every good thing we have in Christ.

PHILEMON 1:6

Jesus said that "'it is more blessed to give than to receive'" (Acts 20:35). Nothing could be truer when it comes to giving away your faith.

My wife and I decided to make our house a neighborhood lighthouse for Jesus Christ. We began to pray for our neighborhood, and we joined some of our closest friends in launching a Bible study. It sounded great in the planning, but the first night it was to happen, I came home exhausted, not having eaten all day.

Just as I sat down to eat, a knock came at our door—forty-five minutes early. When my wife got up to answer it, I challenged her to turn off the lights so that no one would think we were home. All I wanted was a quiet supper—no people!

Thank goodness my wife chose to open the door. Waiting in the chill of the night was a young wife and mother. She said, "I've been sitting in front of your house in my car for two hours. I need God! When I saw the announcement for the Bible study, I thought maybe this was where I could find Him."

As a result of one opened door, Toni Ann accepted Christ. Not only that, but her son, her brother-in-law, and her mother are now saved; her father is working through a Bible study as he searches for Christ; and her Jewish mother-in-law is attending a Bible study in another state.

From experience, I can assure you that making your home a lighthouse will help you have a "full understanding of every good thing we have in Christ"!

LIGHTHOUSE THOUGHT FOR THE DAY

Want to give your faith away to others? You can start by making the commitment to turn your home into a lighthouse for the Lord Jesus Christ.

ROBERT E. RECCORD

The Greatest Commandments

Thou shalt love the Lord thy God with all thy heart, and with all thy soul, and with all thy mind. This is the first and great commandment. And the second is like unto it, Thou shalt love thy neighbour as thyself.

MATTHEW 22:37–39, KJV

What is the greatest sin a person can commit? Is it murder or adultery? Surely "thou shalt not covet" is not as important as "thou shalt not steal"!

To know which is the greatest sin, we need to know which is the greatest commandment. That's why the Pharisees asked Jesus the very pertinent question, "Master, which is the greatest commandment in the law?" (Matthew 22:36, KJV).

Jesus responded by quoting the familiar Jewish Shema, "Thou shalt love the Lord thy God with all thy heart, and with all thy soul, and with all thy mind." Then He quickly added another that is "like unto it," which means just like it and just as important: "Love thy neighbour as thyself." If we truly love God and our neighbors, we will obey all other commandments. Thus, Jesus said, "On these two commandments hang all the law and the prophets" (Matthew 22:40, KJV).

Now, in light of this great truth, it's time for serious self-evaluation. If "love thy neighbour" is the second most important commandment in the Bible, how well are you doing? Do you know the names and needs of your closest neighbors? Are you praying for them, not only by name, but also by need? Are you building loving relationships by doing random acts of kindness so they will "see your good works, and glorify your Father in heaven" (Matthew 5:16, KJV)?

That's what being a lighthouse for Jesus is all about. Prayer-care-and-share is another way of "loving your neighbor as yourself."

LIGHTHOUSE THOUGHT FOR THE DAY

Let's reflect on the two greatest commandments and ask ourselves how we are doing in obeying them.

LARRY LEWIS

Sowing with Tears

May those who sow in tears reap with shouts of joy!
He that goes forth weeping, bearing the seed for sowing, shall come home
with shouts of joy, bringing his sheaves with him.

PSALM 126:5–6, RSV

There is nothing sad about sowing seed. It takes no more work than reaping. The days can be beautiful. There can be great hope of harvest. Yet Psalm 126 speaks of "sowing in tears." It says that someone "goes forth weeping, bearing the seed for sowing." Why is he weeping?

I think the reason is not that sowing is sad or that sowing is hard. I think the reason has nothing to do with sowing. Sowing is simply the work that has to be done, even when there are things in life that make us cry. The crops won't wait while we grieve or solve all our problems. If we are going to eat next winter, we must get out in the field and sow the seed whether we are crying or not.

This psalm teaches the tough truth that, whether I am emotionally up for it or not, there is work to be done, and it is good for me to do it. Suppose you are in a season of heartache, and it's time to sow seed. Do you say, "I can't sow the field this spring, because I am brokenhearted"? If you do, you will not eat in winter.

Suppose you say instead, "I am heartsick. I cry if the milk spills at breakfast or if the phone rings at supper. I cry for no reason at all, but the field needs to be sowed. That is the way life is. I don't feel like it, but I will take my bag of seeds and go into the fields and do my crying while I do my duty. I will sow in tears."

This psalm promises that if you do that, you will "come home with shouts of joy, bringing your sheaves with you"— not because the tears of sowing produce the joy of reaping, but because the sheer sowing produces the reaping.

LIGHTHOUSE THOUGHT FOR THE DAY

As lighthouses for Christ, let us believe the promise that our simple work of sowing will bring sheaves of harvest and that our tears will be turned to joy.

JOHN PIPER, WITH JUSTIN TAYLOR

Reconciliation

All this is from God, who reconciled us to himself
through Christ and gave us the ministry of reconciliation.

2 CORINTHIANS 5:18

The wonderful truth of the gospel of Jesus Christ is that through His sacrificial death on the cross and His resurrection, He provided for us a way to be reconciled with a completely holy God.

This reconciliation gives us peace in how we approach Him and in how we approach our fellow man. God has reconciled us to Himself, and that frees us to be reconciled to one another—regardless of our ethnicity or background.

Sadly, we have seen in our nation divisions between various racial groups, some based on past injustices and others on simple hatred for those who are different from us. But I believe that we are seeing, and will continue to see, reconciliation between the different peoples of our land. As we come to understand what it means to be reconciled to God, people of different groups will continue to work to be reconciled to one another. We will become more like our Savior, who makes no distinction between Jew or Gentile, African or European, Asian or American.

Christ's death on the cross and His glorious resurrection provide us with the forgiving and reconciling power of His shed blood. Millions are desperate and need His church to come to them with the Good News of the gospel. Because we have been reconciled to God, we can be reconciled to one another, and that further empowers the body of Christ to reach out to a lost and dying world for Him.

LIGHTHOUSE THOUGHT FOR THE DAY

As lighthouses for Jesus Christ, we have a message of reconciliation and forgiveness for all people, regardless of their race or background.

BOBBYE BYERLY

The Bottom Line for Leaders

*Now it is required that those who have
been given a trust must prove faithful.*

1 CORINTHIANS 4:2

We are all leaders. We all have our own spheres of influence. And the bottom line for all of us is faithfulness to God. This brings success as God defines it. It makes for a level playing field, as does the fact that God made and gifted us. We had nothing to do it with.

The Word tells us, "For who makes you different from anyone else? What do you have that you did not receive? And if you did receive it, why do you boast as though you did not?" (1 Corinthians 4:7). Further, we read, "We have different gifts, according to the grace given us" (Romans 12:6). We should not boast, but neither should we feel inferior when it comes to our callings.

We may not be as intelligent as some. That's all right; we can be faithful. We may not be as educated or as spiritually gifted as some. That's all right; we can be faithful. We may not be a lot of things. But that's all right; we can be faithful.

We make but one pass through life. We want to do well. Any advice? We can't do better than "Trust in the LORD with all your heart and lean not on your own understanding; in all your ways acknowledge him, and he will make your paths straight" (Proverbs 3:5–6).

When things work well and we have success, we will remember who made us and gifted us and made our paths straight. When we feel less than adequate and endure down days and dark nights, we will remember that we are a creation of God, His workmanship (Ephesians 2:10).

LIGHTHOUSE THOUGHT FOR THE DAY

If we have been faithful to God's dear name, we can go on in faith, knowing that the bottom line is pleasing Him.

BOB RICKER

Fasting and Feasting

This is what the LORD Almighty says: "The fasts of the fourth, fifth, seventh and tenth months will become joyful and glad occasions and happy festivals for Judah."

ZECHARIAH 8:19

Zechariah 8:19–22 describes an amazing worldwide prayer movement for revival and evangelism. In 1984 it was the theme text for the International Prayer Assembly in Seoul, Korea. Since the three thousand delegates gathered for that event, we have witnessed an unprecented groundswell of prayer.

But note, even though the Bible often encourages prayer and fasting, Zechariah's is a prayer movement marked by prayer and *feasting!* Why is that?

For seventy years the Israelites had been in captivity. In every one of those years they had fasted four times annually to mark the four major sieges of Jerusalem that had taken them into Babylon. But now the Israelites had returned to their homeland to rebuild the temple, and Zechariah challenged them to substitute feasting for fasting. Quite simply, God was about to fulfill for them wonderful promises that would touch the nations. So the prophet asked them to start celebrating the breakthroughs even before they happened.

As you gather to pray, pray seriously for your neighbors (and your nation). Fast a meal to concentrate on a season of intercession. Remember, though, it is a confident hope that God will answer that ultimately motivates you to keep on asking, seeking, and knocking. Therefore, you need to "rejoice in the hope of the glory of God" (Romans 5:2), at times coupling your prayers with joyful anticipation—yes, even with feasting. After all, we pray to a God who always does far more than we even dare to dream (Ephesians 3:20).

LIGHTHOUSE THOUGHT FOR THE DAY

Fast one meal today to pray on your neighbors' behalf. Then "feast" a meal to celebrate the mighty work Christ will do in your community.

DAVID BRYANT

The End or Just the Means?

I have become all things to all men,
so that I may by all means save some.
1 CORINTHIANS 9:22, NASB

One day I tried to think of the ultimate sacrifice I could make for needy people around me. I envisioned giving up my career and using my money to buy meat and vegetables for huge pots of soup. I saw myself serving it to a long line of grateful, hungry people as I gave each of them an encouraging word and a smile.

But suddenly the clouds above me parted. Jesus was returning for me! The soup ladle fell useless to the ground.

Eagerly I sought Jesus' smiling "well done," but my expectancy died within me as He looked past me to the crowd that now had stopped eating my soup. Jesus was gazing into their bewildered eyes—knowing He had to leave them behind on their way to an eternity without Him.

I snapped back to reality as tears filled my eyes. "Oh, Jesus," I cried, "never let me substitute a good and kind and even sacrificial means for the end of bringing them to Your salvation. Don't let me keep so busy doing good things for them that I let them go to eternity without You, dear Jesus."

To be sure, I was alleviating these starving people's suffering temporarily, and this is very necessary for now. But what difference will it make for them if they go through hell's gate with full stomachs or clothes on their backs?

Praying for people is a necessary part of personal evangelism. Caring for them is a wonderful part of reaching them for Christ. But if there is no presentation of the person of Jesus Christ, those first two steps will be in vain.

LIGHTHOUSE THOUGHT FOR THE DAY
In your lighthouse, are you letting those for whom you are praying and caring go unsaved into eternity—because you are not sharing the Good News of salvation through Jesus Christ?

EVELYN CHRISTENSON

Living with Assurance

*"I tell you the truth, whoever hears my word and believes him
who sent me has eternal life and will not be condemned;
he has crossed over from death to life."*

JOHN 5:24

A frail, elderly woman attended an evangelistic rally where I was the guest speaker. When I asked people to come forward at the end of the service, she publicly confessed the Lord Jesus as Savior.

"Why didn't someone tell me this before?" she asked. "Why did I have to wait until almost the end of my life?" But then she added, "I'm glad I at least found out in my seventies." Six months later she went to be with the Lord.

This dear lady died knowing that she had eternal life. Why? Because Jesus assured us that "I give them [those who follow Him] eternal life, and they shall never perish; no one can snatch them out of my hand" (John 10:28). Let's look more closely at this triple promise.

I give them eternal life. The Bible says, "God has given us eternal life, and this life is in his Son. He who has the Son has life; he who does not have the Son of God does not have life" (1 John 5:11–12).

They shall never perish. We never need to fear losing the life that God gives us. Why? Because Jesus Christ laid down His life on the cross. What did He die for? "Christ died for us" (Romans 5:8) and "Christ died for our sins" (1 Corinthians 15:3). The result? "The blood of Jesus, his [God's] Son, purifies us from all sin" (1 John 1:7). Therefore, the Christian need not fear eternity.

No one can snatch them out of my hand. Satan opposes all who follow Jesus Christ and tries to plant doubts in our minds. But Jesus gives us the sure promise that if we belong to Him, we are His forever.

LIGHTHOUSE THOUGHT FOR THE DAY

Lighthouses for Jesus need to proclaim God's assurance of eternal life with Him.

LUIS PALAU

A Forgiving Heart

Bear with each other and forgive whatever grievances you may have against one another. Forgive as the Lord forgave you. And over all these virtues put on love, which binds them all together in perfect unity.

COLOSSIANS 3:13–14

It's impossible to pray for someone we won't forgive. Likewise, it's impossible to not forgive someone for whom we pray.

A lighthouse for Jesus Christ must have a heart to forgive. Forgiveness is not to be dependent upon the person asking, for people often won't request it. No, forgiveness takes place in our hearts as an act of obedience.

Jesus told a parable about a man who was forgiven a huge debt but who wouldn't forgive the small debt of another. Eventually, this man was judged with the same harshness he used to judge others. The warning to believers is that we have no right to hold onto other's small debts because we all owe God the unpayable debt of our salvation.

As we seek intimacy with God by receiving His forgiveness daily, then we in turn can help others to know Him. Forgiveness is, literally, a part of our becoming "fishers of men" (Matthew 4:19). By withholding forgiveness from others, we withhold God's kindness—and it is His kindness that leads to repentance (Romans 2:4).

What better way to demonstrate our care for others than to practice the discipline of forgiveness? Our world is filled with people who hold grudges and give conditional love. Demonstrating God's forgiveness is in stark contrast to the ways of our me-oriented world.

LIGHTHOUSE THOUGHT FOR THE DAY

We should ask God to open our eyes to situations where we can be a conduit of His grace through forgiveness.

TOM PHILLIPS

We're His Forever!

For I am persuaded, that neither death, nor life, nor angels,
nor principalities, nor powers, nor things present, nor things to come,
nor height, nor depth, nor any other creature, shall be able to separate us
from the love of God, which is in Christ Jesus our Lord.
ROMANS 8:38–39, KJV

An adopted child has all of the rights and privileges of a child living with his own parents. He calls his adopted parents Mom and Dad and has the same loving relationship with them as children the parents conceived and bore.

The Bible tells us that salvation is a spiritual adoption. The apostle Paul wrote that we "have received the Spirit of adoption, whereby we cry, Abba [literally Daddy], Father" (Romans 8:15, KJV). In Christ you have now become part of God's own family. You are an heir of all He has.

God knew about you before the creation of the world. He planned from the beginning to make you like Jesus (Romans 8:29–30). Not only did God plan that you would be saved and become His adopted child, but He also laid out in advance a plan for your Christian life (Ephesians 2:10).

As you walk with Christ, there will be special times of renewal and dedication—so-called mountaintop experiences, and there will be deep valleys. But God does not depart from you in those hard times. There is no need to be "saved" over and over again. Indeed, it is in those low times when God is often the most real to you. He's there by your side, just like a daddy.

LIGHTHOUSE THOUGHT FOR THE DAY

When God adopts someone into His family, that person's eternal destiny is settled forever. That is the love and devotion of God, which we should take to those around us.

PAT ROBERTSON

Solid Food

Solid food belongs to those who are of full age, that is, those who by reason of use have their senses exercised to discern both good and evil.

HEBREWS 5:14, NKJV

A growing number of Christians today have developed a taste for spiritual junk food. I suppose spiritual junk food is better than no food at all, but it's not a balanced, vitamin-enriched diet. If you munch only tasty, sweet candy to the exclusion of vitamin-packed lean meat and vegetables, you will find yourself stuck in spiritual infancy. What the Christian needs are green beans, but what a lot of Christians want are Gummi Bears.

Let's face it, Gummi Bears are tasty, cute, squishy, brightly colored, and convenient. They've got everything going for them—except food value. On the other hand, green beans are less tasty; they're not so cute; nobody likes them squishy; and they are not brightly colored. The main thing green beans have going for them is their nutritional value. They will help make you strong and healthy. Eating Gummi Bears is a nice treat, but eating green beans is what establishing good growth habits is all about.

When you study God's Word, don't settle for Gummi Bears. When you buy study books on the Word, don't settle for Gummi Bears. When you listen to Christian radio or watch Christian television, check out how much of the content is based on the Bible. When you buy Christian books, look for references to the Word. If they are scarce, the fare may be tasty, but is it what you need to grow?

Develop an insatiable appetite. Don't settle for Gummi Bears. Go for the green beans. Read the Word until you look into the face of God.

LIGHTHOUSE THOUGHT FOR THE DAY

Spiritual maturity, as well as an effective lighthouse ministry, requires that we take in proper nourishment—the Word of God.

WOOD KROLL

Prayer, Then Care

We loved you so much that we were delighted to share with you not only the gospel of God but our lives as well, because you had become so dear to us.

1 THESSALONIANS 2:8

Fervent, consistent prayer for fellow believers and for those who don't yet know Jesus is the foundation of any effective lighthouse ministry. Without it, we will accomplish nothing. With it, there is no limit to what we can do for our Lord.

As lighthouses for Jesus Christ, we need to pray for fellow believers' maturity and consistency in their personal Christian lives (Ephesians 3:14–20; Philippians 1:9–11; Colossians 1:9–12) and that each of us will stand fully assured in all of the will of God (Colossians 4:12). We should pray for the purification of our thoughts and deeds so that we will be fit instruments and channels of God's love (Psalm 139:23–24) who encourage and stimulate one another to love and good deeds (Hebrews 10:24). And we need to lift up one another's individual spiritual, physical, and material needs (Philippians 4:6–7, 19).

Prayer for nonbelievers in your neighborhood is the first step you must take before you attempt to care for or share the gospel with them. One great way to pray for your neighborhood is to "prayer walk" the street—walk up and down the street and pray for each individual in every home.

Be ready to put actions behind your prayers. Take time to chat with folks who are in their yards, driveways, or porches. Learn people's names. As you become acquainted with them and their needs, let them know you are praying for them.

Prayerfully and sensitively look for ways to share with your neighbors. An illness, job loss, or a new baby may be opportunities for you to meet real needs.

LIGHTHOUSE THOUGHT FOR THE DAY

Prayer is the first step in effective lighthouse ministry, and it will give you opportunities to reach out to and care for others around you.

VONETTE Z. BRIGHT

Sowing in Good Soil

I planted the seed, Apollos watered it, but God made it grow.

1 CORINTHIANS 3:6

We've all had those little inner battles with ourselves over whether we should share the gospel of Jesus Christ with someone we know.

They don't want to hear about Jesus now!

I don't want to seem pushy....

I'd just offend them....

It's easy to imagine that there's all kinds of resistance to the gospel. But the reality may be that there isn't any. Neighbors you have prayed for and cared for are more receptive to the gospel than you know. One of them may actually be desperately seeking spiritual answers and ready to hear the Good News.

Salesmen talk about the difficulty of making "cold calls" to sell their products. This means that when all their good sales prospects dry up, salesmen have to start from scratch by calling on people they have never met and who know nothing about their product. It's the most difficult kind of call to make.

However, if you have been praying for and caring for your neighbors, there is no need for "cold calls." You can be assured that the Holy Spirit has been working in their lives so that anything you say will be seed sown in good soil.

There are a multitude of ways to sow the seed of the Good News in your neighborhood. There are tracts, videos, books, and all kinds of gifts that you can use to explain to your neighbors how they can respond to Jesus Christ. But you must sow the seed!

LIGHTHOUSE THOUGHT FOR THE DAY

You have been breaking up the hard ground of your neighbors' hearts with kindness. You have watered with prayer. God has been working in their hearts to prepare them. Now, go plant some seed!

TOM PELTON

Reconciling the New

*"Forget the former things; do not dwell on the past.
See, I am doing a new thing!"*

ISAIAH 43:18–19

I visited a church that had recently introduced some praise choruses into its worship service. As the congregation sang one of the choruses, one lady sat the entire time clutching the old hymnal with a scowl on her face. She wouldn't have sung those choruses if Jesus Himself had directed the choir!

In our churches, new ideas and methods are often met with passionate opposition and fear. People get comfortable with how things are, and they draw rigid battle lines, ready to protect cherished traditions.

In Acts 10, Peter received a vision that released him to go and preach the gospel in the home of Cornelius, a Gentile. A door that had traditionally been closed was suddenly thrown open, and many Gentiles were saved. But, like the lady clutching the hymnal, the people back in Peter's own home church were horrified. Custom said they were not allowed even to speak to a Gentile, much less enter his home.

Acts 11:4 tells us that Peter had to explain everything to the Jewish Christians so they would understand. He told them about the vision and about all that had happened in Cornelius's house. Once they heard, they had no more objections and rejoiced with Peter that so many had been saved.

God still gives visions today that may seem confusing or strange, and sometimes reconciling the new things of God with the old is difficult. Prayer must be the bridge.

LIGHTHOUSE THOUGHT FOR THE DAY

Pray to have a discerning spirit so that you can not only accept, but also embrace the new things God is doing to glorify Himself and bring people to salvation.

DR. TERRY TEYKL

What Hinders Us?

When they saw the courage of Peter and John and realized that
they were unschooled, ordinary men, they were astonished
and they took note that these men had been with Jesus.

ACTS 4:13

There's a story about three devils discussing ways to keep Christians from sharing their faith. One devil says, "I know, let's tell them that there's no heaven, no possibility of reward. That might keep them quiet." The second says, "No, let's tell them there's no hell, no possibility of punishment. That might keep them quiet." But the third says, "Well, let's not be theologically unsound here. Rather than tell them there's no heaven or hell—let's just say there's no *hurry.*"

Deitrich Bonfoeffer once wrote, "To tell people that the cause is urgent, and that the kingdom of God is at hand, is the most charitable and merciful act we can perform, the most joyous news we can bring." So why do we hesitate to share our faith? Our reluctance usually boils down to two things: our doubts and our fears.

"But what if they ask me a question that I can't answer?" you ask. Expect it! Tell seekers you don't know the answer, but you can't wait to research it and get back to them. "What if I offend a seeker when I share the gospel?" you ask. Then say: "I am so grateful for all that God is doing in my life, but will you let me know if I'm coming on too strong?"

Remember, the gospel is perfectly capable of defending itself and does not need our aid in its defense. Our task is to introduce the gospel in the confidence of *God's* power to convince and convert—not ours.

LIGHTHOUSE THOUGHT FOR THE DAY

Pray that God will increase your faith and give you courage to share your faith in spite of your fears.

REBECCA MANLEY PIPPERT

The Shepherd's Care

*"My sheep listen to my voice; I know them, and they follow me.
I give them eternal life, and they shall never perish; no one can snatch
them out of my hand. My Father, who has given them to me,
is greater than all; no one can snatch them out of my Father's hand.
I and the Father are one."*

JOHN 10:27–30

The Good Shepherd gave His life for His sheep, and through His death and resurrection we have been redeemed. He has forgiven our sins, prepared for us a home in heaven, and given us a new life here and now. Jesus said, "I have come that they may have life, and have it to the full" (John 10:10).

As His sheep, we follow our Shepherd. We know Him, but, more important than that, He knows us. There are times when we are weak and would lose our way, but we follow Him because we trust Him. I saw an illustration of this when I took a trip to the Holy Land.

Today, from the Jericho Road to Jerusalem you can see Bedouin shepherds tending their sheep just as their ancestors did two thousand years ago. One afternoon as our tour bus passed that way, I took a picture that reminds me of John 10. On the side of one of the steep, barren hills, a shepherd was walking along, with about fifty sheep following him single file as he led them to water.

The Good Shepherd provides for His sheep and keeps them safe. As His sheep, we are eternally secure. We will never perish. Nothing can remove us from God's hand.

LIGHTHOUSE THOUGHT FOR THE DAY

Nothing can be more liberating than knowing that we are secure forever in our salvation. This knowledge frees us to live for Christ so we can shine out as lights for Him.

DARRELL ROBINSON

Going Fishing

Then He said to them, "Follow Me,
and I will make you fishers of men."
MATTHEW 4:19, NKJV

God often chose for leaders those who were already engaged in activities that gave them a practical outlook on life. For example, both Moses and David were shepherds before God called them to shepherd His people.

A shepherd needs to be alert to the movements of the sheep, keep them from harm, and guide them in the right direction so that there is always enough food and water for them. Shepherding is good preparation for ministering to a congregation because you learn to take care of what is entrusted to you.

Sometimes, however, God doesn't want a shepherd. Jesus did not tell His disciples to be *shepherds* of men, but *fishers* of men. The fisherman is not responsible for seeing that the fish are fed or moving together in a school. His only responsibility is to harvest them from the water.

The difference between a shepherd and a fisherman is the same as that between a pastor and an evangelist. The disciples of Jesus were evangelists. The pastoral image did not apply to their particular calling.

Jesus uses many metaphors to describe the harvest: "gathering the flock," "pulling in the nets," "scything the fields of grain." Yet the harvest with which He is always concerned is people. We must realize where we fit into God's plan and allow His Spirit to direct us in the different phases of His people harvest.

LIGHTHOUSE THOUGHT FOR THE DAY

Know what God has called you to do. If you are going to be a fisher of men, it is not your duty to keep the fish in schools, but to put down your nets where the fish will be and to be ready to pull hard and fast.

MOISHE ROSEN

Pray!

*They devoted themselves to the apostles' teaching and to
the fellowship, to the breaking of bread and to prayer.*

ACTS. 2:42

To lead a successful assault against Satan and his forces, we must pray. If we do not pray, we will not win. God can win the victory without prayer, but He won't.

Consider the biblical account of the Amalekites attacking the Israelites at Rephidim. Moses told Joshua to choose some men and go out to battle. Joshua went to fight, while Aaron and Hur stood atop the hill overlooking the battle with Moses, who held the staff of God in his hands: "As long as Moses held up his hands, the Israelites were winning, but whenever he lowered his hands, the Amalekites were winning. When Moses' hands grew tired, they took a stone and put it under him and he sat on it. Aaron and Hur held his hands up…. So Joshua overcame the Amalekite army with the sword" (Exodus 17:11–13).

There were complementary acts taking place in this scene. Joshua went out with sword in hand to fight the Amalekites, while Moses stayed behind to pray. Exodus 17:16 tells us, "For hands were lifted up to the throne of the LORD." When Moses prayed, the people of God won; when he stopped praying, the enemy won.

It is that way with us today. We should live with hands lifted up in prayer—for our children, our spouses, our churches, our nation, and for our mission to reach a world held captive by darkness. Let's pray for revival, for holiness, for the lost, and for our strategies to do our part in reaching the United States and our mission fields in other nations.

LIGHTHOUSE THOUGHT FOR THE DAY

Fervent, consistent prayer will make the difference between success and failure in our lighthouse ministries.

BOB RICKER

Your Assignment

And, behold, two of them went that same day to a village called Emmaus....
And they talked together of all these things which had happened.
And it came to pass, that, while they communed together and reasoned,
Jesus himself drew near, and went with them.

LUKE 24:13–15, KJV

Several hundred college freshmen sat in the first day of what was called the "Preacher Boys" class. The professor spoke: "Here's your assignment for the entire school year. You are to share your faith with seven people every week. Write a one-page report on each conversation, and turn it in each week."

I was one of those freshmen, and that assignment changed my life and the lives of hundreds of others. A similar assignment could do the same for you!

I would like to challenge you to take on the assignment of setting a goal of sharing your faith with a set number of people each week. You can choose to share with three, with five, or with seven. The second half of this assignment is to keep a journal of the results of this sharing. Write down the person's name, his or her response, and a prayer request.

But how can you find ways to verbally share your faith? Jesus Christ is our model. Walking and talking with people to find out how they think and live will lead to conversations about Him. One great example of this is found in Luke 24, where we read that Jesus appeared to two men who were traveling to Emmaus. At first, the men's eyes were prevented from recognizing Him (v.16). But as Jesus walked and talked with them, their eyes were opened.

It is the Holy Spirit's job to open the spiritual eyes of those you tell about Jesus. Your assignment is to tell those around you about Him.

LIGHTHOUSE THOUGHT FOR THE DAY
You'll be a bright light for Jesus as you consistently share your faith.

DR. CORNELL HAAN

The Cross and the Tomb

And if Christ is not risen, your faith is futile;
you are still in your sins!
1 CORINTHIANS 15:17, NKJV

Once, a liberal theologian was waxing eloquent about Christ's passion. He spoke of it as though it were merely a story, a symbol of hope for renewal and rebirth. A young reporter from *Christianity Today* magazine challenged him with a simple question, "Sir, if you were a newspaper reporter standing outside of the tomb on the third day after Christ's crucifixion, what would you report to your newspaper?" The theologian cleared his throat and answered, "Young man, did you say you were a reporter from *Christianity Today* or Christianity *yesterday?*"

Thank God, the cross and the empty tomb are not merely symbols! They are historical realities upon which the church, the body of Messiah, is securely founded. Our faith is based on facts. When we talk about the cross and the tomb, we are not reminiscing about yesterday's Christianity; we are talking about Christianity today.

I once heard someone say, "I would never wear a cross or a crucifix around my neck. My Messiah isn't hanging on a cross anymore. If I wanted to wear anything around my neck, it would be the sign of an empty tomb."

Well, I've never noticed anyone wearing a symbol of an empty tomb. I'm not encouraging or discouraging the wearing of a cross, but I'd like to point out that the cross and the empty tomb are inseparable. Without the cross, the empty tomb would be meaningless. Without the empty tomb, the cross would be powerless.

LIGHTHOUSE THOUGHT FOR THE DAY

We who gather together around the cross and the empty tomb have a message of hope and life. By proclaiming our hope, we can help transform the destiny of thousands who don't yet know Messiah.

DAVID BRICKNER

Lives of Perseverance

*Endure suffering along with me, as a good soldier of Christ Jesus.
And as Christ's soldier, do not let yourself become tied up in the affairs of this
life, for then you cannot satisfy the one who has enlisted you in his army.*
2 TIMOTHY 2:3–4, NLT

Spiritual growth is a lifelong process that requires perseverance. At times we will be weary and want to throw in the towel. We'll have to endure pain, fear, disillusionment, and a host of other emotions. We may get discouraged if we've been laboring hard but can't see any progress. Nevertheless, the Bible tells us that if we persevere through it all, we will preserve our spiritual gains.

The apostle Paul wrote, "I have learned how to get along happily whether I have much or little. I know how to live on almost nothing or with everything. I have learned the secret of living in every situation, whether it is with a full stomach or empty, with plenty or little" (Philippians 4:11–12, NLT). When Paul wrote these words, he was in a Roman prison waiting to hear if he would be executed. Instead of complaining, he accepted the reality of life's ups and downs without closing himself off from God.

As Christians, we are like soldiers who can win the war only if we fight to the end. Like athletes running a marathon, we must follow God all the way to the finish line. Like farmers, we must do our work in every season and then wait patiently to reap the benefits of our labor.

If we quit before we reach our goal, we may lose the spiritual gains for which we have fought, trained, and worked. But if we endure until we reach the goals God has laid out before us, we will joyously reap the reward.

LIGHTHOUSE THOUGHT FOR THE DAY

Being a light for Jesus will involve setbacks and discouragement, but if we persevere, leaning on our Father for strength, we will see the rewards of success.

STEPHEN ARTERBURN

Think on Good Things

Finally, brothers, whatever is true, whatever is noble, whatever is right, whatever is pure, whatever is lovely, whatever is admirable—if anything is excellent or praiseworthy—think about such things.

PHILIPPIANS 4:8

Some years ago I was at the gate of Golden West Commuter Airlines outside the Ontario Airport in California, waiting for a plane from Los Angeles. As I watched people file off the plane, a very angry elderly woman caught my eye.

She walked from the plane to the gate to meet her daughter, who was standing next to me. I learned that while the mother was in the Los Angeles airport at the American Airlines concourse, she had received erroneous directions to the Golden West gates. She believed that it was a very short walk to the gates when, in fact, it was 150 to 200 yards away. She felt misled, and she stewed on it—probably during the entire flight to Ontario. By the time she arrived, she was so angry that her reunion with her daughter was ruined. Over what? The fact that Golden West was 200 yards away from American Airlines!

Isn't it amazing how we can get so wrapped up in thinking about the negative that we become anxious or angry to the point of hurting people around us? If the woman in this story had just done as it says in Philippians 4:8—thought on the good things—she could have had the peace referred to in the next verse.

How do you respond when difficult circumstances arise in your life? Do you dwell on what went wrong, or do you rejoice in what went right? Do you think on things that are true, noble, right, pure, lovely, admirable, excellent, and praiseworthy? Put your thoughts to the test of Scripture!

LIGHTHOUSE THOUGHT FOR THE DAY

How you think—negatively or positively—will affect your emotions and the quality of the light that shines from you to those around you.

STEVE DOUGLASS

Faithful in Little Things

"'Love the Lord your God with all your heart and with all your soul and with all your mind and with all your strength.' The second is this: 'Love your neighbor as yourself.' There is no commandment greater than these."

MARK 12:30–31

A friend of mine recently brought me up to date on his progress in leading his neighbor to Christ by telling me this story:

"My wife and I have a Sunday morning routine we cherish. Instead of rushing back home after the morning church service, we go to a coffee shop and relax for an extended time. When we began using these times to talk quietly and reconnect with each other after the hectic past week, we began looking forward to them almost as much as the worship services themselves.

"Then, after months of our prayers and encouragement, our previously atheistic neighbor finally started attending Sunday morning church services with us. After our neighbor began to accompany us regularly on our trips to the coffee shop, we found our quiet time threatened. We knew it was good that he wanted to spend time with us, but we felt selfish about this time.

"Then, after several weeks he thanked us for doing 'all the little things you don't really think much of at the time.' He told us, 'You don't have to invite me to church. You don't have to invite me to the coffee shop. But the fact that you do means more to me than you'll ever know.'"

This story says a lot about doing "the little things" to demonstrate Christ's love to our neighbors. It shows how it's often our smallest gestures that reveal Jesus to those around us. May we all be faithful in these "little things."

LIGHTHOUSE THOUGHT FOR THE DAY

We need to give Christ and our neighbors our very best, and sometimes that means doing small things that say, "Jesus cares, and so do I."

MARY L. MARR

The Need for a Destination

May God be gracious to us and bless us and make his face shine upon us,
that your ways may be known on earth, your salvation among all nations.

PSALM 67:1–2

Many of the great prayers of the Bible carry three central themes: focus, fullness, and fulfillment. *Focus* represents requests for a fresh revelation of who Christ is to us and for us. *Fullness* represents requests for a deeper work of Christ over us and within us. *Fulfillment* represents requests that God would equip us for Christ's mission into the world, working through us and going before us.

Prayer is like a sailboat. To get where you need to go on a sailboat, three things must be kept together: a sail, a boat, and a destination. Take any one of those elements away, and you end up going in circles. We need to pray for the sail to fill with wind (fullness) and for God to give us the means (a boat) to reach His goals (fulfillment). But we also need a goal, a destination. What is it?

Whether in worship, in disciple-making, in evangelism, in compassion ministries, in church planting, or in revival—wherever the work of God's power is, there is always just one destination—the revelation to believers and unbelievers alike more of who Christ is and what Christ does.

Psalm 67 is clear about this focus. All of our prayers should sound a little like it. Prayers for friends and neighbors are always "so that" a great increase of God's blessings might come upon many others, "so that" the revelation of Christ's kingdom might spread beyond those for whom we originally pray, care, and share. The gospel spreading to the ends of the earth—that is the destination, the reason for the ship and the sail.

LIGHTHOUSE THOUGHT FOR THE DAY

Ask yourself: What is the ultimate destination of my prayers for my friends and neighbors? Then, restate your prayers. End them with the phrase "so that…"

DAVID BRYANT

I Love You, Man!

"Love your neighbor as yourself."
MATTHEW 19:19

Recently the senior pastor of a large church told the congregation that he loved them. Someone whispered, "He loves me? He doesn't even know my name." You can't love people you don't know.

As a lighthouse for Jesus Christ, you need to get to know your neighbors. That is the first step in the process that leads to sharing the gospel of Jesus with them. Getting to know people takes time and commitment, but it's also as simple as taking a walk this Saturday morning to make contact with them.

When you meet people, try to memorize their names and one thing about them. Ask them about themselves—about their jobs, their families, their interests. Take an interest in them! Care about them before you tell them that Jesus cares about them enough to die for them.

A popular beer commercial on television coined the phrase, "I love you, Man!" The person who said it wasn't expressing a heartfelt emotion; he was trying to get a can of beer. Few people really care about others. That's why Jesus required His followers to love their neighbors as themselves.

Care-evangelism is not befriending someone with an ulterior motive; that would be self-serving. Care-evangelism is doing like Jesus did: meeting people's needs and carrying their burdens because you really care about them. You are the incarnate Christ to your neighbors and friends.

Do you dare to care the way Jesus did? Ask yourself, "What would Jesus do?" Then, do what Jesus did! That means *give*. Jesus cared enough to die for men and women that they might be reconciled to God.

LIGHTHOUSE THOUGHT FOR THE DAY
Your light for Christ shines best in your loving care and concern for others.

DR. CORNELL HAAN

Are You Listening?

"But when he, the Spirit of truth, comes, he will guide you into all truth.
He will not speak on his own; he will speak only what he hears,
and he will tell you what is yet to come."

JOHN 16:13

American Christians like to talk about the Holy Spirit. We have three-step, five-step, and ten-step formulas for being Spirit-filled; we argue about what it means to be filled with the Spirit; we talk about keeping step with the Spirit. In fact, we spend a lot more time talking about the Holy Spirit than we do listening to Him.

We like to think of prayer as a sweet conversation with God. We see ourselves crawling up into our daddy's lap and telling Him everything. But nobody likes being around someone who talks but won't listen. A conversation, by definition, goes two ways. Yes, God wants to hear everything that is on your heart, but He would also like to get in a few words edgewise.

We're comfortable talking to God, but the idea of listening to Him can feel too much like New Age meditation and can scare us off. We have to work on this. Imagine Jesus' disciples talking to Him, but heading home whenever He opened His mouth to teach. How is it any different when the Spirit of Jesus tries to teach us in His still, small voice?

How can you learn to know that voice? By getting to know Him better and better. Asked how she knew the voice of the Spirit, one Christian woman said, "How do you know your husband's step and your child's cry from all others? I cannot tell you how I know the voice of the Spirit, but it is as real to me as the voice of any other person I know."

LIGHTHOUSE THOUGHT FOR THE DAY

Spend some time in "listening prayer" today. When you hear Him, then you really will have something to talk about to your neighbors.

EDDIE AND ALICE SMITH

Sharing Like Jesus!

"You will receive power when the Holy Spirit comes on you;
and you will be my witnesses in Jerusalem,
and in all Judea and Samaria, and to the ends of the earth."

ACTS 1:8

In the popular musical *Camelot,* Sir Lancelot made an insightful remark: "When you lock the world out, you lock yourself in."

In a real sense, that is consistent with the message that our Lord Jesus has for all of us who are committed to follow Him as our Lord and Savior. He has not called us to lock the world of other people out nor to lock ourselves in.

Quite the contrary: He has instructed us to be His witnesses in our own neighborhoods or schools or offices, wherever we live and move and have our being. We shouldn't hide from the world around us: It's hard for light to be effective apart from darkness. And we must not ignore those around us who desperately need the light of Jesus Christ.

We need to be careful not to be satisfied to merely enjoy for ourselves the wonderful benefits that flow from our lives in Christ. If we do that, we will become like the Dead Sea—a stench to others. Spirit-filled Christians who manifest the fruits of the Spirit—love, joy, peace, patience, kindness, goodness, faithfulness, gentleness, and self-control (Galatians 5:22–23)—are a pleasing aroma to those around them and to God.

Those are the qualities our Lord will use in our lighthouse ministry. We need to live in our neighborhoods with the spirit of Jesus, with open hearts and open hands, reaching out with the love and grace of our Lord Jesus Christ.

LIGHTHOUSE THOUGHT FOR THE DAY

We must never lock out people around us, but rather open our hearts and hands to share the love and grace of Jesus Christ with them.

PAUL CEDAR

The Beauty of the Desert

*"See, I am doing a new thing! Now it springs up; do you not perceive it?
I am making a way in the desert and streams in the wasteland."*

ISAIAH 43:19

Barren. Hot. Dry. Mile after endless mile of nothing. Lifeless terrain as forbidding as a remote lunar crater. A torrid climate that bakes the strength from your body and the resolve from your will. A place where nasty little bugs sting and even nastier birds circle ominously overhead, waiting to feast on the carrion of some poor creature that inevitably falls prey to the harsh environment.

Though it is in many ways a fascinating place, a desert is still a heartless, hostile, uninviting environment. If you've ever driven through a long stretch of such an unfriendly wilderness, you know that a sense of hopelessness can engulf you. It seems as though you will never get out of the desert.

Spiritual deserts can be like that as well. They can be lonely, discouraging places in our lives, places where we would give anything for a drink of God's life-sustaining, renewing water.

As uncomfortable as they are, deserts can be fruitful places if we allow God to do His work in us. In the desert—where distractions are few, visions are many, and water is mostly nonexistent—we have no choice but to focus on God and rely on Him to sustain us.

Moses received empowerment in the desert; so did the Lord Jesus. It can be the same with us. Spiritual deserts are places where God can empower us anew by His Spirit, give us a new sense of direction, and refresh us by drawing us near to the river of life.

LIGHTHOUSE THOUGHT FOR THE DAY

Those in spiritual deserts cry out for more of God. That is the beauty of time in the desert.

STEVE FRY

The Upside of Suffering

And we know that all things work together for good to those who
love God, to those who are the called according to His purpose.

ROMANS 8:28, NKJV

Most of us can identify with dark periods of struggle when we find ourselves weary and frustrated. We get tired of toiling and wonder what God's all about in our lives. It's about that time—when we're in the middle of some painful perplexity or shattering disappointment—that a well-intentioned fellow Christian comes alongside and whispers a certain verse of Scripture in our ear.

Usually, what they whisper is my least favorite verse in the Bible: Romans 8:28. I'd hazard a guess that you've had it quoted to you a few times, too.

Frankly, I don't want to hear that verse when I'm in pain. I don't want to hear it when I'm grieving, and I don't want to hear it when circumstances pull the rug out from under me and leave me dazed and disoriented on my backside.

The truth is—and stay with me here—Romans 8:28 is only half a thought. It isn't that much help or encouragement unless you *link* it with the other half of the thought—Romans 8:29. Yes, all things *do* work together, as long as you know what that work is for! Yes, we are called "according to His purpose," *but what is that purpose?* Verse 29 makes it clear: "For whom He foreknew, He also predestined to be conformed to the image of His Son, that He might be the firstborn among many brethren" (NKJV).

So, what is God working at in my life? What's God up to in your life? He's up to one thing, and one thing only. He is making you and me more like His Son. Period.

LIGHTHOUSE THOUGHT FOR THE DAY

God uses suffering in our lives to make us more like His Son. When that happens, we will glorify Him before our friends, family, and neighbors.

RON MEHL

How Can I Pray?

I urge, then, first of all, that requests, prayers,
intercession and thanksgiving be made for everyone.
1 TIMOTHY 2:1

Just before we bowed our heads to give thanks for our meal, I looked at the young waitress and said, "Is there anything that you would like us to pray for?"

She looked astonished, but after a moment of reflection, she said, "My life is really good right now." I told her that we would just thank the Lord for a good life, and tears welled up in her eyes as she thanked us. We prayed, then enjoyed our meal.

When the waitress brought our check, she hesitated and then asked if she could talk with me after her shift. When I talked to her later, she confessed that she had lied earlier and that her life was a total mess and she needed help. I then talked to her about Jesus Christ and prayed with her.

We live in a world where people are very open to being prayed for. It has been estimated that 90 percent of the population believes in a "higher power." Most say they would like to be able to connect in some way to this higher power. This speaks of an openness to God that we Christians need to recognize.

Prayer is a wonderful open door to blessing people around us. Offering to pray for someone not only demonstrates our faith, but it can also give us openings to lead people a step or two closer to Jesus Christ.

When you pray for someone, remember to be specific. Pray for his or her needs, then be ready to watch God work. He might even use you to accomplish something big!

LIGHTHOUSE THOUGHT FOR THE DAY

We should be sensitive, tactful, yet bold when it comes to praying for our neighbors. Be ready to ask if you can pray for someone, then be ready to do it.

DALLAS ANDERSON

The Worship of Giving

"You are the light of the world.... Let your light shine before men, that they may see your good deeds and praise your Father in heaven."
MATTHEW 5:14, 16

If our society seems to be getting darker, it's not the fault of those who are in darkness. As Henry Blackaby has said, it's because those who are supposed to bring the light of Christ are not shining. Light automatically dispels darkness. That's its nature and its power.

A Christian family may be the only light that people in some neighborhoods are ever exposed to. The way we live, the choices we make, and the things we choose to do or not do will determine whether our light is hidden or held up for all to see.

While shedding light on those around us certainly includes sharing the truth of the Word, Jesus made it clear that it also means doing good deeds that others will see and associate with our devotion to God. In Matthew 25:35–36, He lists some specifics: "For I was hungry and you gave me something to eat, I was thirsty and you gave me something to drink, I was a stranger and you invited me in, I needed clothes and you clothed me, I was sick and you looked after me, I was in prison and you came to visit me." In a broad sense, Jesus is talking about meeting the physical and emotional needs of those around us.

This world doesn't show much care for individuals, which may help explain why people are reluctant to reveal their needs. We have to watch for practical ways to shine our light so people will praise the Lord. It could be as simple as retrieving the neighbors' wandering dog or making them a batch of cookies.

LIGHTHOUSE THOUGHT FOR THE DAY
Our families can shine for Christ as we make a fresh commitment to be on the lookout for opportunities to bless those around us.

BILL MCCARTNEY

The Most Excellent Way

Jesus went through all the towns and villages,
teaching in their synagogues, preaching the good news of the kingdom
and healing every disease and sickness.

Matthew 9:35

Jesus was our perfect example of faith and love in action. He didn't ask whether His responsibility was to extend love or to save the souls of the needy people around Him. He just did both. His earthly ministry was a blend of the great commission (preaching the gospel) and the great commandment (loving your neighbor).

We are to do the same. Those who bear the gospel have social responsibilities. Galatians 5:6 tells us, "The only thing that counts is faith expressing itself through love." This simply means we need to put our faith into action by loving those around us.

First Corinthians 12:31 tells us of "the most excellent way," and then leads us into chapter 13, which is called the love chapter of the Bible. The first three verses tell us that what we say and what we do—even in the name of ministry—is a string of zeroes if the significant digit of love is not there.

A powerful part of our lighthouse ministry is caring for our neighbors as well as praying for them and sharing the gospel with them. This takes time and is often not convenient. But if we are to follow our dear Savior, who "so loved that He gave," we will make caring for our neighbors a significant part of our lives.

We have marching orders, and we have the example of Christ to follow.

Lighthouse Thought for the Day

In addition to praying for those around us and sharing the gospel with them, let's follow the example of the Lord Jesus Christ in looking for ways to lovingly care for them.

Bob Ricker

Facing the Turbulence

"I have told you these things, so that in me you may have peace. In this world you will have trouble. But take heart! I have overcome the world."

JOHN 16:33

Imagine you are on an airplane and hear the captain say, "I'm going to ask all of you to return to your seats and fasten your seatbelts. There's turbulence ahead, and it doesn't look like we're going to be able to avoid it." Would you feel helpless?

That's what life without Jesus is like. Sometimes people who have known Christ for a long time forget that life is turbulent for people without Him—which is most of the population. It's a rough ride when you don't know the Lord. Chances are you have a neighbor who even now is on a turbulent trip like that.

Most of us know what turbulence in the air is like. But turbulence at sea is more terrifying still. Having your vessel dashed against the rocks is a horrible prospect. That's why a few generations ago, before modern technology replaced them, lighthouses played such an important role. In all kinds of weather they sent out life-saving signals.

The lighthouse is a perfect symbol for our movement. Let it remind you daily that as a believer you could play a life-and-death role in the lives of those around you. Without your light shining like a beacon, people you see every day could be in serious spiritual trouble. If you are faithful to shine, you may be able to guide them to safe harbor.

LIGHTHOUSE THOUGHT FOR THE DAY

Life is turbulent, even for Christians. Imagine what it must be like for those who don't know the peace of a personal relationship with Jesus Christ. Do all you can to express His love to those around you. Start by letting them know how God has helped you face the turbulence.

DAVID MAINS

A New Song

He put a new song in my mouth, a hymn of praise to our God.
Many will see and fear and put their trust in the LORD.

PSALM 40:3

Many years ago an alcoholic made his way with unsteady step toward his home. As he came within view of the house, he heard through an open window his little girl singing a beautiful melody. When he came in, the music had stopped, and the little girl was nowhere to be found. "Where is Maggie?" he asked his wife.

"Oh, she heard you coming," she answered, "and she was afraid."

Suddenly the drunkard began to weep. He found his little girl and held her in his arms. "Oh, Maggie," he said, "I have spoiled the music, but by the help of God, I will never do it again."

From the time of Creation, God intended harmony and music to fill the physical universe and the human soul. The morning stars sang together, and all the sons of God shouted for joy (Job 38:7). The Creator designed the universe to be a symphony of praise. But one day Satan spoiled the music.

The new birth does more than take away the guilt and shame of the past. It creates a new person with a whole new life. No wonder the song of a soul set free from death is jubilant! It is no longer the song of bondage and fear but of victory and thanksgiving.

If your soul is filled with mournful emptiness and discordant anguish, you need Jesus Christ, the creator of eternal harmony, to erase the music of the past and give you a new song. At that moment, your new song will begin.

LIGHTHOUSE THOUGHT FOR THE DAY

Songs of praise and worship sounding from our lighthouse will draw those around us to our Lord and Savior, Jesus Christ.

CHARLES T. CRABTREE

The Power of the Name

Then they called them in again and commanded them
not to speak or teach at all in the name of Jesus.
ACTS 4:18

I used to think the term *spiritual warfare* referred to the heated debates at church board meetings. I had never received formal training in that area of the Christian faith. In fact, one of my seminary professors taught that the enemy, Satan, did not even exist. I remember thinking, *Whew! What a relief! I was worried about him!*

The truth is, spiritual warfare is a natural by-product of the confrontational gospel of Jesus Christ. It is the result of the clash of kingdoms. Religion is nice; teaching and moralizing are fine; ethical standards are wonderful. But the power and authority of the name of Jesus stirs things up. The grace available to every person through His work on the cross leads to a holy rebellion against the status quo of religion, sin, sickness, and sadness. If we are proclaiming His name, we are bound to encounter spiritual resistance.

In Acts 4:18 the disciples were commanded to stop speaking and preaching in the name of Jesus because things were getting too stirred up. Many people were responding to this radical gospel, and the religious leaders were getting nervous. So the disciples retreated back home to their "lighthouse" and prayed. When they did, "The place where they were meeting was shaken. And they were all filled with the Holy Spirit and spoke the word of God boldly" (Acts 4:31).

The same Holy Spirit who empowered those believers to do battle is available today to help us boldly speak God's word. Prayer is your weapon in the spiritual battle. It invites the Holy Spirit and prepares the way for God to prevail.

LIGHTHOUSE THOUGHT FOR THE DAY

Call on the name of Jesus, and watch spiritual warfare begin. Use prayer with abandon, and watch how God gives you the victory.

DR. TERRY TEYKL

Demolishing Strongholds

The weapons we fight with are not…of the world….
They have divine power to demolish strongholds.

2 CORINTHIANS 10:4

When Jesus spoke about entering a strong man's house and carrying off his possessions, He said it was necessary to first restrain the strong man (Mark 3:27). The possessions that lighthouse keepers seek are the hearts of our unsaved neighbors and acquaintances. They will find Jesus in us as, through prayer, we exercise our authority to demolish strongholds of sin.

An incident in the ministry I direct, Every Home for Christ, illustrates this reality. We chose a large city in Argentina for home evangelism, including showing the JESUS film in strategic areas. Because the city had five times as many satanic worship centers as churches, we decided to prayer walk it first.

The following week we visited five thousand homes, and that Sunday night we showed the JESUS film beneath a huge two-hundred-year-old Ombu tree in the town square. We selected the location because every Friday night satanists held worship services there. Not only did 132 people find Christ that Sunday evening, but the following Tuesday the huge tree mysteriously exploded and split in half. The sound could be heard for many blocks. When they removed the tree, city engineers said that the explosion had been a supernatural phenomenon.

One of the first converts after the incident was a leading sorceress who had used her home as a satanic worship center. Hundreds more have since found Christ. Clearly a stronghold had been demolished.

LIGHTHOUSE THOUGHT FOR THE DAY

"What prayer does is to enable us, not to find a way around the hard thing, but to go straight through it, not to avoid but to accept it and overcome it. Prayer is not evasion; prayer is conquest."—William Barclay

DICK EASTMAN

Bringing in the Sheaves

*He that goeth forth and weepeth, bearing precious seed, shall
doubtless come again with rejoicing, bringing his sheaves with him.*

PSALM 126:6, KJV

In this one verse the psalmist gives us the basic principles for effectively sharing our faith.

First, we must *go*. Jesus used that word often. "Go ye into all the world," He said, "and preach the gospel to every creature" (Mark 16:15, KJV). He gave us the great commission: "Go ye therefore, and teach all nations" (Matthew 28:19, KJV). And He reminded us: "As my Father hath sent me, even so send I you" (John 20:21, KJV).

Nowhere does the Bible command the lost to come to church. But over and over again the Bible commands the church to go to the lost. The Mission America effort to mobilize Christians in America to pray and care for and share the gospel with every person in our sphere of influence is simply a serious effort to fulfill this great commission.

Once we go, we must *sow* the precious seed of the Word of God, "the power of God unto salvation to every one that believeth" (Romans 1:16, KJV). We can sow seed in the form of a gospel tract, a New Testament, a booklet, or a video. The seed may be your testimony delivered personally, on a web site, or in a letter; or it could be a memorized presentation of the gospel. Perhaps your very best witness will be your own life, which has been transformed by the power of God, and your reaching out to others through loving acts of kindness.

LIGHTHOUSE THOUGHT FOR THE DAY

The promise is certain: When we go and sow faithfully, bathing our effort with the weeping that comes from true compassion, we will "come again rejoicing," bringing the sheaves with us.

LARRY LEWIS

Spiritual Exercise

Walk in love, as Christ also has loved us and given Himself for us,
an offering and a sacrifice to God for a sweet-smelling aroma.

EPHESIANS 5:2, NKJV

Maintaining a good spiritual diet, one that will ensure spiritual growth, is much easier than maintaining a good exercise program. But as I have learned—and as doctors, nutritionists, and personal trainers have been saying for years—diet alone is not enough. You need both diet and exercise if you are to be healthy.

Output is equally important as intake. If you want to lose weight, you have to reduce your fat and calorie intake, but you also have to burn more calories. And you know what that means—exercise, exertion, activity.

I'll admit that I don't enjoy exercise. I do it—I just don't like it. I've heard people talk about a "runner's high" and the euphoria that comes with prolonged physical activity, but I've never experienced it. What's more, I'd be more convinced that runner's high existed if I saw smiles instead of strained grimaces on the faces of joggers.

It's difficult to maintain an exercise regimen when we do it only because we know we should. And often we neglect spiritual exercise for the same reason. We feel we ought to do it, but it's not something we look forward to. We have a sense of obligation, but not a sense of anticipation.

Spiritual exercise means we put feet to our Bible study. We should never study the Bible for the sake of becoming a Bible student. We should do it to become fit servants of the One who loved us and gave Himself for us (Ephesians 5:2).

LIGHTHOUSE THOUGHT FOR THE DAY

Prayer, fellowship with other believers, and witnessing are spiritual exercises that are vital for our personal growth and for a successful lighthouse ministry.

WOOD KROLL

Who Wants to Evangelize?

Always be prepared to give an answer to everyone who asks you to give the reason for the hope that you have.

1 PETER 3:15

Ask the question posed by the popular television show, *Who Wants to Be a Millionaire?* and millions would drool at the prospect of acquiring such a financial windfall. But ask the question, "Who Wants to Be an Evangelist?" and the silence would be deafening!

As Christians, we are called to be living epistles to those around us. In other words, we are *all* evangelists. Evangelism is allowing nonbelievers to pick up the book of our lives and read the fine print. In any sustained relationship, people observe our words, actions, and deeds—good or bad. That is how it is with our lighthouse ministries.

When Jesus sent the seventy-two on their mission, He specifically instructed them to take only one set of garments. No money. No food. They were to depend upon the people they ministered to. If they were welcomed into a home, they were to "stay in that house" (Luke 10: 7). Why? Because they had found a spiritual warm spot in the community. Hospitality was a sign of spiritual openness. The Lord says, "He who listens to you listens to me; he who rejects you rejects me" (v. 16). Do you see the point? Those who listen to you are more likely to listen to God.

No one will receive Christ through you who will not receive you first. Those neighbors who respond to you socially are the schooling fish. It's in your home or yard or workplace that people are most apt to respond to the gospel.

LIGHTHOUSE THOUGHT FOR THE DAY

We should always be ready to give an answer to those around us who ask us the reason for the hope they see in us. Are you ready?

JOE ALDRICH

The Paradox of Peace

*"Glory to God in the highest, and on earth peace
to men on whom his favor rests."*

LUKE 2:14

God's angels announced peace at the birth of the Savior, Jesus Christ. But Jesus later said that He "did not come to bring peace, but a sword" (Matthew 10:34).

This is certainly a paradox, but it is not a contradiction. In the angelic announcement recorded in Luke 2:14, the Lord proclaimed that He, through the birth of His Son, had provided a way to make reconciliation and redemption—peace with God—possible for us. The Prince of Peace came to provide a "new and living way" for mankind to have a relationship with God and with one another.

Although Christmas is to be a joyous time of celebration of the peace that God offers, there are many who, because of the heavy weight of sin, don't personally know what that peace means. Even though they strive for peace, their efforts always lead to more strife. The sword of truth that Jesus brought is the only thing that can slice through such strife.

When people yield to truth, they find peace. This causes a ripple effect, for those who have discovered the peace that comes from reconciliation with God pass that peace along to others. But in order to embrace and pursue the new way God has provided, the old ways must be sliced away by the sword of the truth.

As lighthouses for Jesus Christ, it is up to us to lovingly and prayerfully show the hurting, scared people around us that there is a better way. God promises peace to those who will turn to Him through faith in the Lord Jesus Christ.

LIGHTHOUSE THOUGHT FOR THE DAY

We can bring the peace of God to those around us, but only when we wield the sword of truth of God's love through His Son, Jesus Christ.

JACK HAYFORD

When We Are His

*So we make it our goal to please him, whether we
are at home in the body or away from it.*

2 CORINTHIANS 5:9

John Wesley's discovery of "instantaneous conversion and immediate assurance" for himself 250 years ago eventually made an impact on all of Britain. The Lord quickly impressed upon Wesley the mission of preaching the gospel of Jesus Christ, and during the next fifty years he preached forty thousand sermons. His message was always the same: He urged his listeners to make sure of their salvation.

As biographer A. Skevington Wood points out in *The Burning Heart*, "Wesley was firm in his conviction that those who are indeed children of God will not be left in doubt by the Holy Spirit."

The New Testament makes this clear. In Romans 8:16–17 we read, "The Spirit himself testifies with our spirit that we are God's children. Now if we are children, then we are heirs—heirs of God and co-heirs with Christ, if indeed we share in his sufferings in order that we may also share in his glory." The Scriptures also declare that "this is how we know that he [God] lives in us: We know it by the Spirit he gave us" (1 John 3:24).

It's not enough, however, to simply enjoy the Holy Spirit's assurance that we are saved and have eternal life. He compels us to share the gospel of Jesus Christ with others. Like Wesley, may we be fervent and faithful witnesses in our generation to those we know or meet who have yet to trust the Lord Jesus as Savior.

LIGHTHOUSE THOUGHT FOR THE DAY

We can be grateful to the Lord for the witness of the Holy Spirit that we are His. That should motivate us to share the gospel with our family members, friends, neighbors, and coworkers.

LUIS PALAU

Prayer for a Nation

Blessed is the nation whose God is the LORD.

PSALM 33:12

It was God's extraordinary grace that made America great, not her military might, scientific know-how, or even her form of government. Her true source of strength came from her *faith* in God, the Creator and Sustainer of all things. Therefore, if ever her faith waned, her greatness would be at stake.

Today, all signs point to the conclusion that America is squeezing God out of the picture and pressing toward total secularization. Two hundred years ago, the declaration of independence from Britain gave birth to America as a nation. Could the founding fathers have imagined that in just over two hundred years a declaration of independence from God would be threatening to lead to America's downfall?

Satan is doing all he can to tear this country down, spiritually and morally. The only way to reverse this downward trend is through prayer, repentance, and a turning toward God. He has given the church the responsibility of first praying, then sounding the warning and issuing the call of repentance. We do that by reaching one person at a time with the Good News of salvation through Jesus Christ.

I believe that to help facilitate this effort, God has raised up the Lighthouse Movement, which is composed of literally millions of neighborhood prayer-care-and-share ministries across the land. Through this nationwide network, like-minded Christians join hands, encourage one another, and learn from one another as they spread the message of hope through a relationship with Christ.

LIGHTHOUSE THOUGHT FOR THE DAY

A nation turns to God one person at a time. God can use lighthouses for Jesus to achieve that end. We can be part of revival!

THOMAS WANG

Loving the "Unclean"

"It is not the healthy who need a doctor, but the sick."
MATTHEW 9:12

Jesus got Himself in a lot of trouble with the religious establishment when He dined with sinners. The religious leaders of the day believed it was unethical to associate with the "unclean," who were pretty much everybody but them. Jesus responded by saying in effect, "I'm a soul physician—where would you expect a physician to be if not among the sick?"

Jesus knew that the only way to reach those who needed Him was to walk among them. Likewise, we can't bring a message of hope to a hurting humanity if we won't associate with those who desperately need to know the truth that will set them free.

It seems odd that when Jesus met people's physical needs, He often told them not to tell anyone. Why would He do that? Because the word would quickly spread that Jesus was miraculously meeting people's physical needs, when His primary reason for coming to earth was to meet spiritual needs.

So why did He heal the sick, restore sight to the blind, and hearing to the deaf? He did it for the same reason that He dined with "sinners"—because He was moved by compassion. It was His nature to do these things. Likewise, caring for others will become our nature as we conform to the image of God.

People all around us are dying without Christ. Jesus cares about that. Do we? Our neighbors are living in bondage to the lies they believe. Do we care enough about them to lovingly share the truth that will set them free? Our neighbors don't care how much we know until they know how much we care—for them.

LIGHTHOUSE THOUGHT FOR THE DAY

We can't preach the Good News to our neighbors unless we also live it by showing compassion for them.

NEIL T. ANDERSON

Always in His Presence

Let us draw near to God with a sincere heart in full assurance of faith.…
Let us hold unswervingly to the hope we profess,
for he who promised is faithful.

HEBREWS 10:22–23

The assurance *of* God's presence comes from spending time *in* God's presence. The writer of Hebrews urges us to "draw near to God." This means we're to come close to Him, not stay at a distance. When we come to God sincerely desiring to connect with Him, we can do so with the full assurance that God wants to welcome us into His presence.

The assurance of God's faithfulness produces hope within us. This is not some kind of theological rhetoric or mind game. We can have security and hope in our God because these things are anchored in His faithfulness. In short, He can be trusted to do what He says He'll do!

We can depend on God to meet our needs according to the wisdom of His will—though it may not necessarily be our will. Occasionally we need to remind ourselves that God is wiser than we are. He knows best, and we can trust Him—even though we may not understand the way He works and may be tempted to ask or demand an answer to the "whys" of life. We need to submit ourselves and our circumstances to Him and ask Him to work the wisdom of His will.

When we do these things, we can walk in the promises of His Word: "You have made known to me the path of life; you will fill me with joy in your presence, with eternal pleasures at your right hand" (Psalm 16:11).

LIGHTHOUSE THOUGHT FOR THE DAY

As believers and as lighthouses for Jesus Christ, we need assurance of God's presence. We get that by drawing close to Him. When we do that, our lights will shine brighter for Jesus.

BRUCE SCHOEMAN

What's Important

She gave birth to her firstborn, a son. She wrapped
him in cloths and placed him in a manger, because there
was no room for them in the inn.

LUKE 2:7

One of the inherent messages in God's allowing His Son to be born in a barn is that He doesn't need an antiseptic environment in which to do His work.

Over the centuries, the church has developed structures, systems, and philosophies to keep God safe from man's impurity. It is not uncommon, for example, for people in the church to express concern over and take actions against the commercialism that has seeped into the celebration of Christmas.

I do not preach against commercialism. I recognize that the world makes Christmas commercial, but I don't let that ruin my celebration. In fact, I see the commercialism as almost an affirmation of the true beauty and value of Christmas. You see, only valuable things are counterfeited, and that includes Christmas. People counterfeit money, not paper bags, and I haven't stopped using cash simply because there are counterfeits. Neither will I stop celebrating Christmas because of the counterfeit of commercialism.

God's clear statement when His Son was born in a manger was that the Lord remains unpolluted in any situation. So it should be with our celebration of the Savior's birth.

We should celebrate the truth of what came to our lives when God became man and dwelt among us. We should always focus on the life, power, and incredible joy God has given us.

LIGHTHOUSE THOUGHT FOR THE DAY

A lighthouse Christmas celebration focuses on the fact that God became man and dwelt among us in the person of Jesus Christ.

JACK HAYFORD

God Became Man

The Word became flesh and made his dwelling among us.

JOHN 1:14

For thirty-three years Jesus felt everything you and I have ever felt. To think of Jesus in such a light is—well, it seems almost irreverent, doesn't it? It's not something we like to do; it's uncomfortable. It is much easier to keep the humanity out of the incarnation. There is something about keeping Him divine that keeps Him distant, packed, predictable.

But don't do it. For heaven's sake, don't. Let Him be as human as He intended to be. Let Him into the mire and muck of our world. For only if we let Him in can He pull us out.

Listen to Him.

"Love your neighbor" was spoken by a man whose neighbors tried to kill Him (Mark 12:31).

"Pray for those who persecute you" came from the lips that would be begging God to forgive His murderers (Matthew 5:44).

"I am with you always" are the words of a God who in one instant did the impossible to make it all possible for you and me (Matthew 28:20).

It all happened in a moment. In one moment…a most remarkable moment. The Word became flesh.

There will be another. The world will see another instantaneous transformation. You see, in becoming man, God made it possible for man to see God. When Jesus went home, He left the back door open. As a result, "We shall all be changed—in a moment, in the twinkling of an eye" (1 Corinthians 15:51–52, NKJV).

LIGHTHOUSE THOUGHT FOR THE DAY

God became man and lived among us so that we could one day dwell with Him.

MAX LUCADO

No Path to Comfort

"If anyone desires to come after Me, let him deny himself,
and take up his cross daily, and follow Me."

LUKE 9:23, NKJV

The man saw me passing out tracts on a street corner. His greeting was the effusive encouragement of a brother. I tried to greet him in a Christian way, but people were passing by me without the gospel. So I turned away to hand literature to a passerby. When I turned back, I was surprised to see he was still there. He wanted to talk. I stopped for a moment, and he told me about all of the great things that he did in his church. He taught Sunday school, served as a deacon, bought bonds for the building program. I nodded.

When it seemed that he wanted to talk longer than I could afford to listen, I invited him to help me hand out some of the literature. His obvious annoyance startled me. "I don't think I could be comfortable doing that," he said. It was an awkward moment, and he was now eager to leave, so we said our farewells. I wondered about his discomfort at handing out literature.

In thinking about that encounter, it seems to me that Christ didn't come to give us comfort and social acceptance. Jesus was our example of this. To give us eternal life, He came to be crucified. Jesus says to those of us who would be His radical disciples, "Take up your cross, and follow Me."

Instead, we usually choose to take up those things that give us dignity or worldly status. Some of us seek to impress people with our worth and worthiness. Yet there is no such thing as a comfortable cross, and if we are going to serve God, we need to move beyond our comfort zone.

LIGHTHOUSE THOUGHT FOR THE DAY

Jesus didn't choose the comfortable path. He chose the cross. We should do the same daily.

MOISHE ROSEN

Rejoicing in Heaven

*"There will be more rejoicing in heaven over one sinner who
repents than over ninety-nine righteous persons who do not need to repent."*
LUKE 15:7

Jesus contested the thinking of the religious leaders of His day on two counts: First, they cared little for lost and hurting people, and, second, they thought that God hated sinners and rejoiced in their destruction.

Jesus challenged the first wrong attitude with His parable of the lost sheep. He said in effect, "You religious leaders have more concern for dumb animals than for hurting people. If a sheep is lost, you are so concerned that you leave the rest of your other sheep to go find it. You're willing to face danger and hardship, and when you find it, you tenderly carry it home on your shoulders and then call your friends to rejoice with you. But if people are lost, you don't care at all. Instead, you make life even harder for them by accusing and condemning them. You don't lift a finger to help them. In fact, you avoid them. You despise them and call them sinners."

The Jews had a saying that typified their unloving attitude toward those they called sinners. They said, "There is joy in heaven over one sinner who is obliterated by God." Jesus challenged this second wrong attitude by telling them that there is great rejoicing in heaven when a sinner repents.

God's attitude toward sinners is exactly the opposite of what the religious leaders of Jesus' day thought. People matter very much to God. He—and all heaven with Him—rejoice when a sinner turns to Him.

How much do people matter to you?

LIGHTHOUSE THOUGHT FOR THE DAY

Imagine heaven rejoicing over someone you know who has repented and come to faith in Jesus Christ. Pray passionately for that day to come soon.

AL VANDERGRIEND

Seeing As Jesus Saw

When He saw the multitudes, He was moved with compassion for them,
because they were weary and scattered, like sheep having no shepherd.

MATTHEW 9:36, NKJV

Picture yourself on a crowded city street. It's the height of rush hour, and a swarm of people pushes past you, wearing a thousand different faces. What are you feeling right now? Overwhelmed? Threatened perhaps?

How did Jesus feel when He encountered seemingly endless crowds of needy people? He expressed the passion and caring concern of almighty God.

Jesus saw people as they truly were. He saw through their self-sufficient masks, knowing it was all an illusion. He saw needy people in desperate spiritual conditions. He saw them weary and scattered, like sheep without a shepherd.

Sheep are not endowed with a great deal of intelligence. They follow one another blindly, head to tail, even if it means walking off of a cliff. Sheep need a shepherd, someone to guide them and watch out for them. So do people.

If we are to demonstrate the compassion of Christ, we need to see past people's facades to understand them and their circumstances as He sees them. We need to see people who are without Christ as lost and without hope. To open our hearts and care for such people makes us vulnerable to rejection and scorn. However, if we're to be like Jesus, we must take that risk.

If we see crowds as Jesus saw them, we'll be able to show the compassion that He showed during His earthly ministry. When He looked upon them, He did not see a sea of humanity wearing a thousand different faces. He saw individuals, and He cared for each one as a shepherd who sought out one lost lamb.

LIGHTHOUSE THOUGHT FOR THE DAY

Being a lighthouse for Jesus is about caring for people—caring for the lost and having concern for those who are like sheep without shepherds.

DAVID BRICKNER

He Brings Great Joy!

*But the angel said to them…"I bring you good news of
great joy that will be for all the people."*

LUKE 2:10

Few words are more misunderstood, even among Christians, than the word *joy*, for it is often used synonymously with happy. There is often happiness where there is real joy, so the confusion isn't hard to understand. But there is a vast difference between the two, starting with their source and their durability.

Happiness is a positive human emotion, while joy is one of the fruits of the Spirit. Happiness can be very fragile, and the prospect of finding it can be very dim at times. On the other hand, true joy never grows faint, and there is nothing fragile about it because it is a spiritual resource.

Joy is that inner thrill that comes with the certainty of two things. The first is that the things you have deeply longed for are not merely your own idle dreams, and God approves of them. The second is that God has set Himself to bring those things about. A great sense of excitement will well up within you when you begin to see the things He has promised coming to pass.

On that night in the outskirts of Bethlehem, the angel appeared to the shepherds to tell them that the thing they had always dreamed of—the coming of the Messiah—had come to pass.

All joy finds its focus in Jesus the Savior, for He has come to complete God's work in our lives. Knowing this truth brings us great, unquenchable joy.

LIGHTHOUSE THOUGHT FOR THE DAY

The message the angel brought to the shepherds all those centuries ago is the same one we as lighthouses for Christ can bring to our neighbors today: Joy has come for all people in the person of Jesus.

JACK HAYFORD

Sharing the Pain

A friend loves at all times, and a brother is born for adversity.
PROVERBS 17:17

In *A Decembered Grief,* author Harold Ivan Smith makes an interesting observation about our world today: We are obsessed with excitement.

We love the excitement of Christmas, birthdays, and other times of celebration. But for someone who is suffering—over the loss of a loved one, an illness, the loss of a job, a divorce, a teen rebellion, or over simple loneliness—holidays and other times of celebration can be torturous. For that person, hearing "Joy To the World" for the tenth time during the Christmas season can make him or her want to scream, "Stifle yourself!"

Pain is ugly. Pain is uncomfortable. Pain is lonely. Pain is *painful.* One curse of living in a society obsessed with excitement is that few people will intentionally enter into someone else's pain. Everyone goes through painful life situations. Unfortunately, these are times when people are likely to find themselves feeling abandoned and alone.

When your neighbors go through painful times—and that is sure to happen—they will look to see evidence of God's love in your actions. Having been abandoned by all but their most loyal friends, they will be more acutely appreciative of your willingness to lay aside your own desires for fun and excitement and step into their pain with them.

That willingness to share in the pain will lead to opportunities to share the Good News of Jesus Christ.

LIGHTHOUSE THOUGHT FOR THE DAY

There will be times when we care for those around us by sharing in their pain. This is what it means to "love your neighbor as yourself."

MARY L. MARR

A Timeless Truth

I am not ashamed of the gospel, because it is the power of God for the salvation of everyone who believes: first for the Jew, then for the Gentile.

ROMANS 1:16

The world is full of ideas that don't last. But one idea, one truth, one driving force remains the most powerful force for change in the world. It transforms people, nations, and world events. This one truth is the gospel of Messiah. Jesus is the only Savior. His death, burial, and resurrection make it possible for us to receive God's forgiveness for sin and the hope of eternal life.

Why is the gospel so powerful? How has it stood the test of time, outlasting all competing ideologies? How can it cut through emotional and spiritual barriers? The apostle Paul says it is because the gospel is the very "power of God to salvation for everyone who believes, for the Jew first and also for the Greek" (Romans 1:16, NKJV). The Creator of the universe has invested His authority in the gospel message. When we proclaim the gospel, God unleashes His limitless power to save those who hear and believe.

We have been entrusted with a message of extraordinary strength and power. That is why we can confidently share Jesus with the unsaved. We need not argue with people or cajole them. God is at work in the lives of thousands of people who pass by us daily. It is His power that transforms the lives of those who in faith believe the message we bring.

As we are faithful to proclaim this timeless truth, God will reveal His eternal, life-changing power to those who hear and believe the gospel of Jesus. Jews and Gentiles alike, who once had been headed for a Christless eternity, will become new brothers headed for heaven's glory.

LIGHTHOUSE THOUGHT FOR THE DAY

We cannot produce faith in those who hear Christ's message; that is why prayer is so vital. Prayer is the partner of proclamation.

DAVID BRICKNER

It's Never Too Late

The profit of wisdom is better than silver, and her wages are better than gold.
Wisdom is more precious than rubies; nothing you desire
can compare with her. She offers you life in her right hand,
and riches and honor in her left.
She will guide you down delightful paths; all her ways are satisfying.

PROVERBS 3:14–17, NLT

Ideally, every child should receive wise and godly instruction from their parents as they grow to adulthood. Unfortunately, we all know that in real life this is not the case.

Some fortunate people do grow up in families where the parents model and teach wisdom and righteousness. Others are deprived of such guidance and may, as a result, feel shortchanged. They might even feel angry, resentful, or ashamed, asking themselves, "Shouldn't someone have shown me the way?"

But even if no one was there to teach us wisdom, the book of Proverbs is filled with wonderful guidance that we can still utilize. Proverbs 3:13–18 teaches us that happiness comes from having and holding tightly to wisdom and understanding. Regardless of our upbringing, we have a Father in heaven who loves us and is eager to give us the wisdom and guidance we need. James promises, "If you need wisdom—if you want to know what God wants you to do—ask him, and he will gladly tell you. He will not resent your asking" (James 1:5, NLT).

Let me encourage you today to release any lingering resentment you may harbor about the failure of others to teach you wisdom in the past. Godly wisdom is still there for the asking.

LIGHTHOUSE THOUGHT FOR THE DAY

God wants you to think and live in His wisdom. Through prayer and His Word, He will give you the wisdom and sound mind you need for successful living.

STEPHEN ARTERBURN

Encompassing Nations

I looked and there before me was a great multitude…from every nation, tribe, people and language, standing before the throne.

REVELATION 7:9

I have often thought that the truly great promise that Christ gave the church is found in His powerful prophecy that "this gospel of the kingdom will be preached in the whole world as a testimony to all nations, and then the end will come" (Matthew 24:14). This suggests that prayer, to be truly productive, must ultimately encompass nations. True, the model given in Acts 1:8 begins with our "Jerusalem," but it continues to "the ends of the earth."

Interestingly, the ends of the earth have actually come to us. My wife, Dee, in doing research on unreached peoples in the U.S., discovered some startling facts. America is home to more than 500 ethnic groups who speak 636 languages and dialects. Almost forty-two million Americans speak little or no English. The U.S. is home to more Swedes than Sweden, more Irish than Ireland, and more Jews than Israel. New York City alone has more Jews than Jerusalem, more Italians than Rome, and more Puerto Ricans than San Juan.

The nations have indeed come to us. As we pray for our neighborhoods, we are in fact praying for the nations. We recall God's promise to His Son: "Ask of me, and I will make the nations your inheritance, the ends of the earth your possession" (Psalm 2:8). This promise is for us, too. Paul reminds us, "We are heirs—heirs of God and co-heirs with Christ" (Romans 8:16–17).

May our prayers touch not only our neighbors, including the nations God has brought to us, but all the nations of the world.

LIGHTHOUSE THOUGHT FOR THE DAY

Prayers that touch the nations touch the heart of God, for God sent His Son as a sacrifice for the entire world (John 3:16).

DICK EASTMAN

Witnessing

*"Go ye therefore, and teach all nations, baptizing them in
the name of the Father, and of the Son, and of the Holy Ghost."*
MATTHEW 28:19, KJV

We all know what it's like to be around people who are in love—*really*
in love. There is a glow about these people. Everything about them
changes, and they have to tell somebody why! Our witness for Jesus
Christ is a lot like that.

Witnessing means telling others about what you have experienced.
In the context of Christianity, it involves testifying to others of the forgiveness, love, deliverance, power, and peace found in Jesus Christ.

Jesus' last instructions to His disciples before He ascended to His
Father related to witnessing. He commissioned them to go into the
world and make disciples. He promised them that when they received
the Holy Spirit, they would become witnesses of all they had seen and
heard. And He said that He would confirm His Word with signs and
authority (Mark 16:20; Matthew 28:19–20).

When people have been forgiven of their sins, they are enabled to
witness—to give testimony to their salvation through Jesus Christ. This
does not necessarily make them evangelists (Ephesians 4:11), but it
does make them like the witnesses in the early church, who said, "We
cannot stop telling about the wonderful things we have seen and
heard" (Acts 4:20, NLT).

The power to witness is a result of the work of the Holy Spirit
(Mark16:17–20). It is not just teaching Bible truths; it is being a *product*
of those truths.

LIGHTHOUSE THOUGHT FOR THE DAY

As children of God through the salvation of Jesus Christ, each of us is
called to be a witness for Him. We do that by saying what Jesus wants
us to say, being what He wants us to be, and doing what He wants us
to do.

PAT ROBERTSON

Real Joy

When they saw the star, they were overjoyed.
MATTHEW 2:10

The visit of the magi to the birthplace of the Lord Jesus Christ is a classic example of how the joy of finding Jesus Christ can be demonstrated in the life of a believer.

These wise men had set out months before their arrival in Bethlehem, following a star in the north sky. As astronomers who understood the Hebrew Scriptures, they recognized that something unique was about to happen, and when they saw this star, they were "overjoyed." But their joy was just beginning.

When the magi first saw Jesus, they were overwhelmed at being in the presence of the Savior. They bowed down and worshiped the infant, and then presented their treasures to Him. Obviously, these men knew what they were witnessing and whose presence they were in.

These wise men certainly had every cause to celebrate. But we as the church have even greater cause. Jesus has come to redeem us, to save us, and to restore our relationship with the living God.

We should share the joy we have over Jesus' birth. We should worship, sing, and celebrate, for, just like the magi all those centuries ago, we have found the King. Let us celebrate our Savior's birth by reaching out to those around us with words of encouragement or blessing or an invitation to a relationship with Jesus.

Like the magi, we should give of our treasures because we have found the Lord Jesus Christ. He has brought us great joy, and we can worship Him by sharing it with those around us, communicating His great love to the world.

LIGHTHOUSE THOUGHT FOR THE DAY

As lighthouses for the Lord Jesus Christ, we should give all we have in worship of the King of kings.

JACK HAYFORD

A New Kind of Obsession

And the disciples were filled with joy and with the Holy Spirit.
ACTS 13:52

We have a dachshund named Schotze. No matter how discouraged, frustrated, or sad we might be at times, Schotze is always the same. She's eleven years old (seventy-seven in doggy years), yet she romps through the house as though she were still a pup. Schotze is so happy to be part of our family that she follows us from room to room and speaks, sits up, and rolls over on command. Schotze, you might say, is obsessed with us.

Spirit-filled Christians are obsessed with the Lord Jesus, and that obsession transforms their lives with authority, joy, and hope (Acts 13:52). Having experienced the fullness of the power of God, they are hooked on the adventure. Everything about our lives is affected by the filling of the Holy Spirit. How we pray, what we eat, how we witness, where we go, how we talk, and how we act around others will reveal our obsession with Jesus.

An old man was heard to pray, "Lord, fill me with your Spirit," to which a lady sitting nearby whispered, "Don't do it, God; He leaks." It's true, the race of life is a long one, and we will constantly need a fresh refilling of God's Spirit.

Be filled with the Holy Spirit today. Live the adventure! Be alive in Christ! Laugh and sing! Enjoy the Lord! Be obsessed with Him today!

LIGHTHOUSE THOUGHT FOR THE DAY

Life is too short not to enjoy the goodness of God. Always delight in the truth that the one and only eternal God lives in you.

EDDIE AND ALICE SMITH

A Year-Round Celebration

The shepherds returned, glorifying and praising
God for all the things they had heard and seen.

LUKE 2:20

The Church On The Way has a thirty-year history of joyous Christmas celebrations. It has never really bothered me that people might think our celebrations are a little too childlike or simple. What would bother me is if they thought we were just going through the motions of established holiday tradition.

I see tradition as reenactment, but I see our Christmas celebrations as commemorations of the Incarnation, which occurred when Christ came to us in the flesh. Christ's arrival as God Incarnate was the occasion for the shepherds' praises and rejoicing. Their response was consistent with the practice of celebration God had established in His law.

One of the annual celebrations the Lord had ordained for the people of Israel was the Passover feast, which commemorated their delivery from Egypt. Every year the people celebrated God's breakthrough in their national history. Some undoubtedly realized that this should not be just a yearly event, but that the children of Israel should thank and praise Him continually.

Likewise, we should continually praise God for the gift of Jesus. God ordained Israel's celebration of their exodus from Egypt, so it makes perfect sense that He wants His people, the church, to celebrate the arrival of the Savior. But He also wants to plant afresh in our hearts every day the joy that arose from the shepherds' hearts at the announcement of His Son's birth. God desires to bring us fresh joy every day of the year, not just during the Christmas season.

LIGHTHOUSE THOUGHT FOR THE DAY

As lighthouses for Jesus, let us ask our Father to help us walk daily in the same joy the shepherds felt at the Messiah's arrival.

JACK HAYFORD

Hard Choices

I will bless the LORD who has given me counsel;
my heart also instructs me in the night seasons.

PSALM 16:7, NKJV

Scripture says that the Lord Jesus was tested in all things as we are. Does He, then, understand and empathize with the matter of hard choices? If you doubt it, come with me to the Garden of Gethsemane. You'll never doubt it again.

There, the Galilean Carpenter was faced with the hardest choice anyone has ever had to make. Would He, in the prime of manhood, lay down His life that very day? Would He, the One who had never sinned, take upon Himself the sins of all humanity for all time? Would He, who had known an eternity of face-to-face intimacy within the Godhead, behold His Father's back for the first time?

Yes, He *knew* God's will. And yes, He was the Son of God. But we dare not imagine that doing the right thing in that instance was an easy decision for Jesus. The prospect before Him was so agonizing that drops of blood seeped through His skin and fell to the dusty soil as He prayed.

Hard? Yes, *cruelly* hard. But it all boiled down to this: Was He going to do His Father's will—*no matter what*—or wasn't He? It's the same for you and me: Are we going to follow Him as Lord, or aren't we?

How, then, do we make hard choices? The answer is rooted in the Garden of Gethsemane. The Second Adam was God who came to be man. In this garden, He chose the path of suffering instead of the path of comfort. On His shoulders, He bore the harvest of sin that had grown from that earlier garden. In this garden, His torment made possible our paradise. In this garden, He made a decision and then acted on it: "Not My will but Thine be done."

LIGHTHOUSE THOUGHT FOR THE DAY

Jesus is our example of a heart that yields to the will of the Father.

RON MEHL

Get Ready, Get Set, Pray!

> Then He said to His disciples, "The harvest truly is plentiful, but
> the laborers are few. Therefore pray the Lord of the harvest
> to send out laborers into His harvest."
>
> MATTHEW 9:37–38, NKJV

In this passage Jesus points out a problem that is apparent to so many in the church today: *The laborers are few.* He also points out the solution: *Pray.* Why? The harvest is the Lord's, and it is up to Him to send the laborers.

Prayer is the first and real business of any kind of ministry. Too often we treat prayer as a formality, a prelude to our own decisions or actions. Or we treat prayer as a fitting conclusion to the "real" business of ministry. Let's remember that prayer is neither the appetizer nor the dessert—it's the main course!

Conversing with God ought to be a delight and a blessing—yet often we find it a burden. We declare the importance of prayer with our words, but sometimes our actions say otherwise. Our society sets goals, measures results, and evaluates success based on visible accomplishment. Christians do the same, and they have accomplished much good for God as a result. Yet there is a tendency to neglect prayer. We cannot always measure the results of time spent talking to God and listening to God—nor should we! Goals do not change lives. Prayer does.

Our standard in this race should be, "On your mark, get set, *pray.*" Prayer requires commitment, but it also takes a great load off our shoulders. Ministry does not depend on our abilities, but on God's resources. By establishing prayer as the foundation of all we do, we take our burdens and lay them at the feet of our Lord.

LIGHTHOUSE THOUGHT FOR THE DAY

As lighthouses for the Lord Jesus Christ, let's pray today that God will raise up more people to be lighthouses for the Lord so that His glory will shine brightly in our communities and all around the world.

DAVID BRICKNER

Pastoring the Lost Sheep

"If a man owns a hundred sheep, and one of them wanders away,
will he not leave the ninety-nine on the hills and
go to look for the one that wandered off?"

MATTHEW 18:12

Many of my neighbors don't know it, but I'm their pastor. They don't go to church. No one prays for them or looks after their souls. So, I do it. There is really no need for them to join my church or ask me to be their pastor. When I moved into the neighborhood, it became my parish, and they my parishioners.

Many of my neighbors are what I call "not-yet Christians" (I think that is a much more hopeful label than "non-Christian"). But they don't have to be Christians to be part of the flock I pastor.

Some of my neighbors are believers who, for one reason or another, find themselves outside organized religion. They think they would never fit in at church. They expect "religious" people to reject them. They're dealing with divorce, addiction, or other things that would make them feel hypocritical if they went to church. This is all the more reason they need a pastor who can come to them.

Many have never been touched by authentic faith on a personal level. They have either been damaged by religious hypocrisy or have become a skeptical observer of church scandal. They expect Christians to be judgmental, critical, arrogant, and hypocritical.

But these people have a pastor who cares for them, prays for them, and is there to serve them whenever the need arises. I can tell you that this is a calling I have been overjoyed to answer!

LIGHTHOUSE THOUGHT FOR THE DAY

Jesus is looking for people who will leave the ninety-nine sheep in the fold and go for the one that is lost. Will you pastor the lost sheep in your neighborhood?

TOM PELTON

First and Last Words

*"But you shall receive power when the Holy Spirit has come upon you;
and you shall be witnesses to Me in Jerusalem, and in all Judea
and Samaria, and to the end of the earth."*

ACTS 1:8, NKJV

Do you know what the first recorded words of Jesus were? They are found in the second chapter of Luke. On their homeward journey, Joseph and Mary discovered that Jesus was missing. They returned to Jerusalem to find Him, and when they found Him in the temple, Mary said, "Son, why have You done this to us? Look, Your father and I have sought You anxiously" (2:48, NKJV). Then Jesus, just twelve years old at the time, replied, "Why did you seek Me? Did you not know that I must be about My Father's business?" (v. 49).

Before any teaching about the kingdom, before any advice on prayer, before calling His twelve disciples or predicting His death, Jesus said, "I must be about My Father's business."

Do you remember what the last words of Jesus were? The last recorded words of our Lord are found in Acts 1:8. After He had been crucified and raised from the dead, and just before He ascended to heaven, Jesus said to His disciples, "But you shall receive power when the Holy Spirit has come upon you; and you shall be witnesses to Me in Jerusalem, and in all Judea and Samaria, and to the end of the earth."

Jesus' first words were a declaration that *He* should be about His Father's business, and His last words were a declaration that *we* should be about His Father's business. Aren't you challenged by that notion?

LIGHTHOUSE THOUGHT FOR THE DAY

Like the Lord Jesus Christ during His earthly ministry, we are to be about our heavenly Father's business, and that includes being a witness of Him to those around us. That is part of maturity in our relationship with Christ, and it is part of our calling as lighthouses for Him.

WOOD KROLL

But Can You Save?

Mercy triumphs over judgment!
JAMES 2:13

Hypocrites love to judge others because it makes them feel superior. But as a lighthouse for Jesus Christ, it is not to be so with you. You must earnestly seek lowliness of heart.

Many zealous, but proud Christians fail to reach spiritual maturity because they assume they are called to judge others. Our Lord's example says otherwise. If Jesus did not come to condemn the world but to save it (John 3:17), neither should we condemn those around us.

Anyone can pass judgment, but can anyone save? To judge after the flesh requires but one eye and a carnal mind. On the other hand, to redeem and save takes the loving faithfulness of Christ. One act of His love revealed through us will do more to soften hardened hearts than all our pompous criticisms.

One may argue that Jesus condemned sin. Yes, He did! But let us first condemn our own sin, the sin of judging others. If you insist on finding fault with others, beware, because Christ sets a high standard for judges: "He who is without sin among you, let him be the first to throw a stone" (John 8:7, NASB).

Speak out against unrighteousness, but be motivated by the love of Jesus. Remember, it is written, "While we were yet sinners, Christ died for us" (Romans 5:8, NASB). Jesus has set the standard. In the kingdom of God, unless you are first committed to die for people, you are not permitted to judge them. "With the measure you use, it will be measured to you" (Matthew 7:2).

LIGHTHOUSE THOUGHT FOR THE DAY

As lighthouses for Christ, we are not called to judge sinners. Rather, it is our job to lead the "sick" to where they will find the remedy for their sin: the foot of the cross.

FRANCIS FRANGIPANE

Lives of Integrity

*"May they also be in us so that the world
may believe that you have sent me."*

JOHN 17:21

A friend of mine went shopping for a television for his wife's birthday. She wanted a small one for the kitchen, so he bought one with a seven-inch screen. He thought that the box containing the set was unusually large for such a small unit, and when his wife opened the box, she found four smaller boxes inside. What had appeared to be a box for a single television was actually a carton of four TVs.

Neither my friend nor his wife even considered keeping the extra units. They kept the one he had purchased and took the other three back to the merchant. Everyone at the store was amazed at their honesty.

Isn't it sad that people in our world today find basic displays of honesty and integrity so exceptional, so noteworthy? Shouldn't that be the rule, and not the exception?

This is at the heart of what Jesus prayed in John 17. In effect, He was praying that believers would live lives that reflected a commitment to the heart and character of God, and that the world would believe in Him when they saw the difference. When our hearts are abandoned to God, when we consistently do what is right because we know Him, our neighbors sit up and take notice.

Your neighbors may find your honesty and integrity a little strange. Well, so be it! If someone tells you that you are "honest to a fault," smile and tell that person that your honesty and integrity spring from a heart that wants to please your Lord!

LIGHTHOUSE THOUGHT FOR THE DAY

In a dark world, we can shine more brightly for Christ when we live lives of integrity and honesty.

MARY L. MARR

I Love a Parade

For in [Christ] dwelleth all the fulness of the Godhead bodily.
And ye are complete in him, which is the head of all principality and power.
COLOSSIANS 2:9–10, KJV

Spectators lined the streets of Pasadena, California, one New Year's morning years ago. Some had camped out for several days in an attempt to secure for themselves the best view of the Tournament of Roses parade.

Suddenly, amid the marching bands and riders on palomino ponies, a beautiful float appeared. Everyone marveled at its floral artistry. Then, to everyone's surprise, it sputtered and quit. It had run out of gas. Ironically, the beautiful float represented the Standard Oil Company.

We Christians are like that float, in that we have at our disposal all the "fuel" we need to do the things God wants us to do. The apostle Peter tells us that God "has given us everything we need for life and godliness through our knowledge of him who called us by his own glory and goodness" (2 Peter 1:3).

Why is it, then, that we run out of gas so often? It's simple. God is so relational that He created us to be constantly dependent upon Him. We have a small gas tank. Sure, He has given us holiness, power, authority, and more. However, none of these things are automatic. They are available to us only as we deny ourselves (Matthew 16:24), reckon ourselves dead to sin (Romans 6:11), seek Him with our whole heart (Jeremiah 29:13), and allow Him to fill us with Himself daily (Ephesians 5:18).

Let's ask God for the filling of His Holy Spirit so we can make it through today's parade of life.

LIGHTHOUSE THOUGHT FOR THE DAY

Lighthouses for Jesus Christ need to be filled with the fuel of the Holy Spirit if they are to minister effectively to their neighbors.

EDDIE AND ALICE SMITH

Prayer for Ministry

*"May they be brought to complete unity to let the world
know that you sent me and have loved them even as you have loved me."*

JOHN 17:23

Part of our responsibility as intercessors is to pray for those who have dedicated their lives to taking the gospel of Jesus Christ to those in need. Cultivate the habit of praying Scripture for your requests

We should start by praying for unity within the body of Christ and for the evangelization of the world (John 17:11; Acts 4:29, 32; 1 Timothy 2:4). Then, we should pray for the church and church-related organizations. We should pray for pastors, deacons, elders, lay ministers, missionaries, chaplains, teachers, and evangelists, as well as theological schools and for strategic events. We need to pray that God's servants walk in a manner worthy of their calling—showing forbearance to one another in love (Ephesians 4:1–3).

We should pray that God gives His messengers boldness to make known the mystery of the gospel (Ephesians 6:19; Colossians 4:3–4). We must also pray that God's men and women will devote themselves to prayer (Acts 1:14; 2:42; Ephesians 6:18; Colossians 4:2; 1 Thessalonians 5:16–22), cleanse themselves from defilement by the flesh and the world, and live in the fear of God (2 Corinthians 7:1). We need to pray that they will be good stewards of resources and that, as they commit all their financial needs to God, God's people will learn to engage in good deeds to meet pressing needs (Titus 3:14).

Paul gave us a pattern for the kind of prayer that will strengthen our outreach to the world. We observe him praying specifically for the development of the spiritual character of those he loves, rather than for their circumstances (Ephesians 1:18–20; 3:14–19; Philippians 1:9–12).

LIGHTHOUSE THOUGHT FOR THE DAY

"Prayer is not my work but God's work in me." —Andrew Murray

VONETTE Z. BRIGHT

Positives from Negatives

*"As for you, you meant evil against me, but God meant it for good
in order to bring about this present result."*

GENESIS 50:20, NASB

Years ago, I worked as the lead system engineer on a missile control system. Our first model had just come off the production line, and for several weeks, I worked late into the night. A production engineer was assigned to work with me after regular hours, but he called in sick at least once a week. When he did manage to come, he was next to worthless. He also had the obnoxious habit of eating sunflower seeds while I was trying to concentrate. It drove me nuts.

In desperation, I finally asked him if he ever went to church. As I suspected, he didn't. He told me that he and his wife had been considering going, mostly for the sake of their three children. For the first time, we had a meaningful conversation, and I invited his family to come to our church on Sunday.

The following Tuesday morning I got a call from my pastor. He said, "I thought you would like to know that I led your engineering friend to the Lord last night. But there is something else you need to know. He is an alcoholic."

At that moment, I understood why my coworker had been missing work. It made me think about my response to this hurting man. When my frustration had reached its limit, I finally did what I should have been doing all along—being the witness God called me to be.

God has His own ways of getting our attention when He wants to use us to meet the needs of our neighbors. Sometimes those attention-getters come in the form of annoyances. When they do, we should respond to them as Jesus would.

LIGHTHOUSE THOUGHT FOR THE DAY

Your neighbors' negative habits may be what God is using to get your attention so you can fulfill your ministry.

NEIL T. ANDERSON

A Worshipful Home

*Therefore, I urge you, brothers, in view of God's mercy,
to offer your bodies as living sacrifices, holy and pleasing to God—
this is your spiritual act of worship.*

ROMANS 12:1

As the spiritual leader of his family, it's a man's responsibility to make the home a lighthouse for Jesus Christ. One of the primary ways a husband and father fulfills this calling is by leading his family in worshiping almighty God.

The foundation of a worshipful life, family, and home is the example a man sets for his wife and children by daily offering up his body as a living sacrifice to God, by consecrating himself to Christ, and by setting himself apart for the Spirit's use. This happens when he commits his whole heart, mind, will, and strength to serving the Lord and His kingdom—every day. It's the initial way for a man to light up his house and lead his wife and children spiritually.

So what does presenting your body as a living sacrifice mean? It may look something like this: eyes spending daily time in the Bible and not looking at anything "unclean," like pornography; ears being quick to hear what God and others have to say, but refusing to listen to coarse jesting, racial jokes, or negative music; a mouth speaking words of truth and grace and refraining from cursing, slander, gossip, or boasting; a mind thinking the best of people instead of the worst and refraining from negative thoughts, pessimism, and hopelessness; hands touching nothing unholy or illegal, but working hard and with excellence; feet avoiding sinful places, but going instead wherever God sends you to follow Christ.

LIGHTHOUSE THOUGHT FOR THE DAY

Men, dedicate yourself to God as a living sacrifice. Then pray for each member of your family individually, blessing them and affirming their gifts and abilities.

BILL MCCARTNEY

Renewing Relationships

Live a life of love, just as Christ loved us and gave himself
up for us as a fragrant offering and sacrifice to God.

EPHESIANS 5:2

"A loving spirit is a condition of believing prayer," wrote the anonymous author of *The Kneeling Christian.* "We cannot be wrong with man and right with God."

Productive praying, in addition to all else, enhances relationships. Indeed, prayer without forgiveness is prayer without power. Jesus said, "And when you stand praying, if you hold anything against anyone, forgive him, so that your Father in heaven may forgive you your sins" (Mark 11:25).

Interestingly, Jesus gave this admonition in the context of commanding mountains to be removed (Mark 11:22–23). Could there be a direct relationship between a forgiving spirit and removing strongholds? One thing is certain, real prayer leads to true forgiveness and release.

An attitude of forgiveness is especially vital as we envision our lighthouses shining the light of Christ around us. Surely our neighbors know if we've been unforgiving in the past. Voicing forgiveness in specific prayers over our neighbors is a good place to begin. If your past behavior necessitates it, pray specifically that God will open a door for you to ask forgiveness of a particular neighbor and then to share a loving witness of Jesus with that person.

We should also be willing to openly forgive any neighbors who may themselves harbor unforgivingness. Remember: The model of prayer evangelism in Luke 10 begins with first speaking peace (blessing) over those we ultimately desire to reach with the gospel (v. 5). At the heart of speaking peace is the quest for forgiveness.

LIGHTHOUSE THOUGHT FOR THE DAY

Forgiveness is central to spreading the light of Christ about us.

DICK EASTMAN

Gracious Forgetfulness

For as many of you as were baptized into Christ have put on Christ.
GALATIANS 3:27, RSV

I was thanking the Father today for His mercy. I began listing the sins He'd forgiven. My motives were pure and my heart was thankful, but my understanding of God was wrong. It hit me when I used the word *remember.*

I was thanking God for another act of mercy. "Remember the time I...." But I stopped. Something was wrong. *Remember* seemed an off-key note in a sonata, a misspelled word in a poem. It didn't fit. "Does He remember?" Then I remembered His words. "I will remember their sins no more" (Hebrews 8:12, RSV).

Wow! Now, *that* is a remarkable promise. God doesn't just forgive; He forgets. He erases the board. He destroys the evidence. He burns the microfilm. He clears the computer.

He doesn't remember my mistakes. For all the things He does do, this is one thing He refuses to do. He refuses to keep a list of my wrongs. When I ask for forgiveness, He doesn't pull out a clipboard and say, "But I've already forgiven him for that five hundred and sixteen times."

He doesn't remember. "As far as the east is from the west, so far has he removed our transgressions from us" (Psalm 103:12). "I will be merciful toward their iniquities" (Hebrews 8:12, RSV). "Even if you are stained as red as crimson, I can make you white as wool!" (Isaiah 1:18, TLB). No, He doesn't remember.

Do yourself a favor. Purge your cellar. Exorcise your basement. Take the Roman nails of Calvary and board up the door.

And remember...He forgot.

LIGHTHOUSE THOUGHT FOR THE DAY

Our lights will shine all the brighter for Christ when we realize that God has forgiven and forgotten our sin.

MAX LUCADO

Why Spread the Good News?

"While he was still a long way off, his father saw him and was filled with compassion for him; he ran to his son, threw his arms around him and kissed him."

LUKE 15:20

I once saw the great Russian ballet dancer, Mikhail Baryshnikov, dance to Ballenchine's choreographed rendition of *The Prodigal Son*. The most powerful moment of the ballet is when Baryshnikov, playing the Prodigal, returns to beg his father's forgiveness. In the closing moments of the ballet, as the father cradles his son tenderly in his arms, the son rests his head on his father's chest in exhausted comfort. He is home at last, and that is all that matters.

Why does this story, told more than two thousand years ago, still pack such a wallop today? Because Jesus tapped into one of the deepest human anxieties: *There's a child in desperate trouble.* When a child is lost, family relationships are broken, parents grieve, and anxiety abounds. We wonder: *Will the lost child find his way home and be restored? Will the parents' broken hearts be mended?*

Jesus' critics had complained that He associated with the riffraff of society. He answered them by telling a story that revealed God's love for the lost, His yearning for and patient effort in their recovery, and His joy in their restoration.

What is our motive for evangelism? Do we regard unbelievers who have messy lives with the compassion of the Father, or with the judgmental spirit of the elder brother (Luke 15:28)? One way to keep our hearts free of a critical spirit is to thank God that He has shown us mercy despite our sins.

We spread the Good News because people of immense worth to God are lost, and He wants them back home—resting on His chest in exhausted comfort.

LIGHTHOUSE THOUGHT FOR THE DAY

Ask God today to enlarge your heart so that His compassionate love will flow through you to those who have not yet found their way home.

REBECCA MANLEY PIPPERT

No Prayer, No Power

And when he had entered the house, his disciples asked him privately,
"Why could we not cast it out?" And he said to them, "This kind
cannot be driven out by anything but prayer."
Mark 9:28–29, rsv

It is true for individuals and churches. No prayer, no power. Consider the story in Mark 9. The disciples had been unable to cast out an unclean spirit from an afflicted boy. Jesus came on the scene and cast it out. The disciples asked, "Why could we not cast it out?" Jesus answered, "This kind cannot be driven out by anything but prayer." Jesus says there are spiritual forces that are very hard to overcome. His disciples asked why they could not overcome the evil. Jesus answered, "Insufficient prayer!"

What did he mean? Probably not that they hadn't prayed over the demonized boy; it seems that would have been the first approach. Probably he means that they had not lived in prayer. They had been caught in a prayerless period of life or a prayerless frame of mind. Notice that Jesus cast out the demon without praying: "You dumb and deaf spirit, I command you, come out of him, and never enter him again" (Mark 9:25, rsv). Yet Jesus had prayed. He lived in prayer. He spent whole nights in prayer. He was ready when evil came, but apparently the disciples had become weak and negligent in their praying, so they were powerless in the face of strong evil forces.

In other words, without persistent prayer we have no offense in the battle with evil. Individually and as churches we are meant to invade and plunder the strongholds of Satan. But no prayer, no power.

LIGHTHOUSE THOUGHT FOR THE DAY

If we want our lighthouses for Christ to minister for the good of sinners and for the glory of God, we need to make our defense and offense an active, persistent, earnest, believing force of prayer.

JOHN PIPER, WITH JUSTIN TAYLOR

The Path to Peace

*"Peace I leave with you; my peace I give you. I do not give to you as
the world gives. Do not let your hearts be troubled and do not be afraid."*
JOHN 14:27

Many people think that the path to peace is the same as a road to material well-being, or at least to favorable temporal circumstances. It's easy
to understand how someone on that path could think they have peace.

Yet there is another path leading to a deeper peace that is not so
easily understood. It is the road to spiritual well-being, laid down on
eternal realities. It leads to peace that is not visible in our outer circumstances, but rather in how we endure those circumstances. This *shalom*,
this peace, causes calm in the midst of conflict, security in the face of
calamity, rest upon a raging sea.

The world pauses to rest from its warfare and calls such pauses
peace. Jesus promises that although the battles may rage around us,
His peace will reign within us always. The world brings sworn enemies
to the same table to shake hands and calls that peace. Jesus promises
that although every hand be against us, His hand will be upon us to
guide us in the paths of peace. The world restrains wicked men from
doing harm and calls that restraint peace. Jesus promises that although
our foes' fury be unrestrained, we will rest in His peace.

Jesus blesses us with peace that the world cannot give, and it is
therefore a peace the world cannot take away. We have His promise:
Jesus, the Righteous One, conquered sin by His life and death and conquered death by His resurrection. Though we face trouble and distress
"in the world," we can have the courage to face our troubles and
endure them if we are "in" Messiah Jesus.

LIGHTHOUSE THOUGHT FOR THE DAY

May those who search for true and lasting peace see reflected in our
faces the true shalom of God, the peace that comes only through
Christ.

DAVID BRICKNER

Shine His Light on Your World

-Join the Lighthouse Movement-

The Lighthouse Movement
compiled by Dr. Cornell Haan

This book is a complete tool kit on how Christians can be "lighthouses" to their neighbors and reach them with the gospel. It includes thirty-five chapters, each written by a leader respected in his or her field.

ISBN 1-57673-633-4 PA

The Lighthouse Prayer Journal

This essential prayer journal shows you how to be a "lighthouse" for Jesus and pray effectively for those around you. As you record specific requests and results, you'll be inspired by God's hand at work!

ISBN 1-57673-681-4 HD